Classical Indian Philosophy

Classical Indian Philosophy

J. N. Mohanty

ROWMAN & LITTLEFIELD PUBLISHERS, INC.
Lanham • Boulder • New York • Oxford

ROWMAN & LITTLEFIELD PUBLISHERS, INC.

Published in the United States of America
by Rowman & Littlefield Publishers, Inc.
4720 Boston Way, Lanham, Maryland 20706
http://www.rowmanlittlefield.com

12 Hid's Copse Road
Cumnor Hill, Oxford OX2 9JJ, England

British Cataloging in Publication Information Available

Library of Congress Cataloging-in-Publication Data

Mohanty Jitendranath, 1928–
Classical Indian philosophy / J.N. Mohanty.
p. cm.
Includes bibliographical references and index.
ISBN 0-8476-8932-8 (alk. paper).—ISBN 0-8476-8933-6 (pbk. : alk. paper)
1. Philosophy, Indic. 2. Jaina philosophy. 3. Philosophy, Hindu. 4. Philosophy, Buddhist. I. Title.
B131.M54M64 1999
181'.4—dc21 99-36603
CIP

Printed in the United States of America

∞™ The paper used in this publication meets the minimum requirements of American National Standard for Information Sciences—Permanence of Paper for Printed Library Materials, ANSI/NISO Z.39.48–1992.

Contents

Part 2: Metaphysics (*Prameya Śāstra*)

Part 3. Philosophy of Politics, Law, and Morals (*Dharma Śāstras*)

Preface

This is a book that I always wanted to write, but the project had to be postponed up until this stage in my life. Having learned Indian philosophy under two great Sanskrit Pandits—the late Mm. Yogendranāth Tarkavedāntatirtha and the late Pandit Ananta Kumar Tarkatīrtha—I wanted to convey to Western scholars something of the education I had received. Hopefully, I have succeeded in doing so in some measure. There are gaps that I would like to fill, and there are topics on which I would like to elaborate, should there be an opportunity to do so in the future. For the present, I am glad to be able to send this manuscript to the press.

This book could not have been written without the help of Professor Bina Gupta. She helped me in organizing my ideas—and in preparing the manuscript—in effect, overcoming those intellectual and technological infirmities that come with old age.

Śaṃkara and his four disciples: Padmapāda, Sureśvarācārya, Hastāmalaka, and Tōṭakācārya.

Chapter One

Indian Philosophy: A Historical Overview

ORIGINS

According to the Hindu tradition, the various philosophical ideas that were developed in the philosophical systems originated in the Vedas, a body of texts that were composed possibly around two thousand years before Common Era (B.C.E.). While the Vedas contain a myriad of different themes, ranging from hymns for deities and rules of fire sacrifices to music and magic, there is no doubt that one finds in them an exemplary spirit of inquiry into "the one being" (*ekam sat*) that underlies the diversity of empirical phenomena, and into the origin of all things ("was there being or nonbeing at the beginning?"). There are also predelineations of concepts of *ṛta* ("truth" or "moral order"), *karma* and afterlife, and the three qualities (*guṇas*), *sattva, rajas*, and *tama,* constituting nature (*prakṛti*). It is in the Upaniṣads (a group of texts composed after the Vedas and ranging from 1000 B.C.E. to the time of Gautama, the Buddha) that the thinking, while still retaining its poetic flavor, develops a more strictly philosophical character. Among the many different themes belonging to cosmology ("how did the one being become many?") and psychology ("what does the empirical person consist of?") we find attempts to reinterpret, in symbolic terms, the elaborate Vedic sacrifices, and, in the long run, a multifaceted defense of one central philosophical thesis: the identification of the *brahman* (i.e., the highest and the greatest, the source of all things) with the *ātman* (the self within each person). With this last identification, a giant step was taken by the authors of the Upaniṣads, a step that was decisive for the development of Indian philosophy. The Vedas had already decided, famously in the *Nāsadiya Sukta,* that at the beginning of things there must have been being and not nonbeing (for something cannot come out of nothing); now this primeval being was said to be the same as the spirit within. The highest wisdom was intuitively realizing this identity of subject and object (*tat tvam asi*).

How to know this identity was the question? Suggestions range from a contemplative meditation to austere self-mortification. The idea of Yoga and a picture of the yogin make their appearance—possibly having a different origin—and blend with the central thesis of the Upaniṣads. If the real behind empirical nature is the universal spirit within, is then the world merely phenomenal appearance (like the magician's creation, *māyā*), or is the *brahman-ātman* to be construed as the indwelling spirit of all things (*sarvam khalu idam brahman*)? These become the leading disputational questions among the commentators on the Upaniṣads and among the various schools of the Vedānta philosophy.

RISE OF THE ANTI-VEDIC, NATURALISTIC, AND SKEPTICAL THINKING

It was toward the end of the Upaniṣadic period, most probably when the major Upaniṣads had been composed, that in the northeastern region of the Gangetic Plain at the foothills of the Himalaya Mountains, in the present state of Bihar, there was born a most remarkable person, Gautama, the Sākya, of the Licchabi clan (c. 560 B.C.E.), the son of the elected chief of a small republican country. Stories about Gautama's life are many; few things are known with certainty. The story about his experiences of old age, sickness, and death—experiences of existential anguish—which lead him to renounce his princely and worldly life and set him on the tortuous path to enlightenment, is rather well-known. Upon reaching enlightenment, that is, the wisdom that contained his answer to the question of how to escape suffering. Gautama preached, in his first sermon, the fourfold "noble truths," which remain the central belief of Buddhism through all its exuberant growth of sects, schools, rituals and practices. The noble truths are the truth of suffering (existence is marked by suffering), the truth that suffering has a cause (which is craving, *tṛsṇā*), the truth that there is an end to suffering (i.e., *nirvāṇa*), and, finally, the truth that there is a path (*mārga*) to reach that end (the eightfold right path). This path, described as the middle way—avoiding the extremes of sensuous indulgence (which is vulgar, low, and unspiritual) and self-torture (which is painful, useless, and also unspiritual)—consists of eight components: right views, right intention, right speech, right action, right livelihood, right effort, right mindfulness, and right concentration. In his sermons and conversations, Gautama avoided metaphysical questions and insisted only on teaching the path to deliverance from suffering. But Buddhism, very early on, was committed to certain philosophical beliefs: rejection of the Upaniṣadic thesis of *ātman,* a rejection of any permanent substance (of which the no-self doctrine may be regarded as a specific application), a belief in a strict principle of causal dependence (called "dependent origination") to which all existence is subject, belief in *karma* and rebirth, and the belief in the eventual deliverance. Thus Gautama did not totally reject the Upaniṣadic theses. Rejecting the fundamental metaphysics of *ātman,* he still adhered to the other major components: rebirth, *karma,* and *mokṣa* (called "*nirvāṇa*").

Gautama represented a growing revolt against the *brahmanism* as it spread eastward along the Gangetic valley. The revolt was as much against religious theory and practice as against the monarchical state, which the Hindus glorified, a society ridden with priest-craft and caste. But Gautama was not the only, nor was he the first, rebel. The Vedic literature already bears evidence to much skeptical self-criticism. There were skeptics such as Samjaya, who, when questioned as to whether there was an afterlife, said "I do not say there is an afterlife and I do not say there is no after life," thus using, to recall Matilal's words, "illocutionary negation" as contrasted with "propositional negation." This sort of skepticism seems to have had some influence on Buddhism. Among pre-Buddhistic philosophies, one text, Sutrakṛtānga, mentions 363 schools—of which 180 were *kriyāvādins* (believed in the efficacy of action), 84 were *akriyāvādins* (who rejected the efficacy of action), 67 were *ajñānikas* (who claimed not to know, so were skeptics), and 32 *vainayikas* (i.e., believed in salvation by good conduct). These numbers may be exaggerated, but they certainly show intense intellectual ferment. Among the skeptics—besides the famous Saṃjaya—there were those who refused to accept any claim to knowledge owing to the contradictory conclusions and no agreements reached, those who questioned the concept of omniscience, and those who emphasized the difficulty of knowing the other's mind. The Buddha, in the *Sangārava Sūtra,* classifies his predecessors and contemporaries into the traditionalists, the rationalists and the metaphysicians, and the experimentalists who appeal to a personal higher knowledge of the truth. Gautama regarded himself as belonging to this last group.

Of the pre-Buddhistic philosophers who rejected the *brahmanic* belief, especial mention must be made of the Ājivikas, whose leading member was Makkhali Gosala. He believed in strict determinism, rejected freedom of the will, eschewed an atomistic cosmology, and practiced austere asceticism. Other members of the school were Purāṇa Kassapa, Ajita Kesakambali, and Pakudha Kaccāyana. These intellectual rebels had their influence on Gautama as well as on Mahāvīra (599–527 B.C.E.) who founded Jainism. All of these intellectuals rejected sacrificial rituals and Upaniṣadic monism, and all recognized the rule of natural law; they were concerned with the efficacy of *karma* and were skeptical about another world. The two heretical views—*yadṛcchāvāda,* according to which the world is contingent; and *svabhāvavāđa,* for which the world is determined by the nature of things and natural laws—contrasted with *adṛṣtavāđa* and *adhyātmavāđa.* Both of these, in conjunction with tradition, believed in supernaturalism and the spiritual nature of reality.

Of all these, besides Buddhism and Jainism, the one heretical school that is reckoned with in the doxographic literature is Lokāyata, originally one of the branches of Vedic learning, but later surviving as an anti-Vedic materialism. Some trace the origin of Lokāyata to the *dehātmavāda* (the thesis that the self is the body) found in *Chāndogya Upaniṣad* VIII 7-8 (attributed to Virocana). The Jaina author Haribhadra explains the position of Lokāyata to be: "this world extends only to the limits of possible sense-perception."

Founded by Mahāvīra, an older contemporary of the Buddha, who is regarded as the last of the perfected men recognized in the school as prophets, Jainism denied a creator of the universe, looked upon the world as consisting of infinite souls and matter, construed the embodiment of souls as being due to karmic matter (thus having a completely new, materialistic theory of *karma*), and believed in the possibility of the individual attaining perfection through austere practices and contemplative knowledge. Several very sophisticated positions characterize Jaina philosophy: first is the belief that things have infinite aspects (*anantadharmātmakam vastu*), so that no philosophical conceptualization can exhaust its nature. For example, Buddhism is right in its view that things change but wrong in not recognizing that they also have an aspect of permanence. This led the Jaina to develop an elaborate metaphilosophical theory of different possible standpoints (*nayas*) and also a logical theory that rejected the usual two-valued logic and replaced it by a theory of "sevenfold predication" (*saptabhaṇginaya*). For the latter theory—which may be regarded as one of the most outstanding achievements of ancient Indian thought—every judgment, its negation, as well as the conjunction of the two, have an element of truth. Prefix every judgment, the Jaina recommends, with "may be" (*syāt*), meaning there must be a standpoint from which it is true and one from which it is false, another from which it is both, still another from which it is inexpressible. Three more possible "truth values" arise from combinations of these basic four.

Speculations are ripe, if the skeptic Samjaya influenced Mahāvīra, as he, more probably, did influence some of Gautama's skeptical pronouncements. Jacobi proposed that whereas the skeptic Samjaya doubts or denies all four logical possibilities, a Jaina asserts all of them to be true, and that in doing so, Mahāvīra was responding to the skeptic. Matilal suggests that the Jaina sevenfold predication was foreshadowed by the "three-termed" doctrine or *trairāsika* of the Ājivikas, especially of Gosala according to whom everything is of a threefold character (e.g., living, nonliving, and both; existent, nonexistent, and both).

The philosophers and the philosophies reviewed in this section are antitradition, that is anti-Vedic (although some of them, such as the Jaina admitted an eternal self in each living being). To these, we must add another philosophy, which was Vedic, but atheistic, naturalistic in an important sense but admitting an eternal self, one for each individual. This is the Sāṃkhya of Kapila, a legendary figure widely respected for his wisdom even within the Vedic tradition. Already in the Upaniṣads—besides the *ātman-brahman* theory, which later blossomed into the Vedānta school—there was another line of thinking that regarded the world as evolving out of three elements: water, fire, and earth. Even in the technical language of the Sāṃkhya, one Upaniṣad (Śveta V. 7, 8, 12; IV. 5.1.3) describes nature (*prakṛti*) as being three-colored (red, white, and black, standing for *rajas, sattva,* and *tamas,* respectively). It is quite possible that this ancient naturalism was a source of ideas for Buddhism and Jainism. In its mature form, it developed a theory of the evolution of the empirical world out of the original, undifferentiated nature. The three *guṇas,* rendered "qualities," but actually affective components, originally were in a state of equilibrium. This equilibrium was disturbed by contact with *puruṣa,* the self; evolution of nature consists in progressive heterogeneity, in unequal distribution of the three components, and attachment of the self arising out of not distinguishing itself from the psycho-physical complex that is a product of nature. Freedom or *mokṣa,* called loneliness (*kaivalya*), arises from the knowledge that the self is different from nature. While the influence of Sāṃkhya on the religious life is minimal, the Sāṃkhya ideas go into other systems as their components; the distinction between three gunas continues to be an important part of the Hindu view of things, and the Sāṃkhya became the foundation of much of Hindu science, especially of medicine, competing with Vaiśeṣika atomism.

RISE OF THE SYSTEMS: A HISTORICAL CHRONOLOGY UP TO 900 C.E.

The Imperial Mauryas ruled from 322–183 B.C.E.. This is the time of the composition of the *Dharmaśāstras*, more famously of Manu, also of Kautilya's *Arthaśāstra.* In all of these books, the orthodox *brahmanism* sought to preserve and strengthen itself against the anti-Vedic philosophies and their onslaughts. Philosophically more important is Pāṇini's grammar and Patañjali's commentary thereon. It is possible that no other Hindu intellectual achievement has been able to surpass Pāṇini. With the epic *Mahābhārata,* the conception of four ends of life came to be established as an important part of the Hindu view of life. These four ends are *artha*, *kāma*, *dharma,* and *mokṣa,* meaning wealth, sensuous pleasure, righteousness, and freedom from bondage, respectively. The Hindu thinkers then sought to systematize thought about each of these ends, which consisted in defining the goal, laying down the means for achieving it, and classifying the various components as also types of relevant ends and means. Thus arose the *Arthaśāstras,* for example sciences of wealth, *Kāmasūtras,* aphorisms on erotic pleasure, *Dharmaśāstras,* scientific treatises on *dharma,* and *mokṣaśāstra* or scientific treatise on *mokṣa.* Among the latter two, Jaimini's aphorisms on *dharma* and Bādarāyaṇa's Vedānta or *Brahmasūtra* remain the major works, bearing testimony to the Hindu determination to bring order and scientific exposition to unwieldy material in each case. Thus arose the two parts of the Mīmāṃsā system, the system that undertook to interpret the Vedic texts, giving rise to Pûrva Mīmāṃsā and Uṭṭara Mīmāṃsā (or Vedānta), respectively.

It is noteworthy that a new style or genre of philosophical systematization began, one that is very uniquely Indian. This is the genre of the *sūtras* or aphorisms. Out of the disorganized motley of ideas already prevalent, a systematizing genius "formed" a system by composing neatly, systematically, and scientifically a number of aphorisms, brief formulae as they were, easy to memorize and keep one's grip on, however, too cryptic to make clear sense without the aid of explanatory expositions, which soon were bound to follow. It was only natural that whereas the body of aphorisms laid down the general framework of a system, the explanatory expositions or commentaries (*bhāṣya*) made use of and exploited the ambiguity of the aphorisms in order to interpret them in new ways and to let the texts "show" new meanings and interpretive possibilities. Within such adventures, the "systems" or *darśanas,* loosely but misleadingly translatable as "ways of seeing," came into being, seemingly almost from nowhere save the ever-present appeal to the *śruti* or the "heard" texts. Thus we have the *Nyāyasūtra* of Gotama (second c. C.E.), the Commentary of Vātsyāyana (450–500 C.E.); the *Vaiśeṣikasūtra* of Kaṇāda (?), the Commentary of Praśastapada (fifth c. C.E.); the *Mīmāṃsāsūtra* of Jaimini (200 B.C.E.), the Commentary of Bādari (lost) and the Commentary of Śabara (sixth c. C.E.); the *Sāṃkhyasūtra* of Kapila (lost); the *Vedāntasūtra* of Bādarāyaṇa (200 B.C.E.), the Commentary of Śaṃkara and the *Yogasūtra* of Patañjali (200 B.C.E.), the Commentary of Vyāsa (500 C.E.).

Apart from the rise and systematization of the *darśanas,* the period of Imperial Mauryas also witnessed the rise of the *bhakti,* devotional religions. The Greek traveler Magasthenes of fourth century B.C.E. refers to the worship of Vasudeva–Kṛṣṇa: the Pāśupata, Bhāgavata, and Tantra systems come into being. The gods Śiva, Śakti, and Viṣṇu come to the forefront from their minor, sometimes latent, presence in the Vedas. The *Bhagavadgītā,* the song of God, containing Kṛṣṇa's discourse to Arjuna of the Pandava dynasty, emerges from being a chapter of the epic *Mahābhārata* as a major text of Hindu philosophy and religion.

Further development of the systems had to wait several hundred years to take place. What intervened was the Buddhist challenge in the centuries preceding and after the beginning of the Common Era, during the reign of the Kushāna dynasty (first–second c. C.E.) and the Imperial Guptas (320–540 C.E.). During the Kushāna era, the most significant event philosophically was the rise of Mahāyāna Buddhism under the towering genius of Nāgārjuna. Building upon the skeptical questioning of Samjaya, Nāgārjuna may be said to have deconstructed the metaphysical and epistemological concepts and theories of both the Hindus (Nyāya, Vaiśeṣika, Sāṃkhya) and the early Buddhists. His complex dialectical arguments claimed to demonstrate, for one thing, that metaphysics and epistemology presuppose each other, that you cannot begin a metaphysics without assuming an epistemological theory nor can you initiate an epistemological theory without assuming a metaphysics, so that there is no escape from this hopeless circularity. For another, he showed how metaphysical concepts such as rest and motion, part and whole, permanence and change presuppose each other and how each of such concepts involves self-contradictions. The result is a "destruction" of the philosophical–conceptual project *from within,* of philosophy and logic by using their own resources (as a disease is cured by the same poison that causes it, or a thorn is taken out by a thorn). Nāgārjuna was circumspect enough to concede that if his thesis was valid, his own philosophy would suffer the same fate. What will remain is the cognizance of the true intent of Gautama's "silence," of the ineffability of true wisdom, and at the same time of the truth that *nirvāṇa* does not change anything, such that *saṃsara,* the being-in-the-world and *nirvāṇa* are the same.

The age of the Imperial Guptas was a period of intense intellectual activity. In Buddhist philosophy, the Yogācāra school was founded by the two brothers Asanga and Vasubandhu (fourth c. C.E.), and Digñāga laid the foundation of Buddhist logic at the end of the fifth century C.E.. In his commentary on *Nyāyasūtra,* Vātsyāyana not only elaborated the Nyāya doctrines but replied to Nāgārjuna's criticisms of the epistemological project. The *Sāṃkhyakārikā* of Īśvarakṛṣṇa took the place of the not extant *sūtras* of Kapila. *Patañjali's Yogasūtra* came into being. The systems were being consolidated in self-defense.

The seventh and the eighth centuries saw the continuation of the creative work on the foundations laid. In Buddhism, the high point was reached in the works of Dharmakīrti (580–650 C.E.); in Mīmāṃsā, Kumārila's (600–700 C.E.) *Ślokavārttika* made a valiant attempt to meet the Buddhist challenge by defending realism (as opposed to the Yogācāra idealism) and the validity of the scriptures. The period culminated with Śaṃkara, who established his nondualistic Vedānta by interpreting the scriptural texts as much as by systematically refuting the Nyāya-Vaiśeṣika, Sāṃkhya, Buddhism, Jaina, and other competing philosophies. At the same time, Dharmakīrti's logical and epistemological challenges were taken up by Uddyotakara (about 650 C.E.) of the Nyāya school. Vācaspati (900–980 C.E.) and Udayana (984 C.E.) led eventually to the rise of Navya-Nyāya in Mithila under the leadership of Gangeśa Upādhyāya (about 1200 C.E.).

Part 1

Theory of Knowledge (*Pramāṇa Sāśtra*)

Chapter Two

Theory of Knowledge (*Pramāṇa*-Theory)

Every system of Indian philosophy developed its own theory of knowledge. It also developed its own metaphysical theory. It is not often clear which of these two is prior, whether in the logical order or in order of discovery. Expositions by authors differ. In this exposition, the theory of knowledge will be presented first and the metaphysical theory next. As we shall see, they involve and refer to each other.

First, let us start with the key Sanskrit terms. In the earlier prephilosophical discourse, especially in the Upaniṣads, two words were used: *cit* and *jñāna,* both of which are often rendered as "knowledge." In this work, *cit* will be rendered as "consciousness," and *jñāna* as "cognition." Since cognitions may be either true or false, and since only cognitions should be called knowledge, the Sanskrit term for knowledge is not *jñāna* but *pramājñānā* or simply *pramā, apramā* standing for all cognitions that are not true. Whether *cit* or consciousness and *jñānā* or cognition are the same or not is an open question: in some theories such as the Vedānta, they are different, in other theories such as the Nyāya they are the same. We shall return to these questions later on.

The questions that were asked (and that in answering the different systems entered into serious debates) are:

1. What is the ontological nature of consciousness?
2. How is cognition itself cognized?
3. Is *cit* intentional or not?
4. Does a cognition have its own form or is it formless?

Regarding the ontological status of *cit* and cognition, the alternatives that were considered by the philosophers are: it is either a quality of the self to which it belongs, or it is an act of the self, or it is a substance that is identical with the self. The first alternative leaves room for two variations: if consciousness is a quality of the self, it is either an essential quality or a quality that arises only under certain specifiable conditions (and therefore an accidental quality, even if it is true that only a self can have cognitions). Likewise, the third alternative, the view namely that the self is consciousness, allows for various construals, the chief among them being two: the Sāṃkhya-Vedānta view that both self and consciousness are eternal and unchanging, and, in the long run, identical, and the Vijñānavādin Buddhist view that the self is but a succession of cognitive events of various kinds, supported by a deep-lying storehouse consciousness in which the perishing cognitions deposit their traces.

If consciousness were an essential quality of a self, then one had to advance a suitable account of states of deep sleep and swoon when one appears to lose all consciousness whatsoever. This is also a problem for those who identify the self with consciousness. The general strategy adopted by them is to hold that in such states, there is consciousness, only there is no determinate mode of consciousness in the absence of specific objects. There is consciousness of not knowing anything, which makes it possible for a person, upon waking up, to recollect "I did not know anything." But memory requires, for its possibility, traces of past cognitions, and only determinate cognitions, and not consciousness in general, are capable of generating traces. It therefore needs to be explained how a general, indeterminate awareness of nonknowing could leave its traces behind so that one could recollect it. Why not then simply say that upon waking up one simply infers that one did not know anything during the intervening period since one went to bed?

This in fact is the view of the Naiyāyikas and the Vaiśeṣikas: while only the self, of all substances, can have the property of consciousness, the self has this property only when all the necessary causal conditions are satisfied. This happens, when a sense organ is in contact with its proper object, when, in addition, the mind attends to this (technically: the mind is in contact with the sense organ), and the self is in contact with the mind.

If the Vedānta view that the self is consciousness (*cit*) is to be taken seriously, one must nevertheless concede that *cit* is not the same as any specific cognition. Specific cognitions arise and perish depending upon the causal conditions, while, if the Vedānta view is correct, there must be an ever-present (and also ubiquitous) awareness, not identifiable with any determinate state. We seem to be, in that case, getting away from the limits of epistemology into the domain of speculative metaphysics. This perhaps is only seemingly so, for, as we shall see, there is still an important epistemological role of this awareness principle.

Why not then accept the Buddhist view that the self is a stream, or an aggregate, of cognitive events, each such event being a substantive entity, only an instantaneous one? Not unlike Hume, the Buddhist does not find an abiding, enduring self within, and so resolves the putative self into an aggregate of five aggregates (*skandhas*): sensations, feelings, conceptions, traces (of past experiences), and awarenesses. Each of these events, however, is self-cognizing; it shows itself without needing an ever-present *cit* to show or illuminate it. On the Buddhist view, then, *cit* meaning not an ever-present, abiding principle, but the instantaneous event of consciousness, is self-shining.

Regarding question 2, I think one can say that the spiritualistic (*ādhyātmika*) philosophies—the Sāṃkhya-yoga, the Vedānta, and the Buddhist—regard consciousness as self-shining, while the logical (*ānvīkṣikī*) philosophies regard it as an objective property of the self, not capable of showing itself without being the object of another conscious state. Thus we have different answers to the question how a cognition itself is cognized.

On the Naiyāyika theory, a cognition is capable only of manifesting its object, and since it cannot be its own object, it is cognizable only by another cognition, which makes it its object. If the first cognition is called "primary cognition" (*vyavasāya*), the cognition that cognizes the primary cognition should be called "secondary cognition" (*anu-vyavasāya*). A natural objection to this theory is that such an account would generate a hopeless regressus *ad infinitum*, for the secondary cognition, in order to be known, would need a third cognition, and so on. This charge of infinite regress, however, is rejected by the Naiyāyikas. If the primary cognition C_1 is known by C_2, and C_2 by C_3, that by itself does not generate an infinite regress, for C_2 may do its work of manifesting C_1 without itself being cognized. It is not necessary that C_3 be known (unless in each case, possibly excepting in the case of C_1, there is a specific desire to know). As a matter of fact, in accordance with a general rule to the effect that the conditions of outer perception are stronger than the conditions of inner perception, after C_2 one, more often than not, cognizes an external object that is presented to the senses, and so the chain C_1, C_2, ... is interrupted. The decisive point is that C_2, in order to manifest C_1, need not itself be known, and so C_3 need not necessarily arise (unless there is a special desire to have it).

The real problem with the Naiyāyika's theory lies elsewhere. He concedes that C_2 does not *necessarily* follow C_1, that C_1 may do its work of making its object known without itself being cognized. This would be the case if, immediately after C_1, the person, who is the knower, falls into a state of unconsciousness, or possibly dies. C_1 can be followed by C_2 only when there is a desire to cognize C_1. But if C_1, at the time it comes into being, is not itself known (according to the theory under consideration), then how can the subject desire to know it? The very desire to know C_1, by a further act of reflection (which C_2 is), requires, for its very possibility, an acquaintance with C_1, but that would run counter to the theory. There must, therefore, be a pre-reflective acquaintance with C_1 to begin with.

While on the Naiyāyika's theory, C_2 is a reflective, inner perception of C_1, on the theory of the Mīmāṃsakas of the Bhāṭṭa school, C_2 is rather an inferential cognition of the following sort. Once an object O is manifested by C_1 (which is at first unknown), the object O is presented as a known object. In other words, O is presented as having a new property, which may be called "knownness" (*jñātatā*), whereas prior to being known it was merely O. This difference between the mere O and the O as known, for instance, this new property of knownness, needs to be accounted for. One therefore infers that one must have had an act of knowing, in this case C_1, which produced the property of knownness in O. Now, this account of how we come to know C_1 is ingenious, but hardly satisfactory. For one thing, the function of knowledge is simply to manifest its object, and not to effect any change in it, and if that is so the alleged property of knownness is not a real change in O needing a causal explanation. For another, on the explanation given, knownness itself is known, thereby giving rise, in accordance with the theory, to another knownness, and so *ad infinitum*.

A much better theory would seem to be the Prābhākara Mīmāṃsā theory known as threefold perception (*triputi-pratyakṣa*): when I know an object O, the object is known as an *object*, the I is experienced as *subject*, and the knowing is experienced as *knowing*, all at once and together.

The Vedānta of Śaṃkara adds a special dimension to this entire discussion of the question how knowledge is known. The Vedānta brings to the forefront the fact that as one cognizes an object and is aware of knowing it, one is also aware that one was ignorant of that object prior to knowing. Likewise, as one wants to know an object, one is aware of being ignorant of that object now. Thus, awareness of knowing and awareness of ignorance are intimately connected. This awareness should be distinguished from knowledge in the strict sense construed as a cognitive act, an appropriate mental modification (*vṛtti*), which dispels ignorance. Awareness, however, does not dispel ignorance, for we are also aware of ignorance. Of both ignorance and knowledge we are aware. But awareness is self-shining. The Vedānta calls this awareness "witness-consciousness" (*sākṣi-caitanya*). It is the foundation of all knowing, also of nonknowing.

Is consciousness intentional or not? To this question (#3), the Indian philosophers offer different answers. According to the realists, the Nyāya-Vaiśeṣika and the Mīmāṃsā, consciousness is intrinsically intentional (in the Brentano sense), for example, of an object that is really out there. Such a theory naturally has to contend with the fact of error, especially of perceptual illusion. When one mistakes a rope for a snake, that perceptual experience is of a snake that is not really out there. Consequently, the strong thesis of intentionality can be preserved either by holding that the snake that one perceives under illusion is a real snake but not here and now but somewhere else, which one, owing to a special collocation of conditions, perceives here and now (as the Nyāya holds). Or one may contend (as the Mīmāṃsā does) that the snake, which was perceived somewhere else in the past, is remembered now, though the experience is not recognized to be a memory and is not distinguished from the perception of this–there. These theories of error, meant to preserve realism, are beset with many difficulties, which will be discussed in a later context.

The Buddhist, as a consequence, defends a weaker intentionality thesis. A state of consciousness has, as its internal structure, the distinction between an act and its content, *citta* and *caitta*, so that there is no directedness toward an external object. There is only an internal content, or as the Indian epistemologists called it, the *ākāra* or form of a state of consciousness. The perception of a blue jar, as an experience, can then be analyzed into an act of perceiving and a content "blue jar" that internally characterizes that consciousness.

The Advaita Vedānta accepts a compromise position. There are external objects out there. When consciousness objectifies an object, a mental state (called *antaḥkaraṇavṛtti*) assumes the form of that object, and this state is manifested by the self-shining witness-consciousness. Consciousness, in itself, is only self-shining and is not intentional. It is the mind, the inner sense (*antaḥkaraṇa*), which really undergoes modification into the form of the object. Consciousness, as reflected in this modified state, *seems* to be of the object, whereas in reality it is not. Consciousness only appears to be intentional.

We can then say, in response to questions 3 and 4, that:

1. According to Advaita Vedānta, consciousness is intrinsically nonintentional and formless. Intentionality and form or content are superimposed upon it.
2. According to Nyāya-Vaiśeṣika, consciousness is formless, but intrinsically intentional. The object, then, is not a form or content of consciousness, but outside of it, a real other toward which consciousness is directed.
3. According to the Yogācāra Buddhists, consciousness is intentional in the sense that an act-content distinction is internal to it. Other Buddhists, such as the Sautrāntikas, accept the internal act-content distinction, but also admit, over and above the internal content, an external object.

PRAMĀ OR TRUE COGNITION

Cognitions are classified by Indian philosophies into *pramā* and *apramā*, i.e., those that are true (or possess the property called *prāmāṇya*) and those that are not true (or do not possess the property of *prāmāṇya*). Each of these is then divided into various subclasses. Before we consider the proposed types of true and not-true cognitions, we need to ask, What is meant by *prāmāṇya* (or the property of being a true cognition)?

PRĀMĀṆYA: ITS DEFINITIONS

What is *prāmāṇya*? There are three types of views on this question in Indian philosophy. The first of these takes *prāmāṇya* to mean *yāthārthya* (the property of being like the object). A further explication of this latter concept is: "the knowledge of that as that" (*tasminstaditi pratyayaḥ*). It is knowledge that does not deviate from its object. Later authors further refined this mode of defining truth into: "if x is in y in the relation R, then the experience of x as being in y in the relation

R is a true cognition" (*tadvati tatprakārakatva*). This version of what may be called the correspondence theory of truth was considerably refined and improved upon by the neo-Naiyāyikas.

A second type of definition of truth is advanced by the Buddhists: truth is the property of causing successful practical response (*saphalapravṛttijanakatva*). Almost every school of Indian philosophy—except possibly the Advaita Vedāntins, for reasons to be given below—recognized such a pragmatic account as a test of truth, but only the Buddhists advanced it as the nature of truth. A cognition on the Buddhist view is true if and only if the practical response it generates leads to success.

A third type of account of truth is given by the Advaita Vedāntins. They reject a correspondence theory on the ground that when one mistakenly perceives something (i.e., hallucinates a snake where there is none), the object of that misperception is that snake that possesses the predicate "snakeness" and so satisfies the criterion of truth. They reject the pragmatist account on the grounds that when one is thirsty in a dream, and in the dream drinks water, his or her dream thirst is quenched (within dreaming) so that the judgment "that is water" within the dream gives rise to successful practice, and so should be true. For the Vedāntin, therefore, there is no generalized positive criterion of truth. The only workable definition is negative: a cognition is true if and only if it is not contradicted by subsequent experience. This would render—as should be clear—all empirical cognitions only provisionally true. The only definition of truth, which is not provisional, would be "that which, in principle, cannot be contradicted by any experience." On this theory, this strong requirement is satisfied only by knowledge of pure consciousness: to contradict, or to negate it is to affirm it and so makes it incoherent.

TYPES OF *PRAMĀṆA*

Every system of Indian philosophy defended a list of types of true cognition. The Sanskrit word for "true cognition" is *pramā*. *Pramāṇa* means "that by which true cognition is arrived at" (*pramīyate anena*); it may be taken then to be a cause of, or a means for, achieving true cognition. It is a peculiar feature of the Indian epistemologies that this causal meaning of *pramāṇa* is also taken to imply a legitimizing sense so that a cognition is true in case it is brought about in the right sort of way, for example caused by a *pramāṇa*. A classification of true cognition (or *pramā*) is also a classification of the causes of true cognition (or *pramāṇa*).

The following list of *pramāṇas*, as recognized in the different systems of philosophy, would be helpful:

Lokāyata	Perception
Buddhism	Perception, Inference
Vaiśeṣika	Perception, Inference

Sāṃkhya	Perception, Inference, Word
Nyāya	Perception, Inference, Comparison, Word
Vedānta	Perception, Inference, Comparison, Postulation, Word, Nonperception
Bhāṭṭa Mīmāṃsā	Perception, Inference, Comparison, Postulation, Word, Nonperception
Prābhākara Mīmāṃsā	Perception, Inference, Comparison, Postulation, Word

As the foregoing list shows, all schools accepted perception as a true cognition and correspondingly as a cause of true cognition. However, they did not all agree regarding the nature of perception, or, for that matter, regarding any of the others they accepted in common. One major difference that divided the schools concerns the relation between the cognition and its causal conditions. Such schools as the Nyāya, Vaiśeṣika, and Mīmāṃsā sharply separated the causal process (*pramāṇa*) and its result—the cognition itself (*pramā*). Others such as the Buddhists of the Vijñānavāda school and the Jains regarded the cognition itself to be both *pramāṇa* and *pramā*, so in effect rejected that distinction by regarding a cognition to be self-producing. For the present, overlooking this controversy—which has to do with an externalist and causal point of view versus an internalist point of view—let us consider each of the *pramāṇas*.

PERCEPTION (*PRATYAKṢA*)

There are two types of definition of perception in Indian philosophy. First, the definition given in terms of how perceptual cognition is caused; second, the definitions that are in terms of the nature of the cognition.

In terms of how the cognition is caused, the most common definition is that of the Nyāya: perceptual cognition is that cognition that is caused by the contact of the sense organs with their respective objects. The Nyāya adds that for the cognition to arise, two more contacts are needed: namely, contact of the mind (*manas*) with the senses (the sense-object contact, in the absence of attention, may not cause cognition) and contact of the self with the mind (which is absent in deep sleep). Since this definition does not apply to God's perception (the Nyāya believed in God and held that God has no sense organs), later Naiyāyikas advanced a negative definition: perception is that cognition that is not caused by another cognition (that excludes inferential cognition, which has among its causes prior knowledge of the invariable coexistence of the middle term and the major; excludes memory, since memory is caused by past cognition; and also excludes verbal knowledge, which has, among it causes, knowledge of the meanings of words).

Definitions that appeal to the nature of cognition are of three kinds. The first, possibly the earliest such definition, is that of Digñāga, the Buddhist logician: "perception is a cognition which is free from any concept" (*kalpanāpodhaṃ*). Dharmakīrti added the clause "which is unerring" (*abhrāntaṃ*) in order to indicate that in pure sensation we are in touch with ultimate reality. Digñāga had given a list of conceptual constructions (*kalpanā*), which should be excluded from perception. These are proper names, class names, qualities, motions (verbal names), substance-names. These are all "mere names." Perception, excluding as it does all the above, is reduced to the pure sensation, whose object is the unique, ineffable nature of an instantaneous event.

The second way of defining perception in terms of its cognitive features is to be found in the Jaina epistemology. The Jainas define perception in terms of its vividness (*viṣadaṃ pratyakṣaṃ*). Perception manifests its object with clarity and distinctness and manifests it as a substance (e.g., as gold) and also in its modes (e.g., as yellow). It is also conceptual inasmuch as it manifests universal features of objects. Consequently, the Jaina rejects the Buddhist's ineffable, nonconceptual, pure sensation.

A third way of defining perception without bringing in how it is caused is in terms of immediacy. Perceptuality is immediacy (*aparokṣa*). What is immediately apprehended is consciousness. Consciousness as such is perceptual. This is the view of the Advaita Vedāntin. However, in a perception of a definite object such as this book in front of me, the object and my consciousness achieve a certain identity. This happens insofar as—here the account becomes in a peculiar way causal—the inner sense assumes the "form" of the object, and as so "formed" becomes identical with the consciousness of the knower.

It is possible to maintain that each of these definitions relies upon an aspect of perceptual experience, or even that a definition singles out some aspect, or even shows some type of perception. So let us turn to classification of various types of perception.

TYPES OF PERCEPTION

1. There have been since very ancient times two extreme views about perception, and the later theories sought to find room for both while limiting each. These two views were those of the Grammarians, most notably Bhartṛhari, and the Buddhists. The Grammarians held that all cognition, and so all perception, is linguistic. They based this view on the claim that a thing and its name are inseparable, such that to know, be it perceptually or otherwise, fire is to know it as something that is called "fire." (You may know it simply as something bright, then you know it as what is called "bright.") Hence Bhartṛhari's famous statement to the effect that all cognition is penetrated by language. Completely opposed to this is the view of the Buddhist, represented by Digñāga, that perception must be free from

all *kalpanā*, for instance, all conceptuality within which Digñāga also includes "names" (*nāma*). Consequently only pure, ineffable, sensory intake of what is given should be called perception.

Most Hindu philosophies—Nyāya, Vaiśeṣika, Sāṃkhya, Mīmāṃsā, and Vedānta—dealt with this opposition by recognizing that there are two stages of perception, or rather two stages of the unfolding of perception: at first, with the contact of the sense organ with its object, there occurs a purely indeterminate, nonconceptual, nonlinguistic experience which is followed by a conceptual and linguistic cognition more akin to what may be called perceptual judgment. The former is called *nirvikalpaka* perception, the latter *savikalpaka* perception. The Jainas rejected the former, making all perception conceptual; the Buddhists rejected the latter.

But even those who would have both gave different accounts, especially of the first, namely, *nirvikalpaka*. When Digñāga, as said before, defined perception as "free from all concepts," he was obviously defining *nirvikalpaka* perception, and, in his view, that alone deserves to be called perception. But the Buddhist, in so doing, was assuming an ontology of bare particulars. The Naiyāyika, on the other hand, has a more complex ontology: not only particulars but also universals are real. So when my visual sense organ is in contact with an object, say this table before me, it apprehends not only the particular table or the particular brown color that pervades its surface, but also the universals tableness and brownness. Thus the *nirvikalpaka* does apprehend universals as well as particulars. Only, it does not knit them together into a structured whole, it does not know that this table is brown. The latter involves language and a subject-predicate relation, to say the least. Without the former, the latter is not possible. In order to know that A is qualified by B, we ought to be already presented with A and B separately, so argues the Naiyāyika. This view seems to imply that in the prior, indeterminate perception, we apprehend several entities (this table, tableness, this shade of brown, brownness) together but not as related, so that the cognition has the form "A and B and C and D," it is what is called one cognition of various unrelated entities (*samuhālambanajñāna*), though not as unrelated. This first-level perception is prior to the distinction between truth and falsity. It is of the second-level perceptual judgment ("The A that is B is also C and D") that truth and falsity in the strict sense hold good. Besides, for the Naiyāyika, the first-level perception is not a psychological reality, it is not experienced to be so; the only way we can know of its occurrence is through an inference of the following kind: "In order to be able to know that this A is B, we must have already apprehended all the constituent terms separately."

The Advaita Vedāntins also recognize a stage of indeterminate perception that precedes perceptual judgment. But on their view what is apprehended to begin with is no determinate object or feature, but an indeterminate unqualified "something," mere existence (*sat*). We first see something there; this experience is soon replaced by "that is a tree," when the "something" is determined to be "a tree," which introduces a conceptual element. This view has been seriously challenged by Rāmānuja who, in his commentary on *Brahmasūtra* 1.1.1., insists that all perception is of an object as being such and such, and that what is called indeterminate perception is perception of an object the kind of which one is perceiving for the first time (in which case one has not yet learned to categorize it). From the second time onwards, the perception is determinate.

It should be remembered that one's ontology is clearly reflected in one's theory of indeterminate perception, such that whatever one perceives in this way, for example, free from all conceptual intervention, must be *eo ipso* real.

2. The Naiyāyikas, besides distinguishing between outer perception and inner (*mānasa*) perception (of one's present inner states, such as cognition, desire, pleasure and pain, and so on), had to develop an elaborate theory of how all the various types of entities that they hold we perceive are in contact with the sense organs. It is natural to expect that we can sensuously apprehend only particular sensory qualities, and, besides, possibly sensible substances. But for many Indian epistemologies, especially for Nyāya, we also have sensory perception of appropriate universals. According to this theory, if a sensory or qualitative particular is capable of being grasped by a sense organ, so is the universal it instantiates. The universal is also capable of being in contact with the appropriate sense organ. Only, the mode of contact is different. Uddyotakạra, in his *Vārttika* on Vātsyāyana's commentary on the Nyāyasūtras, developed an elaborate theory of "contact" (*sannikarṣa*), making use of Nyāya ontology of relations. According to this ontology, two substances can enter into a relation of "touching" (*saṃyoga*); a quality belonging to a substance has a relation of inherence to the substance, and universals inhere in the particulars that instantiate them. Keeping in mind that a sense organ is also a substance, let us consider a simple case of visually perceiving a blue jar. In this case:

1. The relation between the visual sense organ and the jar is one of simple contact (*saṃyoga*).
2. Since the blue color inheres in the jar, the visual sense organ relates to the color by the relation "inherence in what is conjoined" (*samyukta-samavāya*).
3. Since the blueness inheres in the blue color (which inheres in the jar), the relation of the sense organ to blueness is "inherence in what inheres in what is conjoined" (*samyukta-samaveta-samavāya*).

Thus several relations may be nested together in some order to constitute a complex relation of sense organs to a particular thing such as a blue jar.

3. We need to introduce a distinction that plays an important role in the theory of perception of Advaita Vedānta: this is the distinction between perception as a mental modification (*vṛtti*) and perception by the "witness consciousness" (*sākṣī-pratyakṣa*). On this theory, in the perceptual situation, the inner sense acquires the form of the object, and this mental modification removes the veil of ignorance, which conceals the object prior to its being

known. However, there are objects that do not have an unknown existence, for example, which are known as soon as they exist (or, for whom to exist is to be perceived). Such are pleasure and pain, such are also the mental modifications or cognitive acts themselves. So also is ignorance itself, of which we are never ignorant. Hence the question, how do we know them? We surely seem to know them perceptually immediately. According to Advaita Vedānta, they are directly presented to witness-consciousness without needing a corresponding cognitive act or mental modification as is the case with external objects. Witness-perception, on this theory, underlies all cognition, it is the immediate presentation to consciousness of a cognitive act (which, on its part, manifests its object), also of pleasure and pain, and of ignorance, indeed of all things that do not have unknown existence.

4. The Naiyāyikas also distinguish between ordinary (*laukika*) and extraordinary (*alaukika*) perception. "Extraordinary perception" does not mean such perception that only extraordinarily gifted persons can have. In most cases, it means perceptions that are caused by modes of contact that are not one of the types enumerated under sensory perceptions. Three kinds of such extraordinary perceptions are listed: perception of the *yogis* (which is the only kind that requires special powers), perception of all particulars coming under a universal, and perception mediated by prior cognitive association (the latter two being very frequent occurrences). The *yogis* develop the power of perceiving things far away in space, things in the future, and things that are very small. Not much is said about the mechanism of this kind of cognition. The second kind of extraordinary perception occurs when seeing a cow as a cow, one perceives the universal "cowness," and since this universal is instantiated in all cows, one also has a perceptual cognition (a sort of sensory contact mediated by the universal cowness) of all such instances *qua* instantiating cowness. The third kind of extraordinary perception occurs when on seeing a lump of snow, one also sees that the snow is cold, or when seeing a piece of velvet one sees that it is soft. In such cases coldness or softness, though not proper objects of visual perception, are nevertheless presented to vision by being mediated by prior cognitive association. The second kind of contact is known as "contact through a universal" (*sāmānyalakṣanāpratyāsatti*), while the third kind is called "contact through a cognition" (*jñānalakṣaṇāpratyāsatti*). Those who do not accept such modes of perception do not deny the experiences, but would deny their perceptuality, taking them to be either imagination or memory or simple inferences.

INFERENCE (*ANUMĀNA*)

Next to perception, the most discussed means of knowing for the Indian philosophers is inference. The Sanskrit term for it is "*anumāna,*" etymologically meaning a cognition that follows upon some other cognition or cognitions ("*anu*" = "after"; "māna" = "cognition"). This is the case when upon seeing smoke on the yonder hill, I infer that the hill must have fire.

Leaving aside the materialist Lokayatas, all Indian philosophers recognize inference as a valid means of knowing. The materialist's critique of inference is based on the argument that it is impossible to determine, with certainty, the universal premise stating the copresence of the middle and the major (in the above example, between smoke and fire). This gives rise to the question; How is this universal premise arrived at? This question is different from the question regarding the structure of inferential cognition. It is this part of Indian epistemology that may properly be called "logic." Logic is thus a part of the theory of knowledge or *pramāṇasāśtra*. Inference is studied as a means of true cognition. However, it is possible to carve out of this account of inference a part—separating it from the cognitive and psychological parts—which is concerned with inference patterns and the distinction between sound and unsound inference and so, in a stricter sense, deserves the title of logic.

Logic, in India, goes back to the tradition of debating over religious and moral matters. Rules were laid down for debating. In course of time, rules of evidence and argument were formulated. Gautama's *Nyāyasūtra* presents an account of the structure of a good argument, which, on his view must have five "limbs" (*avayavas*): first, a statement of the thesis to be established ("there is fire on the hill"); second, a statement of reason ("because there is smoke"); third, giving an example of the underlying rule ("wherever there is smoke, there is fire, as in the kitchen"); fourth, "this case is like that"; and finally, affirmation of the thesis as proven ("therefore, there is fire on the hill"). This is the Nyāya account of a sound inference. Other philosophers, such as the Buddhists, proposed to reduce this elaborate structure into a simpler one.

An important step in the history of Indian logic was taken by the Buddhist philosopher Digñāga. Digñāga was concerned with what makes a mark or sign (*liṅga*) a good one (as "smoke" is of "fire"). He laid down three characteristics: the mark (or sign) should be present in the case under consideration, or the *pakṣa* (the smoke must be present in the hill); it should be present in a case (the kitchen) where the inferred property ("fire" in this case) is known to be present (*sapakṣa*); and it should not be present in cases (such as a lake) where the property to be inferred (e.g., fire) is known to be absent (i.e., in a *vipakṣa*). A sign or mark that satisfies these three requirements is said to be nondeviating. Digñāga developed this thesis in a remarkable tract known as "the wheel of reason" (*hetucakra*), the details of which we cannot enter into in this book.

The focus of attention of the Indian logicians, both Buddhist and Hindu, came to be centered on the nature of universal concomitance of the mark or sign or reason (*liṅga*) and the property being inferred (*sādhya*), in our example, between "smoke" and "fire." Let the sign be x and the inferred property be y. On Digñāga's view, to say that there is *vyāpti* (= universal concomitance or pervasion) between x and y is to say that all cases of x are cases of y, and only cases of y are cases of x. Dharmakīrti went further into the nature of this relation and distinguished between two types of *vyāpti*: in one case, y is the own-nature or essence of x, or there is an identity between the two (and the relation is analytic). (The example he gives is "this is a tree, for it is a śimśapā-tree.") In the other case, the relation between the mark and the inferred is one of causality (as in "there is fire, because there is smoke"), in which case the relation is synthetic. The Naiyāyikas reduced all these into one type, and came up with several extensional definitions. Perhaps the best of these is the following. There is *vyāpti* between x and y if:

x is absent in all those instances where y is absent. If x = smoke, and y = fire, then fire can be validly inferred from smoke if there obtains between them a relation such that smoke is absent in all those instances (such as a lake) where fire is absent. This, as we know, is true.

Now, how does inference as a cognition arise? Here, I turn to the Naiyāyikas who give a psychological account. The account runs, in brief, as follows: A person sees smoke on the top of a mountain. On seeing smoke, he remembers the law "wherever there is smoke, there is fire," which he had already learned, and he adduces the instance of his kitchen where this law is instantiated. This memory leads him to see the smoke on the mountain in a new light; he now sees the smoke as that which is always accompanied or *pervaded* by fire. Once this last cognition, known as *parāmarśa* (or "consideration"), occurs, he will necessarily have the inferential cognition of the form "that mountain possesses fire."

This psychological sequence also corresponds to the logical sequence. Logic and psychology coincide; or, rather, if the logic appears to be psychological, psychology of reasoning is also logicized. The logical structure represents not how we ought to infer, but how, as a matter of fact, we do infer.

The subject of inferential cognition, in our example, the mountain—technically called the *pakṣa* or the minor term, the subject term of the conclusion—must, in order to be able to play that role, satisfy certain requirements. If there is certainty that there is fire on the mountain, there would be no inference, unless there is a specific desire to infer (i.e., to establish by inference what may otherwise be already known to be the case). So certainty accompanied by absence of desire to infer inhibits inferential cognition from arising. Consequently, what is necessary for the mountain, in our example, to be the subject (*pakṣa*) of inferential cognition of fire is that there should be absence of certainty accompanied by absence of desire to infer (*siśādhayiṣāvirahaviśiṣtasiddhyabhāva*).

In this psychologistic logic of inference, the so-called fallacies are not errors of inference, but rather hindrances to inference. A fallacy is really a "seeming reason or mark" (*hetvābhāsa*), which, if recognized, would prevent the inferential cognition from arising.

The so-called problem of induction is also discussed by Indian philosophers, the Buddhists and the Naiyāyikas alike. Their question is, How is *vyāpti*—universal concomitance between the mark and the inferred property—ascertained? There are, in short, three sorts of responses. The materialists, such as the Lokāyatas, hold that the universal relation cannot be determined, there being always room for doubt about the unobserved cases. The Buddhists, especially Dharmakīrti, give a metaphysical response: we can determine the relation only if we can determine either the relation of essential identity or the relation of cause and effect between the two terms. But this gives rise unavoidably to the question, How are these latter relations to be ascertained? If by observation, then we resort to the third, the Naiyāyika response. We ascertain the relation of universal concomitance between x and y by perceiving that in all cases the presence of x is accompanied by the presence of y, and not perceiving any instance to the contrary.

ŚABDA OR SOUND (UTTERANCE)

Leaving aside the Lokāyatas, the Buddhists, and the Vaiśeṣikas, all other schools of Indian philosophy recognize that utterances of sentences by competent speakers are a major source of our knowledge, and a *pramāṇa*. Thus a large part of what we know about the world is derived from such utterances (and, by extension, from written texts). Our knowledge of what we ought or ought not to do, and also of supersensible realities, is derived from the scriptural texts. Those who recognize *śabda* to be a distinct *pramāṇa* do so not only because words alone generate much of our knowledge, but also because such knowledge is not reducible to some other kind of knowledge, most plausibly to inference. The Vaiśeṣikas defend the last mentioned reduction of *śabda* to inference. Others not only challenge such a reduction, but also demonstrate that the reduction is not possible. That hearing a competent speaker generates belief is a rather uncontroversial fact. The Indian epistemologists maintained a stronger thesis, namely, that it can, and does, under certain circumstances, generate knowledge or true cognition.

One can distinguish between three sets of conditions that must be fulfilled, so that upon hearing an utterance, one may be able to make a justified claim that one knows that something is the case. These sets of conditions are utterer conditions, linguistic conditions, and understanding conditions. Briefly, they are as follows.

Utterer Conditions

The hearer must be in the presence of the utterer when he makes the utterance. The utterer must be competent (*āpta*). Here "competence" includes intellectual competence (= the utterer must know what he is talking about) and moral competence (= he or she must be sincere and truthful). The utterer must also be known to be competent.

Linguistic Conditions

These are conditions that must be satisfied in order that an utterance is the utterance of a sentence. For this purpose, the traditional Indian philosophers enumerated three requirements: contiguity (*āsatti*), syntactic intention (*ākaṇksā*), and semantic appropriateness (*yogyatā*). The first is that utterances of words must follow each other in close temporal succession (a condition that can be suitably modified to apply to written texts as well). The second requires that utterance of a word must be followed by one from a suitable syntactical category such that the two convey a unified meaning ("close the window" does, but "close the" does not satisfy this requirement). The third requirement is that the succeeding word must not only be syntactically appropriate, but also semantically appropriate ("virtue is green" is syntactically all right, but semantically not).

Understanding conditions

The hearer would be able to know that something is the case upon hearing a competent speaker utter a sentence only if she or he also understands the meaning of the sentence. For this purpose, she or he must understand the meanings of the component words, recognize the syntactical and semantic appropriateness, be able to unify the component word meanings into one related meaning, and be able to disambiguate a sentence, when necessary, by identifying the intention of the speaker (*tātparya*).

It is quite possible that recognition of *śabda* as a *pramāṇa* was felt to be necessary in order to legitimize the claim that the scriptural texts are irreducible sources of our knowledge of supersensible realities and of ethical rules. But the theory was soon extended to include also ordinary linguistic discourse. Thus, one may say, *śabda* is of two kinds, ordinary (*laukika*) and extraordinary (*a-laukika*). Epistemologically, the philosopher must be able to make a convincing case about the former before he can apply it to the latter, and the more controversial, case. Alternately, philosophers were not lacking who conceded that our word-generated knowledge of empirical matter is reducible to inference, while still maintaining that our knowledge of what one ought or ought not to do derives irreducibly from the scriptures or other ethical texts.

THEORY OF MEANING

The chapter on *śabda* is the place where the Indian philosophers invariably discuss the themes of philosophy of language, especially the problem of meaning.

Naturally enough, this problem divides into two categories: word meaning and sentential meaning.

As regards word meaning, we find an array of views ranging from the Mīmāṃsā theory that words designate universals (the word "cow" means cowness) and the Nyāya theory that words mean neither bare particulars nor universals but particulars as qualified by universals, to the Buddhist's theory that words mean exclusion or *apoha* ("cow" means "not not-cow"). The Mīmāṃsā theory makes a strong case for its view by arguing that the word "cow" cannot mean any particular cow (for then the word cannot apply to other cows), nor can it mean all cows, for the totality of cows is an entity that is always changing while the meaning of "cow" is not changing with that change. If the meaning is to be invariable and constant, then it cannot but be the universal cowness whose identity is not affected by changing particular instantiations. Note that for similar reasons the Mīmāṃsā had to uphold the thesis of eternity of words (*śabdanityatva*), and to distinguish the real word from its changing manifestations (utterances, accents, and pronunciations).

But, then, if the meaning of a word be a universal, how then does a sentence like "bring the cow" make sense? The act of bringing can relate only to a particular cow, not to cowness. Consequently, the Nyāya theory prefers to hold that the word "cow" rather means a particular cow as qualified by the universal cowness (*jātiviśiṣtavyakti*).

The Buddhist's theory of meaning is necessitated by his or her rejection of universal entities, as also of individual substances, from his or her ontology. The shared feature by virtue of which the same word "cow" is applied to all cows need not be a universal property called "cowness," it may simply be what they all are not. The negative class "noncow," which is excluded, need not be a real universal, but a constructed concept. This theory, advanced by Digñāga, and Dharmakīrti, has led to various further innovations from Buddhist philosophers and criticisms from the opponents. The chief objection is the obvious point that the idea of "noncow" already implies, and presupposes, the concept of "cow" and so the positive universal "cowness." The Buddhist's response has been that the use of the word "cow" (in "noncow") need not commit us to posit the universal "cowness." The name "cow" alone will serve the purpose. Thus there is an ontological economy but possibly a proliferation of "constructed concepts" to be brought in as needed.

With regard to meanings of sentences, the philosophers were concerned with two different questions: in the first place, does the meaning, even of indicative sentences, consist only in the facts they state, or does the meaning consist in some relevance to possible action that they invoke the audience to undertake? In the second place, and more important, the philosophers ask, Which is prior, word meaning or sentence meaning? In other words, is the sentence meaning compounded of, and constructed out of, word meanings or, is the word meaning derived from the sentential meaning by abstraction so that the sentence is the original home of the word?

With regard to the first question, the Prābhākaras hold the latter of the two alternative positions. They say something like this: if a friend of mine tells me "There is a snake out there in the garden," he is stating a fact because—and this is his intention—he wishes to warn me from going into the garden without a stick in my hand. I think they would have made a more effective case had they distinguished between meaning of the sentence and meaning of the utterer when he or she utters the sentence. Most other Indian philosophers of language either allowed for the distinction between meanings of indicative sentences and meanings of sentences in the imperative mood (reserving the former to be facts and the latter to be possible modes of acting) *or* regarded all sentences to mean some fact or other. This controversy becomes moot in the case of the sentences of the Upaniṣads, which clearly appear to be stating facts, sentences such as "Thou art that," "I am he." As contrasted with these, there are Vedic sentences that have the imperative form, "If you wish to attain such and such a goal, you must perform such and such ritual." The Prābhākaras sought to reduce all to the latter form, maintaining that all the Vedic texts together constitute one text of which the Vedas and the Upaniṣads form only succeeding chapters. The Vedāntins, to the contrary, regarded the Vedas as the *karmakāṇda*, the part devoted to action and the Upaniṣads as the *jñānakāṇda*, the part devoted to knowledge. In this scheme the above cited sentences of the Upaniṣads state an "eternally true" fact (namely, the identity of self and the brahman) and do not recommend a course of action.

More central to philosophy of language is the other question: which of the two—word meaning or sentence meaning—is prior? The Naiyāyikas and followers of Kumārila's school of Mīmāṃsā accorded priority to word meanings and regarded sentential meanings to be constructed out of word meanings. This theory is called *abhihitānvayavāda* or the theory of "relation of designata." Different varieties of the opposite view—namely, that a sentential meaning is prior to word meanings—known as *anvitābhidhānavāda* or the theory that a sentence designates a relational complex, are defended by the Prābhākara school of Mīmāṃsā (and Vedānta). Let us briefly consider the two theories, which may be regarded as Indian equivalents of the so-called composition and context principles of Frege.

The Naiyāyikas argue, in support of their contention, that unless one has prior understanding of a word, one cannot understand the sentences in which that word occurs. Furthermore, if a word is understood only as related to other words in a sentence, it cannot be explained how one could understand a new sentence in which that word occurs. The new sentence would have a new relational meaning, which the auditor has never before encountered. Thus if the word "sky" means the relational complex "sky is blue," the auditor upon hearing the sentence "sky is dark" would not have any understanding of the sentence. Since a word can function in many different sentences, which of the different contexts, or rather, which of the different relational meanings, does the word have? Since the word retains its own meaning in these contexts, would it not be better—so they argue—

to say that a word has its own meaning prior to a sentential context and that in a sentence the word meaning enters into relation with the meanings of the other words figuring in that sentence? The other theory obliterates the difference between the way a *varṇa* or phoneme is a part of a word (the former by itself having no meaning, the word being the simplest meaningful unit) and the way a word is a part of a sentence.

The Mīmāṃsā defenders of the opposed theory argue for the priority of sentential meaning. If the meaning of a word is the contribution it makes to a sentential meaning, it can make that contribution only in conjunction with the other words. A bare word such as "bring" signifies an incompletely qualified action (which is to bring some appropriate object, the meaning becomes complete only in a sentence such as "Bring a cow"). What the theory then amounts to is not that a word's meaning is always related to another specifiable word (like "bring" to "cow"), but rather that a word meaning must be related to another word meaning of an appropriate type. The alleged knowledge of word meaning that is prior to understanding a sentence in which the word functions is really—on the Mīmāṃsā theory—nothing but understanding some other sentences in which that word functions. As against the Nyāya atomism of word meanings, the Mīmāṃsā theorists insist that a sentential meaning could not possibly emerge out of a string of unrelated meanings. What we need is a prior sentential context like "Bring the ____" in which the words "cow" and "horse" could play their roles.

The discussion is carried ahead into the field of language learning. There was no disagreement as to the facts of learning the meaning of a new word through the stages of varying the contexts ("bring a cow," "bring a horse") and introducing a new word ("bring a cow," "take back the cow"). They, however, construed the facts differently.

It may be safe to conclude that the Nyāya was correct in holding that a word has its own meaning, but overemphasized the independence of its meaning. The Mīmāṃsā was right in emphasizing that the sentential meaning is more than a mere set of self-complete word meanings, that the meanings of the component expressions need each other for completion, and that only a sentential meaning is, in the Fregean sense, "saturated." It should be added that the theory of *anvitābhidhāna* (or relatedness-designatum theory) is of two kinds. A sentential meaning is either relatedness to an action (*kāryānvitābhidhāna*) or relatedness to any other meaning. The former is the view of Prabhākara himself and amounts to saying that the meaning of every sentence must relate to some mode of action. In that case there would be no purely existential sentences.

DIFFERENT KINDS OF MEANING

The different kinds of word meaning are rather different ways words are related to the things they designate. First of all, it is obvious that determinate words relate to determinate things. "Cow" denotes cows (it should be added, as qualified by cowness). But what is the relation between "cow" and cow? One view, held by the Grammarians, is that the two are related by "*tādātmya,*" i.e., a relation of such identity as is compatible with their difference. This view is rejected by most other philosophers. Word and thing, they argue, are so different that the word "fire" cannot burn, while fire does. Let the relation between the two then be one of "designatum-designator" (*vācya-vācaka*). The relation is also called "*abhidhā*" or denoting the primary designatum. This is an eternal and natural relation between the two. This is the view of the Mīmāṃsākas.

A third view is that the relation between "cow" and cow is not natural, but conventional, which is based on the desire and the decision of the form "let this word denote that thing." We know that men build a thing to which they give a name. Based on these well-known cases of "giving a name" the Naiyāyikas hypothesize that what underlies and makes possible the relation between a word in a natural language and its primary designatum is a similar decision by God.

Besides the primary meaning of a word (and so of a sentence), many philosophers also recognized a secondary meaning known as *lakṣaṇā*. Thus in the expression "The village on the Ganges," the name "Ganges" means not the stream of water of the famous river, but the bank of that river. Without invoking this secondary meaning, it would not be possible to give the expression a consistent interpretation. Formally, secondary meaning may be defined as what relates to the primary meaning.

The Vedāntins, who made use of "secondary meaning" in interpreting scriptural texts, distinguished between two kinds of secondary meanings of sentences. One is the simple secondary meaning (*kevalalakṣaṇā*) as in the example given above. The other is where the intended meaning relates to the primary meaning through several mediating links. For example, the word "*dvirepha*" in Sanskrit means "having two r's," but secondarily means the word "*bhramara*" (which has two "r's"), but is here intended to mean "bee," which is what "*bhramara*" directly refers to.

The Vedāntins also classify secondary meaning into three kinds: one that refers to a secondary meaning while not using its primary meaning (as when the utterance "Eat poison" is intended to warn the addressee against going to dine with an enemy); the second in which a word refers to its secondary meaning while also exercising its primary meaning function (as in the case of "white jar," where the word white, whose primary meaning is the white color, instead refers to a white thing); the third in which an expression surrenders a part of its primary meaning (as in the case of "Thou art that" (*tat tvam asi*), where the words "thou" and "that" surrender part of their meanings such that the former does not mean the finite person and the latter does not mean the omniscient *brahman*, but both secondarily mean the pure consciousness, which is common to both). The first kind is called *jahat-lakṣaṇā*, the second is called *ajahat-lakṣaṇā*, and the third is called *jahat-ajahat-lakṣaṇā*.

Besides primary and secondary meanings, some philosophers recognize a third meaning called *vyanjanā*. If the word "Ganges" also means the coolness of the water of the river and the sacredness of the river, such meanings, in order to be conveyed, require another relation called *vyanjanā*.

The Naiyāyikas recognize only two meanings: primary and secondary. They want to explain the way "Ganges" conveys the sense of coolness and sacredness by either a sort of "extraordinary perception" called "perception mediated by prior knowledge" (*jñāna-lakṣaṇā*) or an inferential process. The idea of *vyanjanā* being a kind of meaning *sui generis* is used by the Indian aestheticians. We shall briefly expound their theory of poetic meaning in the chapter on aesthetics.

We still have to ask the question, How is the relation between a word and its meaning known? In other words, how do we determine that the word "water" means the tasteless, colorless liquid? On this matter, the theorists agreed that the power of a word to convey meaning is ascertained by grammar, comparison or *upamāna* (e.g., the word "*gavaya*" means an animal that resembles a cow); dictionary, the instructions by those who know; common usage, how sentences end; and further explication. Of these four, the most important is "usage" (or *vyavahāra*). The secondary meaning is ascertained by the determination that without assuming that the word in the case under consideration has this secondary meaning the compound expression or the entire sentence would not make sense.

There remains another question about "word" as a source of knowing, which will be briefly discussed here. That question is, To whom does the meaning relation that obtains between word and thing really belong? Does this relation belong to the word that is uttered by the speaker? The uttered word consists of perishing sounds, which, by the time the last sound is produced, are all gone save the last one; these sounds never form a whole, a totality, which we can call the word to which the power of signification could possibly be ascribed. Faced with this difficulty, the Grammarians distinguish between the word as a type and the token utterances of that type. The type is regarded by them as eternal, which neither is produced nor perishes. This word type is called *sphoṭa*. A similar distinction is drawn in the case of sentences—between a sentence-*sphoṭa* and its utterances. The Naiyāyikas, however, find this idea of *sphoṭa* to be too metaphysical and maintain that although an utterance (of a word) is a succession of sounds, when the last phoneme is uttered, all the previous phonemes are collectively remembered, so that the string of sounds form one word by being the object of one, unitary cognition at the end.

UPAMĀNA OR COMPARISON

A fourth kind of (or means of) true cognition is *upamāna* or comparison. As stated earlier, one of the ways a meaning relation is apprehended is through "comparison." Let us suppose a person wants to know what is meant by the word "*gavaya*." She learns, from another, that a *gavaya* resembles a cow. Now on another occasion she sees an animal resembling a cow and recalls the instruction "*gavaya* is like a cow." So she concludes—knows—that it is this animal that is meant by "*gavaya*." She thus is able to determine a meaning relation between a word and a thing. It is the knowledge of similarity—at first verbal, then perceptual and finally memory—which is the cause of the cognition and so is the *upamāna* as a *pramāṇa*.

The Vedantins use "*upamāna*" in a different sense, while still retaining its etymological connection with "resemblance." A person sees a cowlike animal, for instance, a *gavaya*, so she says "This animal is like a cow." From this cognition arises the cognition "My cow is like this *gavaya*," or rather "My cow possesses resemblance with this *gavaya*." One may want to maintain that this last statement can be inferred from the one preceding it; if it were, then the cognition should be called inference, needing no special *pramāṇa* call "*upamāna*." But the Vedāntins want to argue that in this case an inferential derivation is not possible. For details of this controversy, one needs to consult the chapter on "*upamāna*" in Udayana's *Kusumāñjali*.

It should be noted that the Vaiśeṣikas, unlike the Naiyāyikas, do not regard *upamāna* as a separate *pramāṇa*, and include it, as well as *śabda*, under inference.

In the literature on theory of knowledge, several others are considered as likely candidates to be included in one's list of *pramāṇas*. Of these, two are recognized by the Vedāntins, thereby bringing their list to six. These two are: *anupalabdhi* and *arthāpatti*.

NONPERCEPTION (*ANUPALABDHI*)

Anupalabdhi or nonperception is regarded by the Vedantins to be the way we apprehend an absence. The Nyāya view is that the same sense organ (e.g., the visual sense organ), which perceives the presence of a color in a thing, also perceives the absence of another color in that thing. If x is a perceptible entity, so is the absence of x. To admit perceptibility of an absence, however, is to flout the rule that the appropriate sense organ must be in contact with that absence, which would seem to be absurd. The Naiyāyikas accept that rule only in the case of positive entities. To avoid this and similar problems, the Vedāntins regard nonperception to be the means of cognizing an absence. What they mean is this: when all the conditions for the perception of x are present, and yet x is not perceived, in that case this nonperception would lead to a true cognition of the absence of x.

POSTULATION (*ARTHĀPATTI*)

If a meaning x is not otherwise possible, or cannot be possible save under the assumption of y, then given x, y may be truly asserted (i.e., cognized). The standard example given by the Vedāntins runs like this: suppose that Devadatta is day by day growing fat, but never eats during the day. These two cognitions can both be true only if we postulate that Devadatta eats at night. Thus *arthāpatti* would look like what is called a "transcendental argument," which starts with a given fact x, and then argues that only under the assumption of y is x possible. This is said to be a distinct kind of knowing, and not an inference for technical reasons. It seems not to satisfy the requirements of an inference.

The Naiyāyikas regard it to be a case of inference whose minor term (*pakṣa*) is Devadatta, the major term (*sādhya*) is "eating at night," and the middle (*hetu*) is "growing fat, while not eating during the day." The universal rule that is used is negative, or *vyatirekivyāpti*. Wherever there is absence of *sādhya* (i.e., absence of eating at night), there would be absence of *hetu* (i.e., absence of growing fat, if not eating during the day). The problem is, in that case, to come forward with an agreed example (*dṛṣānta*) in which that rule is instantiated.

There are several other candidates for recognition as *pramāṇas* who do not seem to have had defenders among the major schools. The fact that most writers do consider their claims even if only to set them aside suggests that their claims need to be given serious attention. These are memory, *sambhava* or inclusion, and *aitihya* or tradition. Under "*sambhava*" are included such cognitions as "The number one hundred includes the number fifty." Attempts have been made to reduce such cognition to inference. Knowledge derived from tradition is often reduced to *śabda*, or word-generated cognition. To be noted is that thereby both mathematical knowledge (or at least a part of it) and historical knowledge do not attain the status of distinct *pramāṇas*. A similar negative attitude is more often than not exhibited toward memory. Memory is excluded—with the exception of Jainism—on the ground that it is not an independent *pramāṇa*, it always referring back to prior experience, combined with the criticism that it cognizes by repeating what is already known. It does not let anything that was unknown to be known.

THEORIES OF FALSE COGNITION (*KHYĀTIVĀDA*)

Now that we have surveyed all those modes of knowing that are true or *pramā*, it is time that we also briefly consider the nature of *apramā* or cognition that is not *pramā*. If *pramā* apprehends an object as what it is, and does not ascribe to it a predicate that does not belong to it, *apramā* precisely does that. It ascribes to its object a predicate that, as a matter of fact, does not belong to it. *Apramā* is either error or doubt (*saṃśaya*).

First, as to error, the Indian philosophies were preoccupied principally with perceptual error, or rather with nonveridical perception. Every school of philosophy developed its own theory of error (known as *khyātivāda*) made to fit its epistemology and metaphysics. As a matter of fact, theory of error, or of *apramā* in general, was always an important part of a system's theory of knowledge. Two things need to be remembered to begin with. For a realist, since he believes in the mind-independent existence and nature of the objects of cognition, a theory of truth is easy to produce, but a theory of error is difficult to give inasmuch as in the latter case either the existence of the object of cognition or its nature, or both, do not seem to be mind-independent. On the other hand, if one is an idealist, a theory of error comes easy in hand, just for the same reason (the object of erroneous cognition looks like being mind-dependent), while a theory of truth has to depart from a common sense notion of correspondence. Note that the Vedantin had simply to say: a *pramā* is a cognition that is not yet known to be *apramā*.

With these preliminary remarks, let us begin with standard examples of nonveridical perception. For the Indian theorist, the standard example has been mistaking a rope for a snake. Using this example, we can formulate in general outlines the main theories. Each of the theories will have to satisfy three criteria: first, each theory has to appropriate the fact that the nonveridical perception of a snake and the veridical perception of a snake are exactly alike to begin with. Second, the theory must be able to take into account the fact of correction of the illusion, with which the nonveridical perception first is recognized to be non-veridical. Since the original experience has two aspects—cognitive and conative—the correction of the illusion also has its cognitive and conative aspects (what is now seen as a rope, but not a snake, is recognized as never having been a snake, and the original practical response of running away from the presumed snake is arrested). Finally, the theory must also be able to include a reflective interpretation of the entire experience as it arises, unfolds, gets transformed, then is rejected, but still is recalled and marveled at. Can all these aspects be taken care of by any theory?

The main theories are (the Sanskrit names of the theories and the schools who held them are affixed to each):

1. That what is being perceived, the (illusory) snake, is really nonexistent (*asat-khyāti-vāda*, Cārvākas);
2. That it is really a mental state that is projected outside, the illusory snake, being a mental image (*ātma-khyāti*, Yogācāra Buddhism);
3. That what is being perceived, by itself, is real, error consisting in mistaking a part for the whole (*sat-khyāti*, Rāmānuja's Vedānta);
4. That the supposed erroneous cognition really consists of two different cognitions, a perception and a memory—each, by itself is true, there being no erroneous cognition over and above a failure to distinguish between the two (*akhyāti*, Prābhākara Mīmāṃsā);
5. That (as in 4), of the two component cognitions, the object of one (namely, this) is taken to be the snake, which is the object of the other, the memory (*viparīta-khyāti*, Bhāṭṭa Mīmāṃsā);
6. That the snake perceived (under illusion) is a real snake, only it is elsewhere, not here in front of the perceiver, but is presented through an

extraordinary (*alaukika*) causal process that is mediated by remembrance of past perception of that object (*anyathā-khyāti*, Nyāya); and

7. That the nonveridical perception is as much a unified cognition as is the veridical, only its object (the snake) is neither existent (*sat*), since it is negated by knowledge of the rope, nor nonexistent (*asat*), since it is perceptually presented/encountered and so is indescribable as being either (*anirvācanīya-khyāti-vāda*, Śaṃkara's Vedānta).

Brief Notes on These Theories

1. A nonexistent thing (like a round square or a golden mountain) cannot be perceptually presented. Correction of the illusion does not attest to the object's nonexistence but only to its not being real.
2. Besides the objections to number 1, one needs an explanation of how a mental entity can be perceived to be out there, and to say that it is somehow projected is not to remove that puzzlement. Also, in addition, correction does not testify to the object's status as a mental entity.
3. On this theory, what one sees, under illusion, are still objective features of what is there, namely, the rope. The mistake is due to the fact that there are other features of the real thing that one does not see, so one takes the part for the whole. Correction of error, on this theory, is supplementation of knowledge, one sees more of the thing. Error is partial truth. Thus the theory misses the nature of hallucination, not to speak of nonveridical perception, which is not merely supplemented by more knowledge, but totally negated.
4. The problem with theory 4 is that it gives no good account for why and how one fails to distinguish between a perception and a memory.
5. and 6. These two theories agree that there is a genuinely erroneous judgment, which positively misconnects two different objects of two different cognitions. Theory 5 has to explain how a memory image could be identified with a percept. Theory 6 has to give a credible account of how after all a snake, which is not here before me, can be *perceived* to be here and now. The putative mechanism of "extraordinary" perception known as *jñānalakṣaṇāsānnikarṣa* itself is in need of credible explanation. The experience of correction, in addition, does not show the snake, now rejected, as being elsewhere.
7. The Advaita Vedānta theory claims to be taking into account all aspects of the situation, but pays the price of adding a new ontological category. The snake of our example is neither existent nor nonexistent. Nonexistents like round squares, barren woman's son, or sky-flower are never perceived, even if by mistake. Existent objects are never negated by mere knowledge, and yet it is knowledge of the real entity that leads to the total negation of the appearing snake. The Vedāntin accordingly invents a new category: that which is indescribable either as existent or as nonexistent, otherwise called—precisely in that sense—"false." A definition of "false" is this: a

thing is false if it is negated (for all times, i.e., "never was, is, or will be") in the very same locus where it was perceived. The causal production of such an entity remains a problem—a metaphysical problem, to be sure, which is solved with the help of the Vedāntic concept of positive (*bhāvarūpa*) ignorance.

KNOWLEDGE AND IGNORANCE

The idea of ignorance (*avidyā*) plays a crucial role not merely in the Indian epistemologies, but also in the Indian metaphysical systems. Let us now recall what role "ignorance" plays in Indian theories of knowledge, especially in the Advaita Vedānta. For all Indian philosophies, knowledge manifests its object. Besides, if an object is known (i.e., manifested), there is an *awareness* that the object was unknown before (i.e., an awareness of ignorance). A true cognition or *pramā* arises by destroying the past ignorance of the object being known, and there is an *awareness* that the object was unknown. Likewise, awareness of ignorance also points to the *future*, yet-to-be, *pramā* of the same object. There is thus not only an interinvolvement of knowledge and ignorance, that interplay has a temporal structure—a reference to past ignorance and future *pramā*.

Ignorance is generally understood as absence of knowledge, such that "ignorance of x" is the same as "absence of the knowledge of x." However, the Advaita Vedāntin insists that ignorance is not mere negation or absence, but rather is a positive (*bhāvarūpa*) entity, so that "S is ignorant of x" is to be analyzed into "ignorance as a positive entity, belonging to S's consciousness, conceals the nature (and, possibly, the existence) of x." The Vedāntin holds the view that when I am ignorant of x, there is in me an *awareness* of that ignorance. So also when I know x, there is an awareness of that knowledge. In either case, the awareness is of x—in the one case, of x as unknown, in the other case, of x as known. Hence the well-known thesis asserted by the Vivaraṇa: All things are objects of awareness, either as known or as unknown ("*sarvam vastu jñātatayā ajñātatayā vā sākṣicaitanyasya viṣaya eva*").

Note that the distinction between "awareness" and "knowledge" is important for this thesis. There is not *knowledge* of ignorance, for that knowledge would contradict and so annul the ignorance. But there is an awareness that "I am ignorant of x." The *awareness* is what the Vedantin calls "witness consciousness" (*sākṣī-caitanya*). It is not only not opposed to ignorance, it rather manifests that ignorance. What is opposed to, and removes ignorance (of x), is *knowledge* (of x), when both belong to the same subject. In this sense, knowledge—according to the Vedāntin—is a mental state, an *antaḥkaraṇavṛtti*. Awareness, which manifests both knowledge and ignorance, is not opposed to either.

Empirically real things can have unknown existence (*ajñāta-sattā*). The table on which I am writing exists when no one perceives it. This possibility of unknown existence belongs to the very sense of empirical reality. There are, however, objects that, by the very sense of their being, cannot have unknown existence. According to the Vedāntin, such are pleasure and pain (for them, to be is to be known); illusory objects, for instance, the snake that is perceived where there is only a rope (this false snake has no unknown existence); and also ignorance itself (it is not possible to be ignorant of ignorance). Of all these objects, the Berkeleyan dictum "*esse est percipii*" holds good—but not of (the empirically real) material objects such as sticks and stones.

ARE TRUTH AND FALSITY INTRINSIC OR EXTRINSIC TO KNOWLEDGE?

At the end of this chapter on theory of knowledge, I will introduce now and briefly discuss an issue that is discussed by all schools of Indian philosophy. Besides, the way this issue is formulated and the answers proposed are distinctive of the Indian epistemologies. The question is, Is truth (*prāmānya*) intrinsic (*svataḥ*) to a cognition or is it extrinsic (*parataḥ*) to it? The same question is also asked with regard to falsity (*aprāmānya*). In either case, the question concerns both the "origin" (of truth as well as of falsity) and apprehension of them. Thus we have *four* separate questions.

Consider a cognition K. Assuming K to be true, we can ask: (1) Do the very same causal conditions that give rise to K also give rise to K's truth (which is a property of K)? If they do, then truth is intrinsic (*svataḥ*), with regard to origin, to K. If, besides the causal conditions that produce K, some additional causal factor is needed to make K true, then truth is, with regard to origin, extrinsic (*parataḥ*) to K.

Assuming K to be false, we can ask in (2) exactly the same questions as in (1) about K's falsity: namely, Is falsity intrinsic to K with regard to origin, or is it extrinsic to K with regard to origin?

With regard to the cognition of truth and falsity, we can ask: (3) When K is cognized, is its truth also cognized? Or, is its truth or its falsity cognized later on—subsequently determined on the ground of successful or unsuccessful practice that ensues upon K? In the former case, truth, with regard to its apprehension, is intrinsic (*svataḥ*) to K, in the latter case truth (and falsity) are extrinsic.

For our present limited purpose, we shall leave out of consideration the entire issue insofar as it concerns the origin of truth and falsity. Those, like the Naiyāyikas, who believe that both truth and falsity are extrinsic with regard to origin, believe that for a cognition K to be true (or false), some special causal conditions besides the causal conditions that generate K are needed; for truth, these conditions are called *guṇas* or special excellences, for falsity, these are called *doṣas* or special deficiencies. The latter two concepts are highly controversial, as is the very idea of the "origin" of the properties known as "truth" and "falsity." Into the controversies surrounding these we will not presently enter.

Let us now consider the various answers to questions under (3) above. (a) When K is cognized, it is also cognized as being true, while later on its falsity may be determined on the basis of unsuccessful practice (e.g., upon the failure to quench one's thirst with the mirage water). This position, held by the Mīmāṃsā, combines "intrinsic truth theory" with "extrinsic falsity theory." (b) When K is cognized, it is cognized neither as true nor as false. Both truth and falsity, as the case may be, are determined later, depending upon the success or failure of the practical response to K. This position, held by the Nyāya, combines "extrinsic truth theory" with "extrinsic falsity theory." (c) When K is cognized, it is to be taken as false, unless later experience leads to successful practice when it is judged valid. This view, often ascribed to some Buddhists, combines an "intrinsic falsity theory" with an "extrinsic truth theory." (d) For every K, both truth and falsity are intrinsic. That is to say, K is in some respect intrinsically true, in some not so. This theory, ascribed to the Sāṃkhyā, and possibly to the Jaina, combines an "intrinsic truth theory" with an "intrinsic falsity theory."

In all these proposals, use is made (save in the formulation of [d]) of "cognition of K" where K itself is a cognition. Earlier in this chapter, we discussed the question of how a cognition is cognized? The answer to this question falls into the following patterns: (X) A cognition is self-manifesting, self-revealing, self-intimating (*svaprakāsa*). It makes itself known by its very existence, not unlike, in that respect, the light of a lamp. (Y) A cognition is cognized only by being the object of a subsequent cognition, the latter being of the nature of an inner perception (*anuvyavasāya*). (Z) A cognition is known by a subsequent act of inference that seeks to account for the perceived difference between the known object and the mere object by positing the act of knowing as what produces in the object the property of knownness (*jñātatā*).

Of these, (X) is held in different forms by different schools. These forms are (X_i) that each cognition as it occurs manifests itself. (X_{ii}) that each cognition manifests itself as a cognition, its subject as the knower and its object as the known—all in one act (known as threefold [*triputi*] perception). (X_{iii}) that a cognition is manifested directly by the witness consciousness, while the latter shows itself.

Of these three, (X_i) is the view of the Buddhists, (X_{ii}) of Prābhākara Mīmāṃsā, and (X_{iii}) of Advaita Vedānta.

It should now be clear that if you take into account the diversity of views (X_i), (X_{ii}), and (X_{iii}) as well as Y and Z, and insert them in appropriate places in (a) through (d), you have an interesting range of theories of knowledge and truth, the details of which may be worked out by interested readers for themselves.

To conclude this section, we need to give a brief discussion of the issues involved. A cognition arises, manifesting its object and giving rise to effort either to reach the object if the object is attractive or to shun the object if the latter is repulsive. Now if, as in (c), a cognition is cognized as being intrinsically false, then it cannot give rise to the appropriate practical response. So let us turn to (b). If the cognition K is known to be true only on the basis of another cognition (namely, the cognition that K leads to successful practical response) P_1, then one would want to know how P_1 is known to be true. P_1 can confirm K only if P_1 itself is true, but P_1 itself would need to be confirmed by another cognition P_2. This process would lead to a *regressus ad infinitum*. Furthermore, one may argue that K would not give rise to the appropriate practical response (which may lead to P_1) unless K were already known to be true. To this objection, the supporters of (b) reply in two ways. In the first place, they may agree to ascribe some kind of "intrinsic truth" to the final confirmatory experiences (*phalajñānāni* or *Protokolsätze*) in the weak sense that in these cases there is no room for error and so no room for doubt and so no need for confirmation. The other reply—given by Gangeśa—is that P_1 may very well confirm P_2 without itself being confirmed. A knowledge may manifest an object without that knowledge itself being known to be true. To suppose that this is not possible is to assume that every knowledge, to be knowledge, must be known to be true. But this is to beg the issue (i.e., to assume the position [a]).

Furthermore, Gangeśa rejects the argument that unless a cognition is determined to be true it cannot give rise to appropriate conative response. He prefers a weaker position: a cognition causes appropriate response if it is not known to be false. It need not, over and above that, be determined to be true.

Curiously enough when the Advaita Vedāntin defines "is true" as "is not known to be false," and regards truth in this sense to be "intrinsic" (as per [a] above), he is agreeing with the contention of the Naiyāyika as stated in the preceding paragraph.

Gangeśa has another most interesting argument against the Mīmāṃsā position. "Truth" can be correctly defined only if the definition contains an epistemic property and an ontological property. Truth of a cognition requires that the cognition must have its internal features that correspond to the features of the object. To know that the cognition "This is silver" is true is to know that the *this really* possesses silverness. This ontological fact cannot be known simply by knowing the cognition "This is silver," as the Mīmāṃsā position (a) claims.

Part 2

Metaphysics (*Prameya Śāstra*)

Chapter Three

The Categories (*Padārtha*-s)

LISTS OF CATEGORIES

Indian metaphysicians have always thought of reality in terms of fundamental kinds called *padārtha*-s. The word *padārtha*—literally meaning "the meaning of word"—is generally translated as "category." Since the theory of meaning, in most Indian philosophies, is a referential theory, *padārtha* means "what is referred to by the words," and so the entities that belong to the world. By an understandable extension in the context of metaphysical discourse, it means the most general kinds of things that are, the highest genera of entities. Any discussion of the theory of category in Indian thinking would be facilitated if we start with a provisional listing of categories as is to be found in the Nyāya-Vaiśeṣika—even if there is no reason why we should accept this list to be unrevisable. But it would serve as a good starting point for recovering the basic underlying conceptions, and to review the reasons why many other systems did not accept the list. The list is one of seven categories: *dravya* (substance), *guṇa* (quality), *karma* (action), *sāmānya* (universal), *viśesa* (individuality), *samavāya* (inherence), and *abhāva* (negation). The English words within parentheses are approximate translations, to be made more precise in the course of the ensuing discussion.

A question with which we may begin is, What sort of considerations justify the inclusion of a kind among the list of categories? In other words, in the technical jargon of the system, what can be accepted as a *padārthavibhājaka upādhi*? One answer is that two properties $\emptyset$ and Ψ truly can serve as demarcating categories if and only if $\emptyset$ and Ψ cannot be present in the same locus. In the above list, *dravyatva* (the property of being a substance) and *gunatva* (the property of being a quality) do not inhere in the same thing. The former inheres in a jar, for instance, and the latter in the color of that jar.

But clearly this account is not satisfactory. In the first place, the two properties earthness and waterness do not inhere in the same loci, yet they are not category-demarcating properties. We need to determine which universals do not demarcate a category. We know that "being a substance" or substancehood is a category-demarcating property. Existence is a universal that is present in all those instances in which substancehood is present, but also in more cases. In this sense, existence "pervades" substancehood. Likewise, earthhood is pervaded by substancehood. We may then surmise that if $\emptyset$ is a category-demarcating property, then no property that pervades $\emptyset$, and no property which is pervaded by $\emptyset$, is a category-demarcating property. The above account implies that "existence" is not a category-demarcating property, for there are not two mutually exclusive kinds: being and nonbeing. "Being" is not a category. The next highest universals that are pervaded by "being" are categories, according to the Vaiśeṣikas. The *padārtha*-s or categories are the highest—I should add, following Husserl, "nonformal"—genera under which all entities fall. "Being" does not divide entities into classes. The categories are natural classes of entities. There cannot be an all-inclusive category.

There are further questions about the *padārtha*-s that we need to look into. At this place, I can only formulate one of these, but not immediately proceed to answer it. The question is, are the *padārtha*-s, when they are taken to be natural kinds, "descriptive concepts" or are they speculative concepts? It does appear as though the first three in the Vaiśeṣika list (i.e., substance, quality, and action) are descriptive concepts and the last four are not. But is this initial impression sound? We need, in this connection, also ask, What is the task of a philosophy that intends to deliver a system of categories? Is its task to descriptively ascertain the highest genera of entities? Or, is its task to construct such a system? To such questions we shall return at the end of this chapter. We need also to note and comment upon an initial impression that every student of Indian philosophical writings acquires, namely that the authors are concerned with drawing up and justifying lists of categories (as also of the subtypes coming under them). This textual and rhetorical feature cannot but give rise to the questions, Whence is the list derived, and what sort of justification does it admit of? Naturally, these questions are connected with the question regarding the descriptive versus constructive nature of the systems concerned. But before we are in a position to deal with them, let us go beyond the Vaiśeṣikas and look at other "lists."

OTHER LISTS

The author of the *Vivaraṇaprameyasaṃgraha* gives the following lists of categories ascribed to the various systems of Indian philosophy. Besides the Vaiśeṣikas whose seven categories were listed earlier, we have the sixteen categories of Nyāya that appear to be an odd mixture of epistemological and logical concepts (*Nyāya Sūtra,* I, 1, 1). Leaving these two aside, we have the following lists:

The Old Prābhākaras: *dravya, guṇa, karma, sāmānya, viśeṣa, pāratantrya* (dependence), *śakti* (power), and *niyoga* (duty).
The New Prābhākaras: *dravya, guṇa, karma, sāmānya, viśeṣa, samavāya, śakti, sankhyā* (number), and *sādṛśya* (similarity).
Jainas: *jīva* (individual soul), *ajīva* (non-soul), *āśrava* (defilement), *sambara* (prevention), *nirjara* (destruction), *bandha* (bondage), *mokṣa* (liberation), and *paryāya* (changing states).
Śaivas: *kārya* (effect), *kāraṇa* (cause), *vidhi* (rule of action), *dukkha* (pain).

Besides, we can mention the following lists advanced by some others.

Madhva: *dravya, guṇa, karma, sāmānya, viśeṣa, viśiṣta* (qualified), *aṃśa* (whole), *śakti, sādṛśya,* and *abhāva.*
Vallabha: *kāla* (time), *karma, svabhāva* [28 *tattvas* (principles): *puruṣa/ātman* (self), *prakṛti* (Nature), *guṇas, mahat* (world-soul), *tanmātras* (the simple qualities), *manas*, etc.].
The Bhāgavata: 25 or 26 principles (depending on whether you do not or do admit God and the *tanmatrās*), or 11 [add: cognitive and conative senses] or 6 (5 elements + self) or 4 (3 categories of light—heat, water and earth, and self) or 17 (5 *tanmātras* + 5 elements + 5 senses, *manas* and the self), or 16 (taking *manas* = self). or 13 (5 elements + 5 senses, *manas*, the transcendent and phenomenal selves) or 11 (5 elements + 5 senses + self).

Dasgupta quotes a verse from the *Bhāgavata* in which Kṛṣṇa reconciles these different numbers by referring to "the varying kinds of subsumption of the lower categories under the higher or by the omission of the higher ones or by ignoring some of the successive causal entities." But if, as said earlier, a category must be a highest genus and not subsumable under higher genera, the talk of higher and lower categories must be misleading. So to the Sāṃkhya we may ascribe only two categories: *puruṣa* (self) and *prakṛti* (nature).

Rāmānuja: *dravya, adravya* (nonsubstance)
Caraka: *kāraṇa* (efficient cause), *kārya-yoni* (material cause), *kārya,* (effect), *kārya-phala* (that for which an effect is intended by the agent), *anubandha* (consequence), *deśa* (space), *kāla* (time), *pravṛtti* (effort), *upāya* (means).

SUBSTANCE (*DRAVYA*)

One group stands out in all these categorial systems, and that is the group *dravya-guṇa-karma.* Those who do not include *dravya* in their list of categories propose to reduce it to qualities (*guṇa*-s) and/or actions (*karma*-s). Such reductions are not implausible, but may be faulted for flouting common sense. But if common sense owes its metaphysical insight to the structure of one's language (in this case, of Sanskrit), then this insight is not sacrosanct, and, given another linguistic scheme (such as that of the Hopis) one may find support for reduction of substance to events. To such schemes—as represented in Sāṃkhya and early Buddhism—we shall return. But for the present, let us look at the notion of "substance." Now there is an understandable temptation to compare the Vaiśeṣika *dravya* with the Aristotelian substance. I will not attempt such a comparison here. Let it be noted, however, that the Aristotelian substance comprehends several other concepts—essence, matter, potentiality, final cause—which it is not easy to locate in the Vaiśeṣika. The *dravya*—which perhaps it is more appropriate to translate as "thing" than as "substance"—is defined (1) as the locus of qualities (*guṇas*) and actions (*karma*-s), (2) as the material cause (or "inherence cause") of effects (i.e., that in which the effect inheres). Only a *dravya* can be the *samavāyi kāraṇa* or a material cause. Negatively, a *dravya* is a thing that is not the locus of an absolute absence of qualities (Udayana, *Lakṣaṇāvalī*)—excepting, one may add, at the first moment of its origination (according to Vaiśeṣika theory). *Dravya*-s have to be admitted, argues Śrīdhara in *Nyāyakandalī,* because qualities cannot be without them for then (i.e., if there were no *dravya* underlying qualities), we cannot explain how two or more senses can grasp the same object (i.e., how we can see and touch the same thing). Furthermore, Śrīdhara argues, *dravya*-s are needed to explain why qualities are individuated, for example, why *this* red (of this flower) is different from *that* red (of that flower). Note that on the Vaiśeṣika view, a quality is not a universal, a quality is a particular even if it instantiates a universal. Anticipating the thesis about the relation of inherence (*samavāya*), which we will introduce in this account a little later, we can say, with Karl Potter, that a *dravya* is the only kind of individual (note that qualities are also individuals) that *can* be inhered in without also inhering in something else. Qualities and actions and universals inhere in *dravya*-s, but there are *dravya*-s that inhere in other *dravya*-s (i.e., in their parts), but a *dravya* that is partless does not inhere in anything else. Furthermore, only *dravya*-s, on the Vaiśeṣika theory, can enter into the relation of contact (*saṃyoga*), and one can define a *dravya* as that which can have *contact* as a quality (for, contact, on the theory, is a quality). This last case makes the concept of *dravya* intuitive, but adds nothing to the already given definition that a *dravya* is that in which qualities inhere.

Those who, like the Vaiśeṣikas, admit *dravya* as a category must, in addition, recognize it as the most fundamental category. For, entities belonging to the other categorial kinds, in some way or other, depend on *dravya*-s, and cannot be without either inhering in, or in some other manner being related to, a *dravya*. All others rest upon *dravya*-s.

The theory of *dravya* is further developed by a theory of different kinds of it. *Dravya-s* are taken to be nine in kind: earth, water, fire, air, ether (*ākāśa*), space (*dik*), time (*kāla*), soul (*aīman*), and mind (*manas*). All other seemingly different kinds (of *dravya-s*) are sought to be reducible to one or more of these nine. So one could say, these nine are the only further irreducible kinds of *dravya-s*. Of these nine, the first four are either permanent (if they are incomposite atoms) or impermanent (if composite); the other five are permanent. Of these latter five, ether, space, time, and soul are permanent, being all-pervasive; the last one, mind, is also permanent, being atomic (and partless) in extension. In this chapter, we shall pay some special attention to space and time; and in the next chapter to the "soul." We will not expound the atomic theory, for that belongs to the physics and the chemistry of the Hindus, and not to the theory of categories. To regard space and time as categories is in accord with a dominant mode of thinking in Western thought.

The concept of *dravya* that has been expounded until now is that of the Nyāya-Vaiśeṣika system. Other systems of philosophy that have admitted *dravya* as a category do not often agree with this account. Thus Rāmānuja regards *dravya* as that which has states (*daśāvat*) or as that which suffers change and modification. *Yogasūtrabhāṣya* by Vyāsa regards *dravya* to be of the nature of both generality and specificity (*sāmānyaviśeṣātmaka*). *Mahābhāṣya* regards a *dravya* as that which is a specific kind of conglomeration of its parts.

There are also differences regarding the various kinds of substances. The Nyāya-Vaiśeṣika recognizes, as we saw, nine of these. The Mīmāṃsā of Kumārila added two more: sound and darkness, as against the standard view that sound is a quality, specific to *ākāsá* and that darkness is mere absence of light and so not a positive entity that a *dravya* has to be. The Jaina philosophers questioned if time is a substance. The Madhvas recognize twenty kinds of substances, which include such assorted ones as God, Lakshmi (his consort), *prakṛti* with its three *guṇas* (deriving from Sāṃkhya), time and reflection (*pratibimba*). Clearly, the list is inflated and could be reduced to the benefit of the system. Even the Nyāya-Vaiśeṣikas sought further reductions and wondered—as did Śaṃkara Miśra—if space and time cannot be unified, but rejected this idea on the ground that spatial distinctions and directions are relative to the location of a person while temporal divisions are the same for everyone. Raghunātha Śiromaṇi carries through the reduction by unifying them all in the nature of God.

A few final remarks about the category of *dravya*. First, one should distinguish between two points of view from which the concept of *dravya* can be—or, rather, has been—studied: first, as a cosmological and nature-philosophical concept, and second as a functional-categorial concept. From the former point of view, *dravya* is the *cause* of its qualities; from the second point of view it is the subject of qualities and other determinations such as relations and universals. To define *dravya* as an "inherence *cause*" is to subsume the idea of *dravya* under the idea of cause, and thereby to deprive it of its categorial status. But the Indian philosophers did not see any problem in this possibility, inasmuch as for them there was no strict line of demarcation between ontology as a doctrine of categories and philosophy of nature as empirical explanation of natural phenomena between ontology and natural science. A pure natural science was sought to be deduced from the doctrine of categories.

Whereas Western theories of substance such as Aristotle's and Kant's did not purport to give a list of types of substance and were rather content with advancing general features and roles of substance, the Indian philosophies aimed at, as we noted, producing an exhaustive list of further irreducible types of substance. The theorists consequently, more often than not, ended up with a rather heterogenous list of such types and undertook to demonstrate that nothing can be added to, or taken away from, that list. The list did not simply include "material substance" and "mental or spiritual substance" (as Western philosophers tended to do), but also the natural elements coming together under the former, and "mind" and "soul"—to be clearly separated for all purposes—under the latter—besides space and time, not to speak, as in the case of the Vaiśeṣikas, of a further differentiation—within "space"—between *dik* and *ākāśa.* To define *dravya*—as was often done—with the help of this list, was to blur the distinction between the pure doctrine of the categories and an empirical theory of their exemplifications, a distinction that, as just noted, did not quite exist for the Indian thinkers.

QUALITY (*GUṆA*)

Next to *dravya*, the category most commonly admitted by the various schools of Indian philosophy is *guṇa*, often rendered as "quality," but also meaning what is only nonindependent, nonprimary (*a-pradhāna*). A *guṇa* can be only in a substance, and not by itself. A universal like "cowness" can only be in a substance, in this case, a particular cow. In this regard a universal is like a *guṇa*, but a *guṇa* is a particular that itself may instantiate a universal. Thus the red of *this* piece of paper is a particular quality, but instantiates the universal "redness." Contrary to a predominant view to be found in much of Western thinking, the color of a red thing is not, for example, redness, but a particular red instantiating the universal redness. On the Vaiśeṣika view, in addition, a *guṇa* cannot itself possess a *guṇa*, although as we shall see a number—which is on the Vaiśeṣika theory a *guṇa*—may be ascribed to a set of qualities (e.g., "red" and "green" are *two* colors). In order to avoid this conflict with the thesis that a quality cannot itself possess a quality, Raghunātha Śiromaṇi rightly regards "number" as a separate category, and not as a quality.

As in the case of *dravya,* so also in the case of *guṇa,* one finds an assorted list. This list consists of twenty-four items: color, taste, smell, touch, number, *parimāṇa* (magnitude), *pṛthaktva* (otherness), *saṃyoga* (conjunction), *vibhāga* (disjunction), remoteness, proximity, heaviness, fluidity, *sneha* (viscosity), sound, cognition, happiness, misery, desire, aversion, volition, *dharma* (merit), *adharma* (demerit), and *saṃskāra* (dispositional tendency). Of these twenty-four, color, taste, smell, touch, remoteness, proximity, heaviness, fluidity, and viscosity are qualities of gross material things. Cognition, happiness, misery, desire, aversion, volition, merit, demerit, and sound are subtle (*amūrta)* qualities, or rather qualities of nonmaterial substances. Number, magnitude, otherness, conjunction, and disjunction are qualities of both kinds of substances. Conjunction, disjunction, numbers (from "two" onwards), and otherness reside in more than one thing. The rest (i.e., color, taste, smell, touch, magnitude, remoteness, proximity, heaviness, etc.) reside in one substance each. Some of these (such as color, smell, taste, touch, viscosity, fluidity, cognition, happiness, misery, desire, aversion, volition, merit, demerit, sound) are specific qualities. Others such as number, magnitude, otherness, conjunction, disjunction, remoteness, proximity, and heaviness are common qualities (shared by many). Of sound, touch, color, taste, and smell, each is apprehended by one outer sense organ. Number, magnitude, otherness, conjunction, disjunction, remoteness, proximity, fluidity, and viscosity can be apprehended each by two sense organs—the visual and the tactual. Cognition, happiness, misery, desire, aversion, and volition are apprehended by the inner sense. Merit and demerit are supersensible. Conjunction and disjunction are brought about by action. Remoteness and proximity, numbers such as "two," and otherness are dependent upon cognition.

These features bring some order to the seemingly haphazard list. One may also detect how—by what process of historical development, by what process of appropriating different points of view already prevalent in the tradition—the Vaiśeṣikas arrived at this list of *guṇa*-s. While this is the canonical list, not everyone accepted it. Raghunātha Śiromaṇi points out that these twenty-four have nothing in common. Two of these items in particular come into question: conjunction (*saṃyoga*) and number. Some have added motion to the list. With regard to numbers, Raghunātha assigns them to a separate category, for qualities can also be counted (a desire and a conjunction, can, for example, form two things). What about conjunction or contact? It may quite naturally be regarded as a relation, but the Vaiśeṣika does not have place for a category called "relation." It is as a matter of fact *both* a relation and a quality, or, better, it is a quality that is also a relation. It inheres in *two* substances, not in any one substance, thus it is a relation. Why is it a quality? A quality, on the Vaiśeṣika theory, is what resides only in a substance, and is itself without any quality and action. Conjunction satisfies these criteria and so deserves to be regarded as a quality.

THE OTHER CATEGORIES

Motion or action (*karma*) is the third Vaiśeṣika category. According to one definition, motion is that which, being other than conjunction, is the noninherence cause of conjunction. The term "noninherence" excludes the substances that enter into conjunction, and so are the material or inherence cause of conjunction. Actions are of five kinds: throwing upwards, throwing downwards, contraction, expansion, and moving. There were Naiyāyikas, Bhāsarvajña notably, who classified motion as a quality on the ground that, like *guṇa*-s, inheres in a substance, is momentary, and functions as the noninherence cause of the qualities such as contact.

In the Vaiśeṣika scheme, substance, quality, and motion or action are the fundamental categories. Particulars coming under them constitute the basic particulars. The other four categories are exemplified in these three. In this sense, the ontology of the school consists of an inner circle to which belong substances, qualities, and motions or actions. To the outer circle belong universals, particularities (i.e., "ultimate individuators"), inherence, and "absences." A universal and an ultimate individuator can exist either in a substance, a quality, or a motion *or* in an indivisible substance (such as an atom or a soul). Likewise with absences. The locus of an absence must be a thing that comes under any of the first three categories. The relation of inherence ties together a substance or a quality or a motion with appropriate entities exemplifying the other positive categories: a quality with a substance; a motion with a substance, a universal with a substance; a quality, or a motion, a whole (substance) with the parts constituting it; an ultimate individuator with the ultimately indivisible substance to which it belongs.

Thus inherence (*samavāya*) may be regarded as the ontological glue that ties together entities exemplifying the different positive categories, and makes possible a unified thing as well as a unified world despite categorial differences and a pluralistic ontology.

Very brief remarks may be in order at this point regarding the remaining three categories. A universal is also called *sāmānya,* i.e., what is common to many particulars, often defined as what, though being one and eternal, inheres in many. They are of two different kinds: *parā,* the highest universal, (i.e., being, which is only a genus, but not a species); and *a-parā,* such as "cowness," which, in relation to "animality," is a species, but, in relation to individual cows, is a *sāmānya*.

The "ultimate individuator" (*viśeṣa*) is a category that only the Vaiśeṣikas recognize. Being pluralists, they had to have an account of what makes one cow different from another, despite their shared commonness. In the long run, one has to find an account of why one atom (one earth-atom, in Vaiśeṣika physics, for example) differs from another (earth-atom). Since an atom has no further part, individuation cannot be due to different parts. Each atom must then possess an ultimately individuating feature. The same holds good of the souls that are partless and also individuals.

Negation or absence (*abhāva*) is a category as well, exemplified in negative entities, and apprehended in negative judgments. The Nyāya-Vaiśeṣika distinguished between various types of negations—which can be laid down in the following table:

Table 3–1 Types of Negation.

- Negation
  - Absence ("A is not in B")
    - antecedent nonexistence ("A has not yet come into being")
    - posterior nonexistence ("A is no more")
    - absolute nonexistence ("A does not exist in B")
  - Difference ("A is not B")

We have thus given a sketch of the Vaiśeṣika doctrine of categories. It should be noted that in this theory, beingness, the highest genus, is not itself a category. If it were a category, we would be not only saying what things fall under it but also what things do not fall under it. But the class of all things being coexistent with the class of all things that *are*, "*sattā*," does not exclude anything from its scope. Thus while beingness assimilates but does not differentiate, cowness both assimilates and differentiates. As contrasted with both, "ultimate individuator" differentiates without assimilating.

This canonical doctrine of the Nyāya-Vaiśeṣika with regard to seven categories and many subcategories (nine substances, twenty-four qualities, and five motions) has been, as has already been pointed out, challenged by many. Among those who challenged the doctrine from within the school, reference has already been made to two philosophers. It is time we put together their revisions.

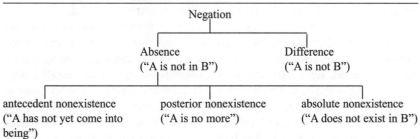

Bhāsarvajña's innovations include appropriating motion to the category of "quality"; denying that number is a separate quality; and also denying that size, separateness, disjunction, farness, nearness, and impetus are separate qualities. Perhaps the most brilliant and original revision was proposed by Raghunātha Śiromaṇi, who reduced space and time to God's nature and so denied to them categorial status. He also reduced "otherness" to "mutual difference;" rejected remoteness and proximity as qualities, rejected "ultimate individuator" as a separate category, and allowed the ultimate individuals (atoms and souls) to be self-differentiating; maintained that "beingness" is not a universal, so that the usage "The jar exists" really means "The jar is *present,*"; and admitted a new category called "moment" (*kṣaṇa*) and another called "one's own" (*svattva*). The latter is especially relevant in legal theory with regard to ownership and inheritance of property. Another new category admitted by Raghunātha is "power" (*śakti*), in this he agreed with the Mīṃāṃsā. He also laid the foundation of an extension of the canonical doctrine of seven categories to a host of others beginning with "contentness" (*viṣayatā*), which arises when a cognition arises. The neo-Naiyāyikas introduced many such abstract entities, chief among which are objectness, contentness, relationness, counterpositiveness, limitorness, and locusness. These, however, are not pure ontological categories, but rather epistemic categories. They arise and are used only in the context of cognition.

The Vaiśeṣika doctrine of categories is neither the most proliferated nor the most austere. Other Indian philosophers introduced many other, putatively irreducible, entity-types. Candidates for categorial status, besides those already mentioned and/or discussed, are causal efficacy, similarity (*sādṛśya*), darkness, self-linking connector, knownness, and many others. An austere doctrine had to take note of such candidates and to "reduce" them to those that must have to be admitted. Let me now turn to the more proliferated, overpopulated doctrines. There is a general distinction among the philosophies between the logico-analytical and the spiritual (*ādhyātmika*). The Nyāya-Vaiśeṣika belongs to the first group. To the second group belong Sāṃkhya, Vedānta, and Buddhism. Of these three, Sāṃkhya and Buddhism exhibit elaborate and richer categorial systems, the Vedānta the more austere doctrine. Being spiritual philosophies, the Sāṃkhya and the Buddhist ontologies are inseparable from their spiritual goals, meditative processes, and ethical ideas. Consequently, the doctrine of categories is not kept separate from epistemological, ethical, and spiritual concepts. In between the Vaiśeṣika and the spiritual philosophies stands the Jaina philosophy, which, like the Sāṃkhya, absorbed into it an old natural philosophy and the eschatological ideas emerging in opposition to the Upaniṣadic idea of *ātman.* The Jaina doctrine, insofar as it concerns us here, may be expounded in two parts: first, a general part and second, a specific part. The general thesis consists in admitting only three categories: substance, quality, and condition (*paryāya*). A substance is that to which qualities and states cling. Qualities have substances for their bearer. The *paryāya*-s are the changing states of a substance. Thus both change and permanence are unified in the substance. Given this situation, the Jaina philosopher distinguished between different conceptual frameworks, which different systems may embody: those which grant priority to substance and those that give priority to qualities or, one may look at all things from the most general aspect of "being." One may alternately consider things from their essential or general aspects as well as from their special traits. As contrasted with these, the Buddhists regard a thing as but a collection of qualities and states. The Jaina instead regard things as having infinite qualities, and all affirmations about a thing to be relative to a standpoint and so partly true, though also partly false.

The specific Jaina theory concerns its ontology. There are five types of existents: space, impulse (*dharma*), hindrance (*a-dharma*), souls (*jīva*-s), and matter, to which was later added "time" (*kāla*). Matter and soul all occupy space in various degrees. Space is one and infinite. *Dharma* and *a-dharma* are construed very differently from other Indian systems—as material atoms that enter into the soul and are the principles of motion and rest, respectively. Matter is insentient and corporeal and is atomic in nature. Souls are incorporeal and spiritual. Into the defects of the cosmology we need not enter. It should suffice to have noted the general nature of the categories.

SĀṂKHYA

For our present, limited purpose, we need not go into the question of the origin, and different strands in the development, of Sāṃkhya. I will mention only the principal structure of the system.

First of all, there are the three realms: the *tattva*-s or ontological principles, the *bhāva*-s or the epistemological and ethical principles, and the *bhūta* or the phenomenal, empirical world.

Although the *tattva*-s or ontological principles are two (i.e., pure consciousness or *puruṣa* and Nature or *prakṛti*), the list develops into twenty-five, all the rest being developments of these two. The twenty-five *tattvas* are:

1	*puruṣa* or pure consciousness
2	*mūlāprakṛti* or the originary Nature (consisting of three constituent qualities: *sattva, rajas,* and *tamas*)
3	*buddhi* or *mahat*, intellect
4	*ahaṃkāra*, egoity
5	*manas*, mind
6–10	hearing, touching, seeing, tasting, smelling (the five sense capacities)
11–15	speaking, grasping, walking/movement, excreting, and procreating (the five action capacities)
16–20	sound, contact, form, taste, smell (the five subtle elements)
21–25	space, wind, fire, water, earth (the five gross elements)

Whereas the *tattva*-s are the ontological and epistemological principles of the world, the *bhāva*-s, eight in number, are the fundamental *predispositions,* or, possibly, the *a priori* tendencies inherent in the intellect (*buddhi*). These are:

dharma—predisposition toward virtue
jñāna—predisposition toward knowledge
vairāgya—predisposition toward renunciation
aiśvarya—predisposition toward power
and their opposite tendencies toward *adharma, ajñāna, avairāgya, anaiśvarya*

The twenty-five principles and the eight predispositions, interacting with each other, give rise to "phenomenal world" or "*pratyayasarga,*" which consists of fifty *padārtha*-s. These are:

five misconceptions or *viparyaya* (taken over into Patañjali's *Yogasūtras*);
twenty-eight "disfunctions" or *āśakti*-s including the perceptual, motor, and mental;
nine contentments (*tuṣṭi*-s); and
eight spiritual attainments (*siddhi*-s).

The spiritual attainments include rational reflection and reasoning; appropriate verbal instruction from a qualified teacher; careful study; thoughtful discussion with peers; an open but disciplined temperament; progressive overcoming of the frustrations of body and mind, of material and social being; and relating to cycle of rebirth and transmigration.

Clearly, these features of the phenomenal world, like the eight predispositions, are not, in a narrow sense, *categories,* if by categories one means either natural kinds or fundamental concepts. But if no description of the world is possible without taking into account the human responses, attitudes, and goals, then these must go into a description of the phenomenal world, and they may be regarded as the most general features of man's being-in-the-world. They would then be *existential* categories.

I will add brief remarks on (a) the Sāṃkhya doctrine of *guṇa*-s and (b) the Sāṇkhya theory of seven types of relations. The idea that nature, nonconscious and material, is composed of three qualitative aspects, each of which is then construed as a process, is a fascinating recognition that even if nature is a process, the process exhibits an intelligible essence, a dynamic aspect and mass or formless inert materiality, in such a manner that the three aspects cooperate and yet each tries to dominate over the other two.

The theory of relations lays down the fundamental relations that the system admits. These are:

1. the relation between the possessor and the possessed (e.g., the king and his servant), which obtains between consciousness and nature;
2. the relation between the root and its transformations (e.g., the milk and curd), which obtains between the original nature and its twenty-three forms;
3. the relation between the effect and its causes (e.g., a wagon and its parts), which obtains between any empirical phenomenon and the three *guṇa*-s;
4. the relation between the efficient cause and its effect (e.g., a potter and the pot he makes), which obtains between the three *guṇa*-s and their predispositional projections;
5. the relation between the source and its offspring (e.g., a tree and its branches), which obtains between the subtle elements (16–20) and the gross elements (21–25);
6. the relation of cooperation and association (e.g., between two friends), which holds between the three *guṇa*-s and their processes;
7. the relation between the killed and the killer (e.g., a snake and a mongoose), obtaining between the way one *guṇa* overpowers the other two.

A scheme such as the Sāṃkhya, one may say, conflates between a cosmology, a psychology, and an eschatology, hence, its seemingly archaic character. Hence also the problem of deciding which part of its theory is a doctrine of categories. On one reading, the system admits only of two categories: pure consciousness and nature. But on the reading favored here, the two *tattvas* give rise to a host of subordinate principles, which may reasonably claim categorial status.

BUDDHISM

In the Buddhist philosophies, a *padārtha* is called a *dharma.* The categories then would be the various types of *dharma*. A *dharma* is generally a point-instant, not an enduring substance. The Vaiśeṣika way of construing the substance-quality relation is rejected. Ultimately, a *dharma* being a simple particular, it is of the nature of a quality. But a complex *dharma* is rather an aggregate of qualities (i.e., *guṇasaṃghāta*). The closeness to the Sāṃkhya nature consisting of three *guṇa*-processes is clear. In different schools of Buddhism, this relation between *dharma*-s and *guṇas* as well as classification of *dharma*-s was differently done.

The early Buddhists, believing as they did that all entities are momentary (*kṣaṇika*), were concerned with the question of whether the past, present, and future have the same or different ontological status. Thus, among the *Sarvāstivādins,* who hold that everything exists (i.e., there are both mental and non-mental *dharma*-s), four kinds of theories came into being. Dharmatrāta held that when the future becomes present, the entity (i.e., the *dharma*), remains the same, it only leaves its future-state (*bhāva*) and assumes its present-state. The *dharma* remains the same—from future through present and past. Ghoṣaka, on the other hand, held that what changes is merely a mark (*lakṣaṇa*), not the entity itself—in the same way as a man, in love with one woman now, becomes free of that attachment later. Vasumitra preferred to say that what changes is rather a state (*avasthā*), not the entity—exactly as the same digit "0" can occupy different numerical places. Finally, Buddhadeva held the view that what changes is the relation, but not the *dharma* itself—just as the same woman is wife, daughter, and sister. As is clear, all these philosophers were concerned with the question, How much of change and how much of permanence is compatible with the nonsubstantiality and momentariness of a *dharma* (i.e., in what sense can we still speak of the same *dharma*)?

Of these four views, Vasubandhu pointed out the first should be appropriated to the Sāṃkhya theory, and in the last the three really coalesce into one. Vasubandhu himself preferred to hold that temporal position depended upon causal efficacy, such that "one depends upon another." A *dharma* thus comes to acquire past, present, and future locations, the structure of "*gata-gacchat-gamiṣyat*" ("will go-goes-is gone"). This, let it be added, is the nature of *samskṛta* or "composite" *dharma*-s.

Dharma-s are either composite (*samskṛta*) or incomposite (*a-samskṛta*). To the first group belong the five *skandhas* to which the Buddhists reduce the putative soul. These five are *rūpa* (visual form), *vedanā* (feeling), *samjñā* (sensation), *samskāra* (traces), and *cetanā* (volition, motivation, action). Each of these titles stands for a series, a *rāsi*, of atomic events. The incomposite *dharma*-s are three: *ākāśa* or empty space, *nirvāṇa*, and a temporary cessation of attention to other objects when the mind is exclusively attending to one. This listing of *dharma*-s shows that the Buddhist categories were psychological rather than cosmological, and yet note that space is one of them. Space is conceived as that which does not conceal and is not concealed, it is the mere absence of *rūpa.*

The smallest aggregation of *rūpa* is called an "atom." It is still not a substance-atom (*dravya-paramāṇu*), but is rather a *samghāta-paramāṇu* (i.e., the smallest *Gestalt*), which is taken to be of four kinds: visual, olfactory, taste, and touch.

Since each composite *dharma* is a momentary event, it has four marks: birth (*jāti*), decay (*jarā*), existence (*sthiti*), and destruction (*anitya*). These are the four primary marks of a composite *dharma.* Existence or *sthiti* is itself also a process. Four additional derivative marks follow: coming into being of birth, decay of decay, existence of existence, and destruction of destruction. The idea seems to be: don't hypostatise any of these stages, each is also a process.

Dharma-s are also classified into those in whom dirt, or evil qualities, tend to accumulate and those that are free from any defilement. Here the ethical, psychological, and cosmological coalesce.

The Vijñānavādin Buddhists severely attacked the Vaiśeṣika theory of substance. The so-called "thing" as an object of knowledge is, according to them, internal to its cognition. Nor are the atoms (of the Vaiśeṣika as well as of the early Buddhists) ontologically real. If an atom is subtle and has no dimension, several of them together cannot generate a gross body. To form an aggregate, the atoms must touch each other, and if they are not to completely coincide, they must touch in one side and not in another, but in that case they must have distinguishable sides and so cannot be "atomic." An atom is not the object of a cognition, for neither its marks nor its form are reflected in the cognition. The Vijñānavādins criticize also the so-called incomposite substances. Space is neither one nor many, so are the "cessations." With the rejection of external reality and the thesis that all phenomenal objects are mere representations, a new concept came to the forefront—that of "*ālayavijñāna,*" which plays the role of the substratum that, as it were, builds itself up by the traces of former experiences, and that contains the potentialities or seeds for all phenomena. It comes to play the role of a category that is at the other extreme from the non-dual consciousness, which the Yogācāra regards as the ultimate reality. Lest this ultimate reality be hypostatised as a substance or *dravya*, it is better to bring in the insight of Nāgārjuna and to regard it as *śūnyatā* or emptiness, and to require of the highest wisdom that it knows the emptiness of emptiness itself. Thus, there is a determined effort on the part of later Buddhism to transcend categorial thinking, not only of the Vaiśeṣikas but also of the early Buddhists as well—to transcend the concept of substance as much as the concepts of process and relationality.

VEDĀNTA

Under Vedānta, we shall discuss only Rāmānuja and Śaṃkara.

Rāmānuja makes an initial distinction between substance and nonsubstance (*a-dravya*). Substance is that which has states, or which undergoes change. The category of "nonsubstance" includes qualities, actions, and universals (which are separate categories in the Vaiśeṣika system). The nonsubstantial entities depend upon substances. The list of such entities includes ten: the *five* qualities of the five elements; the three *guṇas*—á la Sāṃkhya—which characterize matter; *śakti* or power of the cause to produce effect; and *saṃyoga* or contact as it is admitted in the Vaiśeṣika. Substances are six, falling in two groups: matter and spirit. Matter includes *prakṛti* or nature and time, knowledge (which is both a substance and quality of souls); pure (i.e., intelligible matter)—having only the *sattva* quality and without *rajas* or *tamas*; the finite souls; and God. The followers of Rāmānuja such as Venkatanātha expound interesting theses about space and time. Space is not a mere absence (as the Buddhists held) but something positive that we experience even when and where it is occupied by things. Time also is directly perceived as a quality of things that we perceive, it is one and eternal although it may appear to be many. In effect, time is coexistent with God.

There is one fundamental relation that Rāmānuja accepts: the relation of inseparability (*apṛthak-siddhi*), which is neither identity nor identity and difference, but which welds a substance and a quality, or two substances, one of which is dependent on the other, into *one* qualified (*viśiṣta*) entity. In many respects it is like the Vaiśeṣika inherence (*samavāya*), but the idea of dependence is stronger than in inherence. Metaphysically, this is the relation between soul and body, as well as among God, finite souls, and the world.

The Advaita Vedānta, not unlike Nāgārjuna, launched a radical critique of all doctrines of categories. In this exposition, which has to be brief, one can expound the Advaita thesis in two steps. First, the Vaiśeṣika thesis that there are many different types of reals, which are nonetheless related by "inherence" (*samavāya*), that there is an ontological glue that respects differences of type while knitting those entities together, is severely criticized by Śaṃkara. Inherence is defined as a relation between entities which are "inseparable" (*ayutasiddha*). Śaṃkara questions the sense in which a substance and its quality or a substance and its actions, are inseparable while yet being distinct types of entities, and argues that in none of the senses does it hold good. All these lead Śaṃkara to the conclusion that it is best to say that all these entities are, at bottom, identical. The "blue" and the "lotus"—in "the blue lotus"—are fundamentally identical. The quality is of the nature of the substance. It is the substance that, from a different perspective, is called by different names, just as the same Devadatta is sometimes referred to as "the son of Yajñadatta," "the husband of Rukmiṇi," "the father of Rucidatta," and so forth. The *guṇa,* and likewise an action, is really, in essence, the substance (*dravyātmakatā guṇasya*). It would seem, then, that for Śaṃkara there is only one category, namely substance, and one relation, namely "*tādātmya*" ("being its essence"), which is a form of identity that "tolerates" differences (*bhedasahiṣṇu*). The next step in the argument is to show that even this category cannot be coherently stated. It entails "difference"—difference of a substance from other substances, difference of a substance from its qualities and actions, difference between the particular and the universals it exemplifies, difference between the permanent substance and its changing states, difference between the cause-substance and the effect-substance. The philosophers of the Śaṃkara school therefore undertake a dialectical critique of the very category of "difference" in order to show that it involves incoherencies such as infinite regress and self-contradiction. What is called into question is the ontological status and determinability of "difference." Is difference a relation or a quality? If A is different from B, is A's difference from B a quality of A? If so, it is then different from A itself. The same holds good of B's difference from A. If difference is a relation between A and B, one may ask, how is this relation itself related to A and to B? We thus are confronted with infinite regress at all levels. If difference is not a real, then the entire theory of categories—of whichever school—becomes false (i.e., only phenomenally real, having conceptual reality but not ontological reality).

CONCLUDING REMARKS OR REFLECTIONS

Categories may be regarded either as ontological kinds (the highest, not further reducible, kinds) or as concepts (likewise, further irreducible, and of the highest order of generality). The Vaiśeṣika, the Sāṃkhya, and Rāmānuja's theories claim ontological reality. The Buddhist and the Advaita Vedānta theories can at most claim conceptual viability. Whether one is a realist or an idealist, one may nonetheless have to contend with the interesting fact that an identically formulated category may have a *neutrality* as against the larger metaphysical framework in which it may find acceptance. The category of substance is to be found in Aristotle and in Kant; there is a common system-independent content assigned to the category in the two cases. One may find likewise a whole set of categories that are accepted in systems of Indian philosophy that otherwise may differ a great deal among themselves.

Two further features of thinking about categories in the Indian philosophies have been earlier noted, and deserve to be recalled now. In the first place, the Indian systems did not radically separate the categories from the subordinate concepts or kinds that come under each. So the theorists after listing the categories would go on to list the subtypes under each—which Aristotle sometimes, but not always, did, while Kant never would. For the Indian thinkers, such subclassifications, carried far enough, bring us to the domain of the natural sciences. Thus philosophy was not regarded as an *a priori* science, radically cut off from the empirical sciences. The sciences were rather treated as continuous with philosophy.

In the second place, the categories were not often regarded as merely theoretical concepts. Since theory and practice, despite their distinction, were ultimately connected, and philosophical wisdom was supposed to lead to the highest good, sometimes the fully explicated doctrine of categories tended to have psychological, ethical, meditative, and spiritual resonances. This is what they should be, for the categories were the highest concepts of the total structure "man-in-the-world." Not alone the Sāṃkhya and Buddhism, but even the categories listed in *Nyāyasūtra* 1.1.1., testify to this feature of Indian thinking. The sutra clearly lists those categories whose precise knowledge would be conducive to the attainment of *mokṣa*.

We need also to ask, How do the philosophers arrive at a doctrine of categories? Is there a method that they follow in order to be able to discover and list all the categories "systematically and exhaustively" as Kant would insist? Aristotle did not make clear the precise method of discovery. Kant did raise the question and also sought to answer it in his chapter on "Metaphysical Deduction of the Categories." The Indian philosophers are almost always silent regarding their methodology. They would, more often than not, appeal to the tradition of the school, the *sūtra*-s or some ancient text or other. The real method, however, is not spoken about. They excelled in defending, modifying (or destroying, in the case of the opponents) the list. To be sure, the method was never *a priori*.

Even in the case of the realists like the Vaiśeṣikas, is it plausible to claim that their categories are meant to be descriptive? That may well be so. But it is one thing to claim that they were intended to be descriptive, quite another to say that, as a matter of fact, they were constructive in nature, proposing a conceptual framework that, to their satisfaction, best captured certain aspects of experience. Such a reading would collapse the distinction made earlier between categories as ontological kinds and categories as conceptual generalities.

It has also been noted that although many Indian philosophers recognized "being" (*sattā*) as the highest generality, they did not regard "being" as a category. This confirms our interpretation that insofar as Advaita Vedānta regarded the *Brahman=Ātman* as pure being, it transcended categorial thinking, but nonetheless it opposed Being (*sat*) to *a-sat* (and *mithyā*), and tended to regard Ignorance (*avidyā*) as the womb of all categories.

Besides the "material" categories such as substance, quality, action, and so on, there are also the "formal" categories such as "identity" and "difference," and "relational" categories such as "causality" and "inherence." I will briefly bring out their place in Indian thinking. To begin with the latter group, we have seen the role inherence plays in Vaiśeṣika, and "inseparability" in Rāmānuja and *tādātmya* in Advaita Vedānta. Curiously enough, although the causal relation plays a crucial role in all Indian metaphysical thought, causality was never included in the list of *padārtha*-s, not even by the Vaiśeṣikas and the Sāṃkhya who were very much concerned with it. One cannot but ask, why? Only the Śaivas included "*kārya*" and "*kāraṇa*" (effect and cause) in their list, and so did the medicine school of Caraka (whose concern, as is understandable, was with ascertaining the *cause* of a disease, and the healing *effect* of a medicine). The reason for not including "causality" in the list of *padārtha*-s is, not that the philosophers did not assign to it its central importance in metaphysics, but that the relation of "causality"—stripped of the notion of "power"—was analyzed into (a) a substance or a quality or an action, and (b) the relation of "invariable temporal precedence" (*niyatapūrvavartitva*). In the case of a material cause, one has a substance (the matter) in which the effect inheres in the relation of *samavāya*. In other cases, we have the noninherence cause (as e.g., the quality of parts causing the quality of the resulting whole). In Sāṃkhya and Vedānta, the causal thinking is no less fundamental, but believing as they did that the effect was already contained in the cause prior to effectuation, the relation between cause and effect was either one of pure identity or of identity-in-difference.

Now the formal categories of identity and difference did play a crucial role, however. The Buddhist glorified difference, reducing identity to systems of differences; the Nyāya-Vaiśeṣikas recognized both identity and difference as equally real (difference being subsumed under negation [*a-bhāva*] as one of its subkinds, i.e., as "mutual negation" [*anyonyābhāva*], expressible as "A is not B, B is not A"). In the Grammarian philosophy, the aspect of identity in all entities i.e., pure being, is the only reality. The Sāṃkhya stands in between the Nyāya-Vaiśeṣika and the Grammarians. The former regards the universal as a mere *dharma,* but not as *dharmī,* as a property but not as a substance. For the Sāṃkhya, the universal—as with the Grammarians—is the ultimate reality; but unlike the Grammarians, the Sāṃkhya regards the specific differences as also real. The pure being, the highest universal, according to the Vaiśeṣika, belongs to all things, but nothing belongs to it; it is not the *locus* of anything. The Vedāntin and the Grammarians, however, regard it as the locus of all beings. In Sāṃkhya, the universal that permeates all effects, all phenomenal beings, is indeed the ultimate cause. The universal is the cause, particulars are effects. This universal cause is the *prakṛti.* Other metaphysicians, on the ground that time pervades all effects, regard time as the ultimate cause.

Philosophers, especially of the Vedānta school, differed among themselves regarding which of the formal relations is fundamental: "identity," "difference," "identity as qualified by difference," "identity and difference." Others, more dialectically oriented thinkers such as Nāgārjuna, recognized—like Plato in *The Sophist*—that identity implied difference, and difference entailed identity, but unlike Plato, concluded from such arguments that categorial thinking was incoherent.

Chapter Four

The Self (*Ātman*)

The category *ātman* is exemplified not in the omnipresent *ātman* of the Upaniṣads, but in the finite individual selves (and souls) and in the theistic God. While it is plausible, and usual, to translate *ātman* as "soul," a more appropriate translation may be "self." Reasons for this suggestion will be clearer as we proceed (although we shall use both the terms as needed). Now, in *Nyāyasūtra* (hereafter cited as N.S.) 1.1.9, Gotama gives a list of *prameyas* or objects of true knowledge—the list includes only those objects of true knowledge, whose knowledge leads to attainment of the highest good. This list begins with *ātmā,* and continues with body, sense organs, objects (of those senses), cognition (*buddhi*), mind (*manas*), action (*pravṛtti*), defects (*doṣa*), the beginningless series of birth and death (*pretyabhāva*), fruits (*phala*), suffering, and *mokṣa* or complete freedom from all pain and suffering. This list is in addition to the Vaiśeṣika categories such as substance, quality, actions, and so forth.

Commenting on this *sūtra* 1.1.9, Vātsyāyana writes:

> Here, the self is the seer of all things, enjoyer of all things, omniscient, experiences all things. Body is the place of its enjoyment and suffering. The sense organs are the means for enjoyment and suffering. Enjoyment and suffering are cognitions (of pleasure and pain). The internal sense or *manas* is that which can know all objects. Action (*pravṛtti*) is the cause of all pleasure and pain; so also are the *doṣas* (defects), that is to say, passion, envy, and attachment. The self had earlier bodies than this one, and will have other bodies after this one—until "*mokṣa*" is achieved. This beginningless succession of birth and death is called "*pretyabhāva*." Experience of pleasure and pain, along with their means, i.e., body, sense organs, etc., is "fruit" (*phala*). "Pain" is inextricably linked with "pleasure." In order to achieve *mokṣa* or *apavarga,* one needs to consider all happiness as pain—whence will arise detachment and in the long run freedom.

After this list of entities in N.S. 1.1.9, the next *sūtra* proceeds to tell us how "self" (or *ātman*) is known. The self, being too "subtle," is not perceivable by any of the senses, and even if one experiences the self in such judgments as "I am happy," this is not a knowledge of the true nature of the self. Consequently, the question arises, How is the self known? Is it known only through the scriptural texts? The purpose of N.S. 1.1.10 is, according to Vātsyāyana, to answer these questions. The *sūtra* states that the self can be inferred from a series of marks: desire, hatred, effort, pleasure, pain, and cognition. From these marks one can infer the existence of a self that is eternal and different from the body. These six marks are specific qualities (*guṇas*) of the self. The self can be defined as what possesses these qualities. Of these six, the presence of the three, desire, effort, and cognition, is common to both finite selves and the infinite self, that is, God. Two, hatred and pain, are present only in the finite selves; regarding the one remaining quality, God may be regarded as having eternal happiness, while the happiness of finite individuals is noneternal.

The "body" is defined, in N.S. 1.1.11, as the locus of three things: activity (*ceṣṭā*), sense organs (*indriya*), and object (*artha*). This definition needs some explanation. *Ceṣṭā* is explained by Vātsyāyana as any activity that is intended to attain what is good and to avoid or shun what is harmful. Such activity does not belong to nonliving things such as a jar, it can belong only to the body of a finite soul (*jīva*). Likewise, the sense organs belong only to a body. Lastly, by saying that the body is the locus of the object (*artha*) of the senses, the *sūtra* means by *artha* not the objects themselves, but the pleasure and pain they bring about. Such pleasure and pain belong to the body. To say that pleasure and pain have the body as their locus is to say that pleasure and pain belong to the self only as limited (*avacchinna*) by the body.

Pravṛtti," or "activity," means such actions—good or bad—that give rise to *dharma* and *a-dharma,* or merit and demerit. Such actions are either produced by body or by words or by the mind (*manas*). Good or meritorious actions belonging to these three groups are (i) helping the other, hospitality and charity; (ii) truth, doing good to the other, doing what pleases the other and studying the scriptures; and (iii) kindness, nondesiring, and faith (*śraddhā*). Their opposites are the ten actions that produce demerit.

Doṣa is defined, in N.S. 1.1.18, as what causes *pravṛtti* or activity. These *doṣas* or faults incite the self to action, good or bad. These are three: attachment (desire for objects), hatred, and mistaken idea (i.e., *rāga, dveṣa,* and *moha,* respectively). Of these, the last is the most fundamental. Attachment and hatred arise in a person who lacks right knowledge, and incite him or her to perform actions, good or bad.

By "fruit" (*phala*) is meant the consequence—pleasure and pain primarily—of action and the *doṣas* (N.S. 1.1.20).

Duhkha is defined (N.S. 1.1.21) as suffering (*bādhanā*). Without body and the sense organs, there is no suffering. Objects that cause suffering are also called *duhkha* in a derivative sense. *Mokṣa* is complete freedom from suffering.

A next step for the philosopher is to argue that cognition (*buddhi*) is a quality of the self. Cognition cannot be a substance—or a manifestation of a substance, as a pot is of clay—because it is partless and yet not eternal. A substance that is partless, such as an atom, is eternal. But a cognition—such as perception of the flower on this table—comes into being and then ceases to be. It is not, therefore, a substance. Nor is it an action, for an action involves motion in space, and a cognition has no spatial movement. Not being a substance or an action, and yet being a particular, it can only be a quality. But whose quality is it? There are four possible answers to this last question. A cognition is a quality either of a self, or of the body that the self inhabits, or of a sense organ belonging to that body, or of the mind (*manas*). The Naiyāyikas have argued in great detail in order to demonstrate that the last three alternatives have to be rejected, so that only the first is tenable. Another argument often advanced in favor of the thesis that cognition is a quality runs as follows: cognition is a quality, for while being noneternal it is apprehended only by one sense organ (i.e., only by *manas,* the inner sense), as is "color." Cognition cannot be a quality of mind, so argues N.S. 3.2.19, because only the self is a knower; the sense organs, outer and inner, cannot be knowers for they all are dependent while only the self is independent. Furthermore, desire, aversion, activity, pleasure and pain must belong to the same locus as cognition, for the same thing that cognizes a thing also desires to acquire it or shun it; it also acts to possess or shun it, and on reaching its goal experiences pleasure or pain. Body, which is material, cannot be the locus of that structure, all those elements can belong only to a conscious self (N.S. 3.2.35–6).

So far we have been expounding the view of Nyāya-Vaiśeṣika system. This position differs substantially from the views of the "spiritual" (*ādhyātmika*) systems such as Sāṃkhya and Advaita Vedānta. First, a terminological difference. As N.S. 1.1.15 states, on the Nyāya view the words *buddhi, upalabdhi,* and *jñāna* are synonymous. On the Sāṃkhya and Advaita Vedānta view, *buddhi* is a modification of the first evolute of *Prakṛti* (i.e., *mahat,* or the cosmic intelligence), while "*jñāna*" or consciousness is the nature of the self (or *puruṣa*). "Knowledge" (such as perceiving a jar) is a modification (*vṛtti*) of *buddhi,* in which consciousness is reflected. The Naiyāyikas reject this picture of our cognitive life. For them there is no consciousness as such; there is of course a universal "consciousness," which is instantiated in every cognitive state or occurrence. "Consciousness" stands for all such particular cognitive states of all selves. Each such state—a perceiving, an inferring, a remembering, and so on—is called either a *buddhi,* a *jñāna,* or an *upalabdhi* (i.e., a cognition, which arises in a self when the appropriate causal conditions are present). When it was said earlier that a self is a "conscious" substance, what was meant is not that a self has consciousness always and under all circumstances (for it is not conscious when it is in a deep sleep, or in a coma), but that only the self can have consciousness. It is the ability to have consciousness that essentially belongs to a self.

It should be added that for the Nyāya-Vaiśeṣika—as also for the Vedānta—desire, aversion, pleasure and pain, effort, and activity are not themselves "conscious" states. They are, like cognition, qualities of a self, but they are not themselves *eo ipso* cognitions. They rather become objects of cognitions that objectify them. To have a pleasure is not, on the Nyāya view, *eo ipso* to know that one has a pleasure. To know that one has a pleasure is to have a reflective cognition, which objectifies that state of pleasure as occurring in one's self. On the view of Advaita Vedānta, though, pleasure and pain, by their very occurrence, are directly manifested by what the Vedāntins call "witness consciousness" (which the Nyāya does not admit).

What, then, distinguishes a consciousness or a cognition, as distinguished from the other qualities of a self (or, on the Advaita Vedānta view, from the modifications of the inner sense)? It is here that we find two sharply contrasted positions in Indian thought. One of these takes the defining character of "consciousness" to be its self-illuminating feature. Just as the light of a lamp manifests an object but also manifests itself (we do not need another lamp to show the light of the first lamp), so does consciousness, while making its object known, makes itself known without needing to be objectified by another cognition. This is the answer given by the Sāṃkhya, Yoga, Vedānta, and Buddhism. The other position, defended primarily by the Nyāya-Vaiśeṣika, locates the distinguishing feature of consciousness in its function of manifesting, making known, or showing, whatever happens to be its object. In effect, consciousness has the property of having an object (*saviṣayakatva*). There is no objectless consciousness. Besides, having an object is to manifest that object to its knower. If S has a cognition C of an object O, then S knows O. In a certain sense, this amounts to recognizing that consciousness is characterized by its intentionality. In holding this position, the Nyāya-Vaiśeṣika rejects the first position stated above, for example, the view that consciousness is self-revealing. If no object is known, prior to becoming the object of a cognition, the same holds good of a cognition as well. A cognition is known only when it becomes the object of another cognition. Thus we have two extreme positions: (1) consciousness is self-illuminating; and (2) consciousness is intentional.

Now, (1) and (2) are not prima facie inconsistent. However, many philosophers have felt that you can choose only one of the two possibilities. Of the Indian philosophers, Śaṃkara seems to have felt that if consciousness is self-shining and the object is manifested by another, the two must be opposed to each other like light and darkness, and so they cannot be "together," suggesting that consciousness' being of an object must be a "mystery" and can only appear owing to "ignorance" (*avidyā*). Opposed to this is Rāmānuja's view that consciousness is both intentional and self-shining, furthermore, that it is self-shining insofar as and precisely then when it is intentional. An error opposite to Śaṃkara's is committed by the Naiyāyikas when they argue that consciousness, being of an object, cannot be of itself, so that if a consciousness C_1 is to be manifested, it needs to be made the object of a subsequent reflective consciousness C_2. What they need to recognize is the possibility that being self-shining may be the essence, *svabhāva,* of consciousness, and what is true of other things, say, of a jar, need not be true of consciousness. What is needed is a middle position in between complete objectivist with regard to consciousness and complete reflective self-transparency, namely, a prereflective transparency, which reflection presupposes and may further clarify.

Consciousness is both intentional and prereflectively, nonthetically, transparent. I want to claim that this "prereflective, nonthetic transparency" is what is meant by the Advaita Vedāntin's expression "*avedyatve sati aparokṣavyavahāra-yogyatva.*"

Now we can raise the question, Are not the other specific qualities of the self, such as desire, aversion, pleasure, pain, effort/activity also intentional? The standard Nyāya view seems to be that only cognitions have intrinsic intentionality (i.e., *svābhāvika viṣayapravaṇatva*). First defining cognitions as object-manifesting (*arthaprakāśa*), Vallabhācharya, in *Nyāya-līlāvatī,* argues that the object is internal to the *buddhi,* the cognition is given *together with the object.* Pleasure and pain, on this view, do not have their *intrinsic* objects. An object becomes the object of pleasure and pain by first becoming the object of a cognition. Their intentionality is *derivative.*

The text that Vallabhācharya has in mind is not easy to translate. However, in order to clear up the issues, let us distinguish between (i) being the cause of pleasure (and pain), and (ii) being the object of pleasure (and pain). The point that was made in the preceding paragraph is that the object (*viṣaya*) of pleasure and pain must be a known object, while the cause need not be known. In that case, it would be reasonable to claim that when one feels happy about good news that one has just received, the object of that feeling is that news as received (i.e., as the object of a cognitive state). But precisely that object is intrinsic, and not derived, for that feeling. So instead of saying that the object of pleasure and pain is derivative, it would be better to say that the object of pleasure and pain is *founded* on the object of cognition. If a cognition K_1 has an object O, let us say, the object as cognized is $K_1(O)$. Now the happiness, which arises upon that knowledge, has for its object precisely $K_1(O)$. When that happiness is cognized (by K_2), then the object of K_2 is $H[K_1(O)]$. While thus we have a founding-founded relation, the intentionality, in each case, is intrinsic.

This seems to be more in accord with the overall framework of the theory being expounded—a theory that posits an interconnected structure of agency (*kartṛtva*), being the subject of enjoyment and suffering (*bhoktṛtva*), and being the subject of knowledge (*jñātṛtva*). By knowing, one is led to act; by acting, one enjoys or suffers the consequences; by enjoying or suffering, one acquires knowledge of what is to be shunned (that which causes unhappiness or suffering). In this interdependency, all three must be intentional and goal-oriented: knowledge, action, and feeling, yet it may be that knowledge is basic to all, and accompanies them all.

While thus arguing for the thesis that cognition, action, and feeling all have their intentional objects, we may still hold the Nyāya view that only cognition is, by definition, consciousness, while action and feeling are not states of consciousness, but rather possible objects of consciousness. Since on the Nyāya view, consciousness is definable as what manifests its object (and not as self-illuminating), neither cognitions (which is consciousness) nor noncognitive states (of the *ātman*) are self-manifesting, they all are manifested by a cognitive state that objectifies them. What cognition alone can do—for that precisely is its function—is to manifest its object. An action is also directed toward something (e.g., what is to be done, the goal to be achieved, the means to be adopted) and thus is intentional, but it does not manifest, or make known, those objects (i.e., one may pursue a goal without knowing that goal). One may have pleasure and pain, which have their intentional objects, but by themselves—not being states of consciousness—do not manifest those objects (i.e., one may be happy about an object and yet not know about it). That we, more often than not, know our goals and what we are happy about is due to the cognition supervening and manifesting those objects. The advantage of this theory, as compared with a theory that uniformly makes cognition, actions, and feeling all states of consciousness—as with the Buddhists—is that it makes room for unconsciously motivated actions and unconscious pleasures and pains. The Vedāntin totally excludes this last possibility, since it posits a witness self (*sākṣicaitanya*), which "manifests" all internal states. The Nyāya detaches intentionality from self-manifestation; the Advaita Vedāntin also detaches the two. For the Vedāntin, intentionality belongs to the *vṛtti,* "self-manifestation" belongs to consciousness, and their "being together" causes the appearance of cognitions being both. The ever-present "witness" prevents any unconscious internal object. The Nyāya allows for that possibility. One possible mediation is to admit of degrees of consciousness, of degrees of "transparence," and thus to explain the so-called "unconscious" not as *a-cit,* but as still *cit* though with a low degree of transparency. This was implied by the statement that consciousness is both intentional and prereflexively, nonthetically, transparent.

It is at this point that we turn to another major question connected with all that has gone before. This concerns the nature of the body and its relation to the self.

BODY

The reason the question of "body" and its relation to *ātman* is so crucial in our present context is that some of the qualities that are ascribed to the *ātman* seem to be also dependent upon the body. This is especially true of pleasure and pain, and of activity. But it may also be true of cognitions. Let us recall: the specific qualities of an *ātman* are cognition, pleasure, pain, desire, aversion, effort, merit, demerit, and such traces of past experiences as give rise to memory. Each of these is dependent on the soul's being in relation to body. None of them could arise in a purely disembodied soul.

Earlier, we mentioned the Nyāya definition of body. Body has been defined as the locus of activity, sense organs, and pleasure and pain. It is also the locus of all enjoyment and suffering that the self experiences. All activity aiming at attaining the good and warding off the evil or the harmful is located in the body. Action is not mere physical movement. It is goal-directed and belongs to the body. Perceptual cognition depends upon sense organs, and sense organs are located in the body. Inference and *śabda* depend upon sensory perception.

This consideration brings to light a certain tension in the theory that, on the one hand, recognizes the *saviṣayakatva* or intentionality of the specific qualities of the self, and, on the other, is forced to the admission that not the pure self, by itself, but only the self as embodied exhibits intentional properties. The relation of "embodiment," the connection between body and the self is generally brought under the relation or quality of conjunction or *saṃyoga.* But *saṃyoga* is an external relation which cannot adequately do the job of that intimate relation of "embodiment."

In order to emphasize the uniqueness of this relation, let me give below a series of definitions of "body" given in a Vedāntic work *Darśanasarvasvam* by Śaṃkaracaitanyabhārati.

1. The thing which a conscious subject can entirely use for its own purpose is its body (*yasya cetanasya yaddravyaṃ sarvātmanā svārthe niyantuṃ śakyaṃ tattasyaśarīraṃ*).
2. X is the body of Y if X is used in Y's actions and X's movements are regulated by Y's efforts (*tadīyakṛtiprayukta-svīyaceṣṭāsāmānyakatvarūpam tanniyamyatvameva taccharīraṃ*).
3. A thing which a conscious subject can entirely hold for itself is the body of that consciousness (*yasya cetanasya yaddravyaṃ sarvātmanā dhārayituṃ śakyam tattasyaśarīram*).
4. X is the body of Y if Y's fall, owing to Y's movement, is hindered by X's conjunction with Y (*tadīyakṛtiprayuktasvapratiyogikapatanapratibandhakasamyoyga-sāmānyakatvaṃ taccharīratvaṃ*).
5. The thing which entirely and uniquely belongs to a conscious subject is its body (*yasya cetanasya yaddravyaṃ sarvātmanā śeṣataika-svarūpaṃ tattasya śarīraṃ*).
6. X is the body of Y if X is always inseparable from Y and is an adjective of Y (*yasya cetanasya yadavasthamapṛthaksiddhaṃ dravyaṃ viśeṣaṇaṃ dravyam tat tasya śarīraṃ*).
7. X is a body if (i) being an ultimate whole, i.e., not a part of another whole, it possesses effort to act; or (ii) being an ultimate whole, it is the locus of sense organs; or (iii) being an ultimate whole, it is the limitor of suffering (and enjoyment); or (iv) it is the cause of the application of the word "body" (*yattu antyāvayavitve sati cestāvattvaṃ, antyāvayavitve sati indriyāśrayatvaṃ, . . . bhogāvacchedakatvaṃvāśarīrapadapravṛttinimittamiti*).

The last one is the Nyāya definition we expounded earlier. The sixth definition is expressed in the language of Rāmānuja's system (i.e., in terms of "inseparability").

In these definitions, we are told, consciousness uses and rules over the body; that consciousness holds its body; that a body by virtue of its conjunction (*saṃyoga*) with a conscious self prevents the free fall of that conscious entity; that a body uniquely belongs to a consciousness; and that a body is inseparable from consciousness and functions as the latter's adjective. But these accounts are not free from difficulties. The idea of a fall is inappropriate. A conscious soul can fall in space only because it is embodied; so to say that the body prevents this fall is incoherent. A body is not inseparable from consciousness, for in case of death, the body remains, but consciousness leaves it. To say that a living body is so inseparable is true, but then a living body is definable as one that is potentially conscious.

The idea that the conscious self rules over the body and regulates its movements is widely held and seems quite plausible. On this view, what is really and originally intentional is the soul or *ātman,* or rather its consciousness, while the seeming intentionality of bodily movements is due to the presence of consciousness in the body. One may even want to say that the intentionalities of consciousness cause bodily movements and lend the latter a semblance of intentionality. I find this account unacceptable, not merely because it is as such not a sound philosophical position but also because it is not the general Indian point of view. It is true the Nyāya-Vaiśeṣika philosophers often speak of the contact (*saṃyoga*) between the soul and the body; the soul being of infinite extension on their view is in contact with all other things. But "contact" is too external a relation, which is better captured by Rāmānuja's "inseparability" (*apṛthaksiddhi*); in case one prefers the Vaiśeṣika *samavāya,* one needs to be able to say that the soul inheres in the body. The reason intentionality of consciousness, on the Vaiśeṣika view, could not be construed as causing intentionality of body is that without the relation to a body the soul by itself does not come to possess all those special qualities that exhibit intentionality. A much better way of conceptualization of the situation would be that there is a sort of identity between intentionalities of consciousness and intentionalities of the body. Experienced from within by a soul itself, and as self-ascribed ("I know," "I desire," "I am acting"), the intentionality is "inner" (i.e., of the specific state of the soul, not still of the pure soul but of the soul as limited [*avacchinna*] by the body). At the same time, as experienced from without and as ascribed to the other ("He knows," "He desires," "He is acting"), intentionality is of the body (i.e., of the specific bodily states, not still of the body as a lump of matter, but of the living body as limited [*avacchinna*] by the relation of belonging to that soul).

Who then is the agent, the subject, of intentionality? Who is Devadatta? His body, his soul, or their conjunction, or the body conjoined with the soul, or the soul conjoined with the body? This is how Prabhācandra formulates the issue in his *Prameyakamalamārtanda.* It is easy to argue that Devadatta cannot be identified with any of these. To say that Devadatta is his body is first to be able to say what "his" means without circularity; second, to be true, the sentence "Devadatta is his body" requires that by "body" we mean conscious, living body; and, third, if by "body" we mean simple nonliving, nonconscious matter, the sentence is false. Devadatta cannot simply be his soul, for the sentence "Devadatta is cooking rice" cannot mean "Devadatta's soul is cooking rice." Devadatta cannot be the conjunction of a body and a soul, for, in the first place, one must in a noncircular manner be able to identify which body and which would make up Devadatta; second, it is absurd to say that the conjunction of two things is cooking rice, or going to the market, or riding a horse. One needs a relation between the two—the body and the soul—such that the two form a whole that would be one individual whole, where the two "limit" each other, the body is the "limitor" of the soul, and the soul of the body, the two are one thing experienced once from within, and once from outside. Of this one thing, cognitions, desires, efforts, actions, pleasure, and pain are intentional qualities, but not merit and demerit, for these two should be able to cling to the soul after the body perishes.

ACTION

Consider the framework for a theory of action that is expressed in the following verse:

ātmajanyā bhavedicchā ichhājanyā bhavetkṛtih
kṛtijanyā bhaveccesṭā cesṭājanyā bhavetkṛiyā

"*Ichhā* or desire is caused by the soul (meaning by *ātmā,* here "knowledge"), desire to do leads to the will to do, the will to do leads to effort, effort leads to action." Now, there are two kinds of desire: desire for the fruit (which is either pleasure or absence of pain) and desire for the means to achieve the fruit. For the first kind of desire, what is needed is simply knowledge of the fruit. For the second kind of desire, what is needed, in addition, is the knowledge that the goal is capable of being reached (*iṣtasādhanatājñāna*).

Desire is of various sorts. One classification is into eight kinds: *kāma* (desire for erotic pleasure), *abhilāṣaḥ* (eagerness to possess something), *rāgaḥ* (desire to enjoy a thing again and again), *samkalpaḥ* (resolution), *kāruṇyam* (desire to eliminate the other's pain, in complete disregard of one's own interest), *vairāgyaṃ* (desire to give up all objects, owing to realization of their faults), *upadhā* (desire to cheat), and *bhāvaḥ* (desire deeply concealed within oneself).

Agency may be defined, following Vācaspati (*Tātparyatīkā* on N.S. 3.1.7), as the coinherence of knowledge, desire, and effort. One who wills to do (*cikirṣannapi*) but is ignorant of the means and their operation is not truly an agent; likewise, a person who is ignorant and does not desire, as also one who desires but, owing to laziness, does not make an effort—neither one of these is an agent.

A special case of intentional action is moral action. Moral action, performed in accordance with a moral injunction of the form "one ought to Ø," raises special questions regarding what could *incite* a person to do Ø. We know, for example, in Kant's philosophy, even if a moral action is performed both in accordance with duty and out of a sense of duty, what incites a person to follow the moral law is a *respect* for the law (i.e., a feeling and not rational considerations alone). The Indian thinkers, on the other hand, held in general—irrespective of the school of philosophy to which they belonged—that an action follows from some cognition. What they differed among themselves about is regarding what that cognition must be of. The question that concerned them, in this context, is, What must be the precise object of a cognition, such that the cognition can produce the will to do through the mediation of producing the appropriate desire?

On the Old Nyāya view, three cognitions jointly bring about the desire. They are the cognition on the part of the agent that he or she can achieve the desired good by performing the action, the cognition that he or she can perform the action, and the cognition that no greater harm will befall the agent for performing the action.

The New Naiyāyikas simplify the matter by requiring that what is required is knowledge of the meaning of the imperative sentence ("one ought . . ."); the latter when uttered by a competent speaker assures the auditor of the achievability of the desired good by doing the action.

The Mīmāṃsakas of the Bhātta school reduced all to one requirement: the imperative form of the verb ("ought" or "should" in Sanskrit), the *vidhiliñ*, has the power to produce the inspiration (*preraṇā*) to make the mental effort needed. This is what the Mīmāṃsakas call *śābdibhāvanā,* meaning the *bhāvanā* or thought produced by the form of the words alone—a thought such as "this wants me to do Ø." Knowledge of the speaker's intention, over and above the efficacy of the imperatives themselves, is not needed for this purpose. In the case of words of the scriptures (e.g., there being no speaker at all or, if there is one we do not know who he is), the words themselves lead the auditor to act. While the form of an injunction, if it is believed to be the words of a competent author, can incite a person to act, the "Ø" (in "one ought to 'Ø'"), refers to a specific action (such as "speaking the truth") that is to be performed to reach a specific goal. This part was called *arthībhāvanā* or thought about the specific content. The relative weight of these two thoughts—the general thought of "ought" and the specific thought of a course of action as conducive to reach a goal—became the subject matter of considerable debate among the schools of Indian philosophy, especially the Mīmāṃsakas. The Prābhākaras emphasized, often exclusively, the role of the verbal form, while the Bhāttas emphasized the conduciveness to a goal.

INTENTIONALITY

The expression "intentionality" and "intentional act" used here need further explanation. There are two senses in which "intentional act" is used. In one sense, more in conformity with ordinary use, an act (physical, mental, or verbal) is intentional if it is purposive (i.e., goal-directed). In this sense, all actions by individual selves, on all the Indian theories we have reviewed, are intentional, being goal-directed. In the other sense, cognitive acts, or rather, cognitive experiences, are intentional inasmuch as they have an "object" of their own (i.e., are *saviṣayaka*), although they may or may not be intentional in the first sense. Many philosophers have tried to subsume the first sort of intentionality under the second. They have maintained, in other words, that if an act is directed toward the goal X, then that act may be said to have that goal X as its object and to have that object in the specific manner of entertaining that object as its goal. Others maintain that in trying to know an object O, one is directed toward the goal of reaching O, and when that goal is achieved, one is said to know O. We can say, in this latter case, having an object is a way of aiming at a goal—which would be tantamount to reducing the second sort of intentionality to the first.

Here, when we have spoken of intentional acts, we want this expression to be understood in either or both of the two senses. Some are purposive or goal-directed; some are of some object or other. The general philosophical abstract form "intentionality" includes both. By "act" in this context one should not mean "activity." It is used as a technical term signifying any experience that is characterized by intentionality. Some of these are activities in the literal sense, some are not activities. Cognitive acts are not activities, but are cognitive experiences of whatever happens to be their objects. In the technical vocabulary of the Nyāya-Vaiśeṣika, those cognitive acts are not *karma*-s but *guṇa*-s of the soul.

One of the issues that arises in the context of intentional acts is how these acts fit into a causal order. The Indian philosophers generally accepted a causal order of things. The intentional acts also belong to this order (i.e., they are themselves caused, and they cause their effects). They do not stand outside the causal order. A cognitive act is caused by appropriate causal conditions, just as the cognitive act itself gives rise to appropriate volitional acts and, in the long run, activities directed toward acquiring and shunning some things. Therefore, the opposition between the causal and the intentional, which plagues Western thinking, does not appear in Indian thought.

There is, in much of Western thinking on these matters, one feature of intentionality that also is absent in Indian thinking. This is the way "intentionality" is connected to the idea of sense (as distinguished from reference). Intentional acts not only are about something, but also are about something *qua* such and such. This theory of sense is just absent in the mainstream Indian philosophical thinking whose theory of meaning is referential. It is interesting how, in the absence of a theory of sense, there could yet be a fully developed theory of intentionality, and just because of this the intentional acts could be inserted into an overall causal order. In the standard (Western) theory, the *Sinn* refuses to be integrated into a causal nexus.

I think, to the end remains the theory that these intentional acts belong to the *ātmā* (or soul) as its qualities—a theory that on the one hand rejects the Advaita

Vedānta theory of the *aīmā* as a nonpersonal undifferentiated consciousness and the naturalist theory, which identifies the self with the body.

GOALS (*PURUṢĀRTHA*-S)

The Indian tradition recognized four goals of life, pursued *de facto* by persons who are embodied souls living in the world and members of a community (i.e., who are beings-with-others and beings-in-the-world). These four ends, viz., *artha* (wealth), *kāma* (sensuous pleasure), *dharma* (righteousness), and *mokṣa* (spiritual liberation from the bondage of the world, embodiedness, and karma-rebirth structure) are desired, striven after, though not always with success. Several things need to be noted regarding this rather well-known doctrine, reduced by repetition to a cliché.

First, in our present context, these goals, as desired and striven after, are features of desires, strivings, and activities that are, on the theory expounded, qualities of the selves. So it is literally true to assert that the souls desire, strive after, and perform actions to achieve the appropriate goals. (On the Advaita Vedānta view, you can say this only obliquely, not literally, for desires and strivings and actions cannot be literally ascribed to *ātman.*) But in order to have these *guṇa*-s, the souls must be embodied, must be in the world and with others. Why this should be so is easy to see. Pursuit of *artha* presupposes social, economic, and commercial institutions through which alone one can acquire wealth. As a matter of fact, the idea of "wealth" presupposes intersubjectively accepted social institutions. Pursuit of *kāma* presupposes corporeality, sexuality, and sensitivity to pleasure and pain. The very idea of *dharma* is the idea of approved (by the scriptures) practices, all of which presuppose the corporeality of the person as well as the existence of being-with-others: duties are, to a large measure, if not in entirety, directed toward others. All three goals thus arise, function, and can be pursued within the context of corporeality and sociality. The same is true, though not so easily recognizable, even in the case of *mokṣa*.

Second, while pursuing these goals—as people always do—one is functioning within a historically constituted tradition. The doctrine of four goals or *puruṣārtha*-s is a part of the Hindu tradition, and it is only within this and allied traditions that one perceives (and interprets) oneself as well as others as pursuing any of these goals (which is not saying that people belonging to other traditions do not pursue these goals). This is especially true of *dharma* and *mokṣa.*

The reason for pointing this out is that, while the soul (*ātmā*) is an a-historical entity, and even if the qualities ascribed to it (in the foregoing exposition) are ahistorically conceived (in the sense that any soul, anywhere, at any time, can have, and generally has, these qualities), the actual, particular qualities (the cognitions, desires, efforts, strivings, actions) that a soul acquires are historically determined and occur within a tradition.

Thus, for example, every person, embodied and living in the world and with others, pursues goals that enhance material prosperity. One undertakes trade, commerce, business, agriculture, and other well-known means for gathering riches and thereby acquiring happiness. But to bring all these pursuits under an overall category of *artha* as referring to one of the four general goals of life is already to use a large idealized concept that itself is achieved within a tradition. (The very same pursuits may be alternately brought under the concept of search for "power".)

For the Indian tradition, these four goals become the themes of four basic sciences: *arthaśāstra* (science of political economy), *kāmasūtra* (the aphorisms on erotic pleasure), *dharmaśāstra* (the science of ethics), and *mokṣaśāstra* (the science of spiritual freedom). Other possibilities of exploring those goals still remain. The idea of four sciences, also made use of in the tradition, namely *trayi* (the science of the [first] three Vedas), *vārtā* (the science of agriculture and animal husbandry), *dandanīti* (the science of criminal justice), and *ānvīkṣikī* (philosophy) does not quite coincide with the other fourfold scheme. But *trayi* may be correlated to *dharma, vārtā* to *artha, dandanīti* provides conditions necessary for all pursuits including philosophy whose goal is emancipatory wisdom.

These sciences, then, have their foundation in idealized concepts of the goals of human strivings, which are, ontologically considered, "qualities" of the finite soul as embodied and as being in the world.

Chapter Five

Central Metaphysical Issues

THE PROBLEM OF CAUSALITY (*KĀRYA-KĀRAṆA-SAMBANDHA*)

Early Beginnings

Questions about causality were being asked already in the Vedic hymns in connection with the origin of the world. One fundamental question seems to have been unresolved there: the question, namely, regarding the priority of being or of nonbeing. Thus in *ṚgVeda* X.72, we hear "Existence, in an earlier age of gods, from nonexistence sprung." The hymn goes on to speak of "the productive power." The hymn X.129, known as the *nāsadīyasūkta,* makes an indecisive speculative effort: "Non-being then existed neither, nor being," and the one, by "its inherent force," also "by force of heat" came into being. "Creative force was there, and fertile power: Below was energy, above was impulse." The one desired to be many ("Desire entered the One in the beginning"). Hindu thought moved toward according priority to being. How can being come out of nonbeing? became a refrain in the questionings of the philosophers.

The Svetasvatāra Upaniṣad I.1 asks, "What is the cause of the world? Whence are we born?" The next verse suggests various possible answers. "Time, or inherent nature, or necessity, or chance, or the elements, or a womb, or a person," or a combination of all these? Clearly, there were those who held that things arise by fixed inherent nature; again, those who held that things arise by chance; or, again, those who held that things arise in accordance with laws. There were again those who said that things arise from an original womb in which all things were *in potentia,* or also those who said that the ultimate atoms, the elements, combined to produce all things. Thus we have the indications of the Sāṃkhya, the Vaiśeṣika, the Cārvāka, and the Buddhist views.

From the time of the Upaniṣads, two cosmological pictures seem to have captured the Hindu mind. One is the picture of things of the world arising out of combination of indivisible atoms. The other is the picture of things arising out of the womb of a primitive, undifferentiated, One Being. The former is conceptualized in the Vaiśeṣika and early Buddhism, the latter in Sāṃkhya and Vedānta. The latter, again, finds different expressions in the texts. On one account "Desire entered the One in the beginning" (*Ṛg Veda,* X.129). The One wanted to be many. "Would that I were many! Let me procreate myself! So he desired . . . and created this whole world" (*Taittirīya Upaniṣad,* II.6). On another account, "At that time, the world was undifferentiated, It became differentiated just by name and form" (*Bṛhadāraṇyaka Upaniṣad,* I.IV.7).

Later Developments

If the things of the world arose out of combinations of atoms, the perceptible, experiencable things are effects whose material causes are the atoms together with a certain relation (such as mutual contact or *saṃyoga*). The efficient cause, on the Vaiśeṣikaa theory, is of course God. In the case of entities like a piece of fabric, the effect (i.e., the fabric) is produced by a host of threads put together in a certain relation by the weaver. The first thing to note about this account is that what is produced, the fabric for example, is a new thing, over and above the aggregate of its parts. It has properties and functions that the parts do not have. It is a new product, which did not exist, even potentially, in its causes (in the parts—atoms or threads). The theory, therefore, is known as the theory that the effect (*kārya*) was nonexistent (*asat*) prior to its production (*asat-kārya-vāda*), also as the theory of new beginning (*ārambhavāda*).

The second thing to note in this account is that the threads form the material cause, the parts in which the newly emergent whole inheres; they are also called the inherence cause (*samavāyikāraṇa*). But the threads alone cannot produce a fabric. They must be brought into a certain relation. That relation is also a cause, but not one in which the product may be said to inhere. It is therefore called non-inherence cause (*asamavāyikāraṇa*). Hence three kinds of causal conditions are needed: efficient cause, inherence cause, and noninherence cause. If one of the latter two is destroyed, the product is also destroyed.

The Vaiśeṣikas also recognize, besides these three, some causes that are common to all causation (which invariably precede *all* effects). These are eight in number: God, God's knowledge, God's desire, God's effort; the unseen merit and demerit (as forces); the antecedent nonexistence of the effect; space and time. All these eight invariably and unconditionally precede any effect whatsoever. What we generally regard as the cause of an event or entity is not any of these but the specific cause of it. As regards the specific (*asādhāraṇa*) cause of something, the Vaiśeṣikas single out something that plays a special role among all the causal conditions. This is called the *karaṇa* (whereas the other conditions are all *kāraṇas*). A *karaṇa* is that which, together with a process or the final condition, known as *vyāpāra,* immediately results in the production of the effect. Some authors use *karaṇa* for both, for the last condition that is immediately followed by the effect. Thus the word *karaṇa* or cause sometimes stands for any causal condition or for their totality. The cause is defined as that which exists uniformly before the effect but saying this much is not enough. For there are things that exist uniformly before an effect, but we do not count them as causes. For example, the color of the threads exists before the fabric to be woven, and yet it is not taken to be a cause. We therefore need to add some other requirement: the cause must be "nonirrelevant." What exactly "relevance" (and so "nonirrelevant" in this context) means needs much more elaboration, which we cannot undertake now.

It must be mentioned, however, that the Naiyāyikas, in order to make a causal relation universal of the form "whenever A, then B," want to insert into its formulation the concept of "limitor." To say that fire causes burning is to regard fire as limited by fireness (*vahnitvāvacchinnavahni*) to be the cause (but not fire as limited by its color). The "limitor" functions as an intensionalist device for recovering a universal quantification and so to avoid the Humean probabilistic formulation. The Vaiśeṣikas do this without positing a causal power (*śakti*) as an ontological entity, as opposed to the Mīmāṃsā school.

The Vaiśeṣika theory, so far discussed, known as *asatkāryavāda,* has been rejected by the mainstream tradition of "spiritualist" (*ādhyātmika*) philosophies such as Sāṃkhya, Yoga, and Vedānta. If a cause can produce something that was nonexistent, then it remains utterly inexplicable how what was nonexistent comes into existence, and also gives rise to the worry why then does A (the putative cause) and not C cause B when neither A nor C contains B within it. If the oil seed that, when pressed, causes oil to flow, did not contain, prior to pressing, oil within it, then why cannot chips of stone (which also do not contain oil within them) be pressed to produce oil? The plausible answer would seem to be that A causes B, but C does not, because B is already contained—implicitly, *in potentia*—within A, but not within C. Something cannot come out of nothing. What is utterly nonexistent cannot become existent. Such considerations lead to the opposed theory known as *sat-kārya-vāda* or the theory that the effect (*kārya*) was already existent (*sat*) within the cause. On this theory, causal production is not bringing into being a new entity, but making explicit what was already implicit, rendering actual what was potentially there, or giving the preexistent stuff a new form (as in the case of making jewelry out of a lump of gold). Such arguments logically lead to postulate an original stuff, the so-called *Urnatur,* the *mūlāprakṛti,* in which all empirical phenomena were contained, and out of which they emerge.

Although the Vaiśeṣikas admit existence (*sattā*) as a universal that permeates all entities, they regard this universal existence to be a property (*dharma*) that is located in all entities, but not as by itself an entity (*dharmī*). The Sāṃkhya philosophers, on the other hand, regard the universal as the locus, the stuff, underlying all particular entities. Consequently, in the Sāṃkhya system, the material cause is the *dharmī* or the substance, while its effects are *dharma* or properties of that substance. Thus things like pots and jars are properties belonging to the stuff, clay, which, as the *dharmī,* underlies them all as their locus or substratum. The properties or *dharmas* are of three sorts: they are either arisen (*udita*) as when a jar has come into being, or disappeared, i.e., past (*śānta*) as when the jar that came into being is now destroyed, *or* yet-to-arise, i.e., in the future (*avyapadeśya*). It is the universal substratum clay that persists through these changing states as their cause. In this sense, the universal is the cause of particulars. That this is so is shown, for the Sāṃkhya philosophers, by the fact of recognition that "this too is clay" (*sa evāyam mṛt*) in which "clay" refers not to any particular state of clay, but to the universal stuff. As one pursues the universal substratum of particular modifications, it becomes more and more supersensible the more universal it is. Where this process of universalization stops, we reach the last cause of all things, the original *prakṛti*, which for that very reason is furthest removed from all sensuous perception.

In this way, the Sāṃkhya cosmology and the Vaiśeṣika cosmology move in opposite directions. The former stops with the most ubiquitous substance, the latter with the smallest discrete entity. As regards destruction of an entity, the Sāṃkhya does not, while the Vaiśeṣikas do, admit destruction without any remainder inasmuch as according to the former the effect dissolves back into its cause whereas according to the former the effect, being a new entity that was, prior to production, nonexistent becomes nonexistent after destruction.

This Sāṃkhya theory is generally known as *pariṇāmavāda* or theory of transformation (a variety of *satkāryavāda*), i.e., the effect is the cause in a new form. Between the two, cause and effect, there is a relation of identity-and-difference (*bhedābheda*)—identity of stuff but difference of form. Both identity and difference are real. The Vaiśeṣikas affirm just difference between the cause and the effect and argue that it would be a self-contradiction to affirm identity as well as difference between the same two things. The Sāṃkhya philosophers argue that identity-cum-difference is sometimes apprehended by a *pramāṇa,* as in "blue lotus" (contrast "horse cow" where only difference is presented), and what is presented through a *pramāṇa* cannot be self-contradictory.

This theory of identity-cum-difference (between cause and effect) is upheld by—in addition to the Sāṃkhya—many other schools of philosophy such as Bhāṭṭa Mīmāṃsā, Yoga, Bhāskara's Vedānta. Among those who reject it are the Vaiśeṣikas, the Prābhākara Mīmāṃsā, and the Buddhists.

In the *Yogasūtra* (3/13), three sorts of transformation are distinguished. These are transformation of a stuff (*dharmī*) into a property (*dharma*); transformation of a *dharma* into a mark (*lakṣaṇa*) and transformation of a mark (*lakṣaṇa*) into a condition (*avasthā*). The first, known as *dharmapariṇāma*, occurs when a lump of clay is made into a pot; the second, known as *lakṣaṇapariṇāma,* occurs when the pot, at first future and not-yet, becomes present, and then past. The third, known as *avasthāpariṇāma,* occurs when the present is at first "new," then becomes "old" and gradually "ancient'; likewise when the "past" becomes "long past," and so on, or the future is at first "distant future," then becomes "near future" and so on.

The early Buddhists took over many of these ideas, and sought to bring about a reconciliation between the Sāṃkhya and the Vaiśeṣika, taking from the former their thesis that things are always undergoing transformation, and from the latter the thesis that destruction is total without any remainder. This combination leads to their theory of instantaneousness (*kṣaṇikatva*) of all things.

The transition from the Sāṃkhya theory of transformation to the Advaita Vedānta's theory of "illusory transformation" or *vivartavāda* is logical and a rather short step. If the Sāṃkhya rejected the Vaiśeṣika theory of origination of new entities as incomprehensible on the ground that what was nonexistent could not come into being, the same sort of question may be raised against the Sāṃkhya theory itself. How can the Sāṃkhya, on its own grounds, assert that a new form emerges with the transformation of the underlying stuff? Shall we not require—if nothing new can ever arise—that the form too was already there prior to transformation? In that case, neither matter nor form could ever be new, that there cannot be new origination, nor any new transformation. The primal stuff, *prakṛti*, alone is real, the productions and destructions, arisings and perishings of phenomenal things and events would be mere appearances. We now move on from the theory of real transformation to the theory of illusory transformation. Cause alone is real; effect is different from the cause only in appearance.

Returning to the thesis of identity-cum-difference (*bhedābheda*) of the Sāṃkhya, we can now say that on the nondualistic Vedānta view, both identity and difference cannot belong to the same order of reality. Identity is really real; difference is only apparently real. The appearance of difference is superimposed upon the underlying identity.

Thus the nondualistic Vedānta assigns to the idea of transformation of *prakṛti* into the phenomenal world a provisional status while it totally rejects the Vaiśeṣika's atomic theory. Only he regards that original *prakṛti* to be false and so to be the same as what he calls the original ignorance (*avidyā*). With this changed designation (and ontological shift), the Vedāntin can affirm that the phenomenal world is a transformation (*pariṇāma*) of ignorance, but a false appearance (*vivarta*) of the *brahman*—as also a creation of God (*Īśvara*). These three theses can be held together by virtue of a complicated theory as to the relation among the three terms: "*brahman,*" "*Iśvara,*" and "*avidyā.*"

Finally, let us take a quick look at the Buddhist theory of causality. It has already been mentioned that the early Buddhists combined elements from the Sāṃkhya with elements taken from the Vaiśeṣika. From the Sāṃkhya they incorporated the idea of constant and incessant transformation of reality; and from the Vaiśeṣika they took over the idea of destruction without remainder (*niranvayavināśa*). The result is the idea of instantaneous events, of which as one perishes the succeeding one arises. It is closer to the Vaiśeṣika theory that the effect *was* not existent prior to its production, and adds that the cause must have to perish so that

Figure 5–1 Temporal Structure of Events

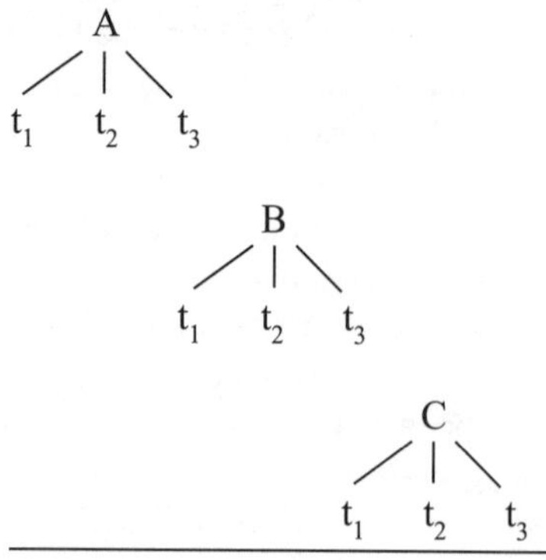

the effect may arise. If the event A is the cause of the event B, and the event B is the cause of the event C, and since each event's life consists of three instants (*kṣaṇa*), one for arising, another for being, and the third for perishing, then the temporality of the three events may be represented in Figure 5–1.

If the cause is what immediately precedes the effect, the Buddhist position seems to imply—as Śaṃkhya pointed out—that not A but the cessation of A causes B. This last thesis would seem to entail that a negative entity—the subsequent nonexistence of A—can cause B, which as so formulated, seems to be absurd. In order to avoid this seemingly absurd consequence, one may take recourse to (1) either admit that such is indeed the case, namely, that the cause must cease to be before the effect arises; *or* (2) hold that a cause is the positive entity immediately preceding the effect, which would rule out the absence of A from being the cause of B; *or* (3) distinguish between the three states of "perishing of A"—arising of perishing, being of perishing, and perishing of perishing—and so also between three states of "arising of B," and rewrite Figure 5–1 above as follows (see Figure 5–2).

In this scheme, arising of B arises with the arising of perishing of A. What causes, as the immediate antecedent, the arising of B is the arising of perishing of A.

The resulting Buddhist theory of causality, also known as the thesis of dependent origination (*pratītya samutpāda*), has certain interesting features. The *Samyutta Nikāya* lists the following. First there is a regularity of sequence in the sense that specific effects arise depending upon determinate conditions. Second, there is lack of irregularity in the sense that given the causal conditions it is never the case that the specific effect fails to occur. Nor is it ever the case, third, that the effect arises from other than its own specific conditions. Fourth, there is no plurality of causes; one effect cannot be due to many different causes on different occasions.

Besides these four, the following also hold good of the causal relation. The cause perishes when the effect arises, such that there is no underlying unity

Figure 5–2 Further Refinement of the Temporal Structure

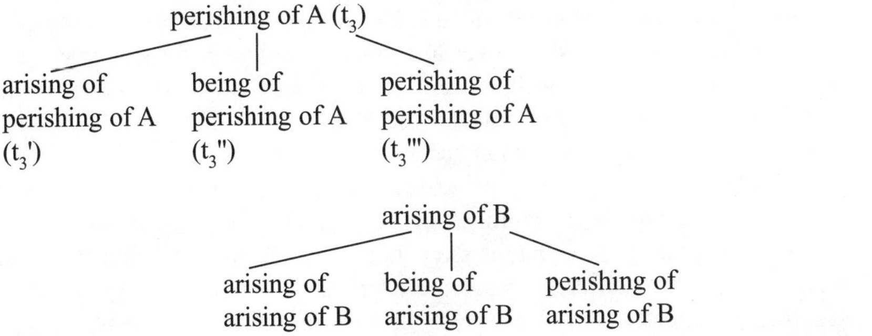

through the process. Also to be noted is the Buddhist view that no activity is exercised, there is only regularity of succession. It is not necessary to posit an active agent. To be fair, since on the Buddhist view to exist is to be causally efficacious, what denial of activity means is that we need not posit an activity in addition to the being of the cause-event. Thus both extremes—noncausality or *ahetukasiddhi* and determinism or *niyativāda*—are mistaken. The result is a view that there is a sort of determination of the effect by its specific causal conditions—a necessity that is not a mechanical, external necessity between two unrelated entities. The relation is rather intrinsic, though it obtains between two distinct entities.

Furthermore, the cause is always an aggregate of various conditions, so also is the effect. When it is said that the cause and the effect are two distinct events, that is said only for the sake of analytic simplicity, or also due to the predominant interest of the speaker. In addition, the causal relation is to be ascertained empirically, and never *a priori*.

RELATIONS

From causal relation, let us move to other relations.

Samavāya or Inherence

The Vaiśeṣika recognizes only one fundamental ontological relation to be a distinct category. This is inherence or *samavāya*. We have already discussed its nature and role earlier in this chapter. To recall what has been said: inherence holds good between entities belonging to different ontological categories—between a substance and its qualities, a substance and its actions, a particular and the universal it instantiates, and an ultimate, further indivisible particular (an atom, a soul, e.g.) and its particularity (*viśeṣa*). Only in one case it obtains between entities that come under the same category. This is the case with a whole substance that inheres in its parts that are also substances. A distinctive feature of inherence is that in all these cases, there is a certain, rather one-sided inseparability (*ayutasiddhatva*) between the relata: the quality is inseparable from the substance in which it inheres, the universal from the particular, for example. This relation serves the Vaiśeṣika well, it preserves pluralism and also makes possible a unified thing. It is accepted only by the Nyāya, Vaiśeṣika, and Prābhākara Mīmāṃsā. The other systems do not accept it.

The Vedāntins undertake a critique and refutation of *samavāya*. They question the underlying idea of "inseparability," and wonder how two quite different entities could be cognized as having the same locus. It is uncontroversial that in "the pot and the jar," two different things are cognized but *not* as having the same locus. If a substance and its color are also likewise very different entities, the cognition "blue lotus" ought also to be like "the pot and the jar." Furthermore, the Vedāntins state: assuming that the two entities "blue" and "lotus" are related by inherence, there are two possibilities. Inherence relates the two either by itself being related to each of the two relata or while itself remaining unrelated to them. The latter seems absurd, if inherence can relate the two relata even if it is not related to any, then any other unrelated entity, not to speak of any other relation such as conjunction, should be able to do so, and inherence would be a useless entity. The former alternative would lead to an infinite regress, for then we would need to posit relations between inherence and each of the relata, and the same questions may be asked about these new relations as well.

The Vaiśeṣikas want to stop this alleged infinite regress by saying that inherence is indeed related to both the relata by a relation that is self-linking, which they call *svarūpa* relation. We will return to this kind of relation later. The Vedāntins do not accept such a relation that is self-linking and that constitutes the nature of one of the terms (i.e., of inherence). But do not the Vedāntins hold that all phenomenal things have their essential nature in the *brahman*, thereby hypostatising the relation of "having that as its nature" (*tādātmya*) in the same manner?

The Vaiśeṣikas also regard this relation of inherence to be numerically one and eternal: one, because were there many instances of inherence, they would be instances of the universal "inherenceness" and this universal would inhere in those particular inherences that would lead to an infinite regress. Furthermore it is eternal, for it also obtains among entities that are eternal, as for example between individual souls and the universal "soulness" (*ātmatva*). The question whether inherence is perceptible or merely inferred divides the schools, which admit inherence as a fundamental relation.

Self-Linking Relation (*Svarûpa*)

We have just seen that, when faced with the prospect of landing in an infinite regress, the Vaiśeṣikas admit a self-linking relation where the dreaded regress ends. This occurs in many different cases. We have examined one case, namely, that of inherence. If B inheres in A, or AIB, then I relates to A and to B by a self-linking connector, which is nothing other than the self-nature (*svarūpa*) of the I itself.

Other such cases are "There is an absence of pot on the floor," "absence of pot," "an absence whose counterpositiveness (*pratiyogitā*) is limited (*avacchinna*) by potness," and "the cognition whose objecthood (*viṣayatā*) attaches to the pot." In each case, the expression within quotes designates a relational structure, but none of the familiar relations such as conjunction and inherence is there. Hence the need for recognizing the presence of a self-linking connector. An absence can be on a floor only as self-linking, so that the relation is of the nature of the bare floor. In "absence of pot," the absence can only be related to the pot (which is absent) in such a self-linking relation. So also is the relation between absence and its counterpositiveness (in the third of the above expressions, potness), or also the relation between a cognition and its object. Gangeśa defines a self-linking relation as what can give rise to a predicative cognition without the need for postulating another relation.

Many neo-Naiyāyikas such as Raghunātha Śiromaṇi do not admit such a relation.

Nondifference (*Tādātmya*)

This is the fundamental relation according to Advaita Vedānta. But nondifference is the absence of difference. How can an absence function as a relation? To show that it may function as a relation, consider the sentence "A blue lotus is blooming." In this case, a unified meaning is possible only if "blue" and "lotus" are understood to be nondifferent. In verbalization of an apprehension, a relation is not mentioned but only understood. The nondifference is to be posited. This nondifference is posited by semantic expectation (*ākāṇksā*), according to the Naiyāyikas. The Prābhākara Mīmāṃsākas on the other hand hold that a word always presents a related entity, so that the words "blue lotus" by themselves can present a relational structure. But they have no good account of *which* relation is it that they signify.

All relations presuppose difference among the relata. How can then nondifference be a relation? To this the Vedāntins reply that owing to difference of the words "blue" and "lotus," one posits difference in their designata, and *then* asserts their nondifference on the ground that otherwise they could not designate a unified meaning.

Contact (*Saṃyoga*)

We have briefly discussed contact as a *guṇa* in chapter 3. This is the view of the Nyāya-Vaiśeṣikas. Here a few other matters of philosophical importance regarding contact will be mentioned. It has been said in that context that contact is regarded by the Vaiśeṣikas as being both a quality and a relation. No substance, if it is not eternal, can arise without contact. All substances, if they are caused, presuppose, on the Vaiśeṣika's theory, contacts among atoms. Can we then say that contact belongs to all substances? We have to bear in mind that contact always obtains between two substances—not in one substance by itself, nor among more than two. Besides, each contact is a particular property, so that in the Vaiśeṣika ontology there are infinite number of contacts. Every substance then becomes the locus of an infinite number of contacts—space, time, God, and finite souls are all regarded, in the Vaiśeṣika, to be all-pervasive. They are therefore in contact with all things, and with each other.

Furthermore, contact is the relation between two things that were previously unrelated. There is no contact, in other words, which has no beginning. Contact can never be eternal. It can come into being either by movement (*kriyā*) or through another contact. The former sort may be either brought about by movement of one substance or by movement of both. Examples of each kind of contact may easily be found. I will give an example of the sort of contact that comes into being through another contact. When I touch a tree with my hand, the contact between my hand and the tree brings about contact between my body and the same tree. Contact with a part brings about contact with the whole.

There are two other features of contact that are worth mentioning. Some relations are such that they make one of the relata to be in another. These relations are technically called "determinant of being in" (*vṛtti-niyāmaka*). Inherence is one such relation. One of the relata of inherence is a color and it is *in* the other (i.e., a substance). But contact is sometimes "determinant of being in," sometimes not. Thus if I place my hand on a table, there is contact between the two such that my hand is on the table (the table is not on my hand). But if I join my two palms to greet a guest, there is contact between the two palms such that none of these is the locus of the other's being.

Contact, in addition, does not pervade its locus. It is with a part of it, while there is absence of contact (with the same thing) in the same thing, only as limited (*avacchinna*) by another part. If a monkey is sitting on the top of a tree, there is contact with the monkey in the tree as limited by the top part, but there is absence of the same monkey in the very same tree at the same time in another part. In Nyāya's technical vocabulary, inherence is *vyāpyavṛtti* (pervades its locus) while contact is *avyāpyavṛtti* (does not pervade its locus).

Part (*Avayava*) and Whole (*Avayavī*)

One of the issues that divides the realistic philosophies of Nyāya Vaiśeṣika and Pūrva Mīmāṃsā from the Buddhist is, Is a whole a new entity that is produced when its parts come together, or is the whole *nothing but* an aggregate of (its) parts? Is a pot, or a jar, or a cloth, nothing but an aggregate of pot shards, or of jar-parts, or of threads (or, in the long run, of appropriate atoms), or is it a new thing that comes into being as a result of putting its parts together? When the

Buddhists preferred to say that a thing is nothing but an aggregate of its parts, they had in mind the metaphor of a heap of sand. The heap is not an additional thing over and above the grains of sand that are in it. The Hindu philosophers, who preferred the other answer, had in mind the case of a pot or a piece of fabric that arises only when its maker—the potter or the weaver—functions as an efficient cause. The new thing that is produced clearly has properties and exercises functions that do not belong to the parts. What is philosophically significant is that the whole is perceived, while not all the parts are, and also when some of the parts may not even be perceptible. If there is no genuine whole, but only a mere aggregate—then I will not be perceiving the aggregate in case I am not perceiving all its constituent parts. What is probably the case is that based on the presentation of parts that I do see, I *infer* those I do not. The consequence is that we do not strictly speaking perceive physical objects, for physical objects are, on the Buddhist view, aggregates of parts not all of which are perceptible. My alleged perception of the tree over there must then be in truth inference. Only the simplest, not further analyzable, element would be perceptible. This is what the Buddhist calls *svalakṣaṇa,* and its perception, or rather sensation, is truly *pratyakṣa*.

As opposed to this view, the Nyāya-Vaiśeṣika and the Pūrva Mīmāṃsā hold that physical objects, as genuine wholes, are perceptible, and argue, in opposition to the Buddhists, that perceiving physical objects is different from inferring them. What is more, you can infer objects that are perceptible. Since the whole, on the theory of the realists, is a new thing over and above the parts, it is not a necessary condition of perceiving that whole that we also perceive all its parts. To the contrary, it is quite plausible that given some of its parts, one can on the basis of that presentation, perceive the whole, a tree for example.

The issue then about the irreducibility of the whole or the *avayavin* is crucial to epistemology. It is also crucial to metaphysics, especially to admitting the idea of God as the creator of the world. The usual causal argument, as advanced for example by the Naiyāyika Udayana, attempts to prove of the world that it is made by an intelligent maker, as is the jar. The Buddhists, in reply, argue that the *pakṣa* or the minor term "world" is not an entity, but an aggregate of such entities as sticks and stones, which themselves on their part are some sort of aggregates. In that case, there is not only the fallacy of *asiddhapakṣa* (i.e., a minor term whose existence is doubtful), but also no possibility of adducing an agreed upon example (*dṛṣṭānta*), in the present case, a thing whose being made by an intelligent creator is uncontroversial.

Thus it is fundamental to Hindu realism that there be wholes that are more than mere aggregates, as it is to Buddhist phenomenalism that there are no such wholes. If the Nyāya distinction between part and whole—*avayava* and *avayavin*—is a most valuable means of rehabilitating the realism of physical objects, we still need to ask what precisely is the nature of the unity of the *whole*. The Nyāya tells us two things on this point: for one thing, as we have noted, the whole is other than the mere aggregate; and for another, the whole resides in each of its parts in the relation of inherence (*samavāya*). This last thesis runs counter to the common sense understanding that the parts are in the whole. The parts, since they are prior to the whole, have an independent being, but the whole, not having an independent being of its own, exists only in the parts.

EXISTENCE OF AN EXTERNAL WORLD

Connected with the above discussion is the denial of an external world by the Yogācāra Buddhist and affirmation of the external world by the Nyāya-Vaiśeṣika and Pūrva Mīmāṃsā. The Yogācāra Buddhist argument for the thesis of *vijñapti-mātratā* or "cognitions alone" may be formulated in four steps as follows:

(1.) Things are but aggregates of parts.
(2.) The ultimately simple parts of [the allegedly external objects] are qualities such as *blue*.
(3.) If two things are never to be found apart (i.e., whenever one is experienced, the other is experienced too), then they must be identical. (This principle is called "*sahopalambhaniyama*".)
(4.) Blue and sensation of blue are such. Whenever we experience blue, there is sensation of blue and vice versa. Therefore they are identical. Blue, therefore, is a content of a cognition. It follows that things are but cognitions, and their putative externality is only an appearance.

Step (2) is established by arguing against the Vaiśeṣika atomism and by replacing the atoms by phenomenal, simple qualities. In this connection, the Buddhist raises some pertinent objections against the Vaiśeṣika thesis that perceptible physical objects arise out of conjunction of atoms. Step (3) is formulated and sought to be established by Digñāga. This step is challenged by many. Even if two things are always found together, they need not be identical. A flower and its perfume are just such entities. Step (4) is challenged by the Naiyāyikas on the ground that it presupposes the Buddhist doctrine that every cognition cognizes itself. Since, on the Nyāya view, a cognition does not cognize itself, when blue is presented, the cognition of blue is not. Therefore, there is no "coexperiencing" (*sahopalambha*) between the two. Moreover, blue cannot be, contrary to the Buddhist, a content of a cognition. A cognition, on the Nyāya view, is formless (*nirākāra*). It has no content. Since a cognition does not manifest itself, but only shows its object, whatever is initially presented by a cognition, for example the color blue, must fall outside the cognition, and cannot be the cognition's own content (for, *ex hypothesis*, the cognition does not show itself).

Indian realism, in its strong form, as it is to be found in Nyāya-Vaiśeṣika and Mīmāṃsā, is based upon two philosophical premises: one, that a cognition is totally formless, so that any form (or content) that appears in a cognition must fall outside that cognition; and two, a cognition only shows its object, but not itself; it is not *svayamprakāśa* or self-manifesting. From both premises, it follows that whatever form is presented in a cognition must be external to the cognition. The Buddhist who denies external things denies both these premises. It subscribes to the theory that cognitions have their own forms (*jñānasākāravāda*) and the theory that cognitions cognize themselves. Both together make realism hard to prove.

Śaṃkara's nondualistic Vedānta regards the phenomenal world to be a mere appearance. Nevertheless, Śaṃkara defends an empirical realism and so takes the Yogācāra to task for denying external objects. If, according to the Yogācāra, there are really no external objects, things only appear as if they are external, Śaṃkara asks, How can anything appear *as if* it were external if in fact there were nothing external? (A rope appears like a snake, since there are real snakes.) To quote Śaṃkara's inimitable sentence, "No one can say Visnumitra appears to be the son of a barren woman."

To be noted is that despite the strong realism, the Nyāya school emphasizes that existence (*astitva*) and knowability (*jñeyatva*) [and also nameability (*vācyatva*)] are coextensive properties. Whatever exists is knowable and nameable. The three properties, however, are different. Their coexistence holds good, but not necessarily. What is asserted in saying "Whatever exists is knowable" is this: if the causal conditions for knowing an object exist, then it will be known. But this knowledge need not be perceptual. It may be inferential. "Knowability," for the Nyāya, does not mean "capable of being perceived."

The nondualist Vedāntin holds that all things are objects of what he calls "witness-consciousness," either as known or as unknown. This thesis makes room for things that I do not know of; they are nevertheless objects of consciousness but as unknown. Those that are objects of consciousness as known (i.e., as manifested by an appropriate cognitive state), logically have *had* unknown existence. Thus the nondualistic Vedānta saves empirical realism by its doctrine of positive ignorance (*bhāvarūpa avidyā*), which conceals a yet-to-be-known object and confers on it the status of "unknown existence" (*ajñātasattā*).

IS THE WORLD UNREAL?

The nondualistic Vedānta of Śaṃkara nevertheless proceeds to maintain that the world (adding "empirical" to "world" is superfluous) is unreal, despite its empirical (*vyavahārika*) reality. This is denied by most of the schools of Indian philosophy—by the Nyāya-Vaiśeṣika, the Mīmāṃsā, the Sāṃkhya-Yoga, schools of Vedānta other than Śaṃkara's, the Jaina, and the early Buddhists. The question, then, "Is the world unreal?" became a most pervasive disputational issue. To understand the issue it is necessary to recall what precisely Śaṃkara means by the falsity of the world (and, consequently, of the finite individuals). To be sure, he does not want to say that the world is simply nonexistent like a rabbit's horn or a round square. He regards the world as being false (*mithyā*), and the false is not the nonexistent; *mithyā* is not *asat.* On the contrary, in his elaborately developed theory of illusion, the nondualistic Vedāntin defines the false as that which is "indescribable either as *sat* (existent) or as *asat* (non-existent)." Indescribable (*anirvacanīya*) in this context means only "cannot be determined. . . ." The false cannot be said to be *asat,* for unlike such nonexistent entities as a rabbit's horn or son of a barren woman, the illusory snake is presented to perceptual experience as the yonder object. What is perceived cannot be *asat.* In the same way, the false is not existent (*sat*) either, for anything that could be removed from existence by a cognition could not be said to be existent (*sat*). The illusory snake just ceases to be there, is not seen any longer, as soon as one has true cognition of the thing over there as a rope. The false object, then, can be characterized as that which becomes the object of negation "for all three times" (it never was there, is not there, will not be there)—*traikālikaniṣedhaviṣaya*—in the very same locus where it was presented (*pratipannopādhau*). The world and finite individuals have precisely this paradoxical nature. That is the thesis of nondualistic Vedānta, but we still have to ask, How is this thesis established? How is it established, in addition to appealing to scriptural texts, that the world and finite individuals are objects of negation "for all three times"?

The sort of philosophical arguments that the nondualist advanced in support of his thesis may be called "a critique of difference." The empirical world consists of differences. Differences are of many different kinds. A preliminary classification would be into homogenous difference (or difference between things belonging to the same class, the difference, for example, of one cow from another), heterogenous difference (or difference between two things belonging to two different classes, the difference, for example, between a cow and a horse), and internal difference (or difference among parts of the same thing, for example, between the top and the legs of a table). When the Sāṃkhya asserts the distinction between consciousness and nature, it makes use of the second kind of difference. When the Sāṃkhya again asserts the difference between many selves, each being a pure consciousness, it makes use of the first sort of difference. When the Buddhist holds that the alleged self really consists of series of changing states, arising and perishing, he makes use of the third kind of difference (i.e, difference among the constituent parts of a whole). The nondualist then launches a severe critique of the very category of difference, and tries to show that it involves circularity, infinite regress, and self-contradiction. The demonstration, in brief, would run like this: let A and B be different. A then has the property of being different from B. The two then, A itself and its difference from B, must be different. Then we have fresh differences leading to infinite regress. Likewise, with B and its difference from A. Applied to causality, the cause and the effect must be different. If the effect is different from the cause, how could then cause produce the effect? According to *satkāryavāda,* which the nondualist accepts, cause and effect must be identical; any difference between them must be a mere appearance. The familiar kinds of negation that a pluralist accepts suffer from the same defect. If a thing does not exist prior to its origination, one needs to answer the question, how could that which does not exist come into being? If there is a negation (i.e., absence of a thing after its destruction), one would want to know if what exists can become nonexistent.

From such criticisms as these would follow that consciousness has no real other (for any such other would fall within consciousness as its content), no real origination and destruction, no internal differentiation, no homogenous differences either (i.e., no difference of my consciousness from yours). As a result, consciousness must be one, beginningless endless reality without any real difference of any kind. That indeed is *brahman.* All differences must be mere appearances.

Given such a conclusion, one still needs to answer the question, What makes the one appear to be many? The appearances are not grounded in the nature of reality, they must be superimposed *ab extra* upon reality, as is the illusory snake appearance superimposed upon the real rope. This superimposition (*adhyāsa*) must be due to ignorance (*avidyā*) that, on the nondualist theory, is a positive and beginningless principle. To say that ignorance is a positive entity (*bhāvarūpa*) is to say that it is not mere absence of knowledge. It has two functions: concealment of the real and projection of the false appearances.

The system is threatened by its admission of two principles: the *brahman* and ignorance. The nondualism is still maintained inasmuch as what we have is not a dualism of two reals, but rather a dualism of the *brahman*, the only reality and ignorance that is false in the sense defined above. Various difficulties arise in the system, the chief among them being the following. What is the locus (*āśraya*) of ignorance (i.e., to whom does it belong)? What is the object (*viṣaya*) of ignorance (i.e., what does it conceal)? Ignorance can belong only to a consciousness, to one who also knows. But a consciousness is either a finite individual or the infinite *brahman*. If ignorance belongs to a finite individual, there would be a vicious circularity, for the same finite individual, on the nondualistic Vedānta, is a product of ignorance. What is a product of ignorance cannot be its locus. On the other hand, if ignorance is said to belong to the *brahman*, there would be a self-contradiction, for the *brahman* is, according to the thesis, all-knowing and so could not harbor any ignorance in its own nature. The same sort of difficulties arise with regard to the object of ignorance. What are we ignorant of? Only two possibilities are there: it is either the world or the *brahman*. The world cannot be the object of ignorance for it is, on the nondualistic theory, a product of ignorance. Moreover, the world is not self-manifesting, it is manifested by consciousness. The purpose of concealing the world is better served by concealing the source of its manifestation, viz. consciousness. Suppose then that the object of ignorance is nothing other than consciousness as the *brahman*. But if that is the case, if, in other words, ignorance is so powerful that it conceals the *brahman,* then who would have the power to destroy this ignorance? The prospect of no escape from the clutches of ignorance, and so the fearful impossibility of *mokṣa* would be the consequence.

The followers of Śaṃkara differed in their responses to these and many other criticisms formulated chiefly by Rāmānuja. Vācaspati, the author of the commentary Bhāmatī, favored the view that the locus of ignorance is the finite individual, and responded to the charge of circularity, which seemingly arises from this view, by saying that since there is a succession of lives of a finite soul, the ignorance I harbor now will produce my next incarnation while I am the product of my ignorance in my past incarnation. There being two series—the series of individuals lives of the same soul and a series of ignorances—the alleged circularity does not arise.

However, the view that possibly captures best the original intention of the Master is defended in the commentary *Pañcapādikā* and *Vivaraṇa* on it, according to which the *brahman* is both the locus and the object of ignorance. This thesis amounts to saying that ignorance tries to conceal the very same reality that also sustains it and supports its being. That being but for whom ignorance would not be known and recognized for what it is, is consciousness. Consciousness manifests ignorance as when one says "I am ignorant." And yet ignorance seeks to conceal that very consciousness that is none other than the *brahman.*

If ignorance conceals consciousness, it is obvious that it does not succeed fully in the task, for were consciousness fully concealed, nothing would be known, the world would be in darkness, and ignorance itself would remain unknown. However, since I am aware of my own ignorance as when I say "I am ignorant of such and such thing," my consciousness manifests that very thing which wants to conceal it. The object and the subject of ignorance are the same consciousness.

We turn now to the question, What then could destroy the all-powerful ignorance when consciousness of the nature of the *brahman* cannot do that? In order to answer this question, we need to bear in mind that pure consciousness (which is the *brahman*) is not a destroyer of anything. It manifests, and in that sense supports, everything, including ignorance itself. Just as the sun rays nourish all plants and vegetation on Earth, while the same sun rays if focused through a lens would burn a blade of grass, so does consciousness, while manifesting all things including ignorance, destroy that ignorance when processed through an appropriate mental state or, technically speaking, a *pramāṇa.*

Ignorance is destroyed not by the original consciousness but rather by a *pramājñāna* or a true cognition of the object of ignorance. Applied to our present case, the *brahman*-consciousness does not, as such, destroy ignorance. What destroys ignorance is the cognition of the *brahman.*

Schools of Vedānta, other than the nondualistic, assert the reality of the world and finite individuals, while maintaining the basic monistic position. This requires various ways of interpreting the Upaniṣads, as well as various conceptual frameworks. To some of these frameworks we may turn next.

IDENTITY AND DIFFERENCE IN VEDĀNTA

The nondualistic Vedānta, as we saw, critiqued and "refuted" the ontological status of the category of difference. As a consequence, nondualistic Vedānta accepted pure identity or *tādātmya* as the only ontologically valid principle; the *brahman* is this identity underlying, and unaffected by, all differences. Differences are mere appearances, the underlying identity being the only reality. The differences are not differences, or rather self-differentiations, of that reality. They are rather superimpositions on it.

Earlier we have seen how the Nyāya Vaiśeṣika took differences to be real, while recognizing the reality of universals and of a basic ontological relation called "inherence," which unifies the disparate elements to form a unified world.

In this section we shall follow different ways the exponents of Vedānta undertook this task. Leaving out Madhva, who explicitly defended a Vedānta based on difference as the ultimate ontological category, all the others admit a sort of monism. For all of them, the reality is the *brahman*. But they also recognized the reality of the finite individuals and the empirical world. How to reconcile these two claims? We shall briefly state three major answers: those of Rāmānuja, Vallabha, and Nimbārka. They all consist in different "mixtures," in different proportions, of the principle of identity and difference. Let us restrict the discussion to the specific question of the relation between the *brahman* and finite individuals.

Rāmānuja, in his Viśiṣṭādvaita, argues that both pure identity and pure difference are false. Since all knowledge necessarily involves discrimination and differentiation, it is impossible to know an object in its undifferentiated form. He concurs with Śaṃkara that the *brahman* is real. However, whereas for Śaṃkara the *brahman* as pure identity is without any difference, Rāmānuja's *brahman* is identity-in-difference (*bhedābheda*). Identity-in-difference implies identity of one substance existing in two real forms (*prakāra-dvayāvasthitatvāt sāmānādhikaraṇyasya*). The *brahman* is an organic unity, a unity that is characterized by diversity. Soul and matter, though equally real, are absolutely dependent on the *brahman*.

Rāmānuja rejects the notion of complete identity between the *brahman* and the individual selves. The individual selves are finite and cannot be identical to the *brahman* in every respect. As the existence of a part is inseparable from the whole, and that of a quality is inseparable from the substance in which it inheres, similarly the existence of a finite self is inseparable from the *brahman*. In the Upaniṣadic statement "that thou art," "that" refers to the *brahman* the omniscient, omnipotent, all-loving creator of the world and "thou" refers to the *brahman* existing in the form of I-consciousness, the finite human consciousness. The identity here should be construed to mean an identity between the *brahman* with certain qualifications and the individual soul with certain other qualifications. To put it differently, the *brahman* and finite selves are one and the same substance, although they possess different qualities (*prakāradvaya viśiṣṭaika vastu pratipādena sāmānādhikaranyaṃ ca*). Hence, the name of the system, Viśiṣṭādvaita ("qualified nondualism" or "nondualism with certain qualifications").

Nimbārka, in his Vedānta, like Rāmānuja, also argues for a kind of identity-in-difference (*bhedābheda*) insofar as he regards both identity and difference to be real. He, like Śaṃkara and Rāmānuja, takes the *brahman* to be real; however, the *brahman,* for him, actually becomes the many. The *brahman* is at once the light and that from which the light emerges. The relation between the *brahman* and the individual selves is explained on the analogy of life (*prāṇa*) and its differentiation into many conative and cognitive sense functions. Just as *prāṇa* differentiates itself into many functions, similarly on account of his *cit* and *acit śakti-s,* the *brahman* differentiates himself into the finite selves and matter without jeopardizing his integrity. Finite selves do not have any existence apart from the *brahman.* The individual selves as part of the *brahman* are identical with it; however, as the nature of the finite selves is different from the *brahman*-nature, individual selves are also different from the *brahman.*

Vallabha argues for pure nondualism (*Śuddhādvaita*) undefiled by *māyā.* The *brahman* as an independent reality is identified with Kṛṣṇa, who is smaller than the smallest and greater than the greatest. Existence, consciousness, and bliss constitute the *brahman's* essence. He is at once the one and the many. He manifests as many on account of his power, *māyā.* Manifestation is neither *vivarta* (as with Śaṃkara) nor *pariṇama* (as Rāmānuja and Nimbārka argue); it is real. It is a natural emanation from God, who is changeless (*avikṛtapariṇāma*). He replaces the notion of material cause (*upādānakāraṇa*) by inherent cause (*samavāyīkāraṇa*) to underscore the point that the material cause is identical with its effect; no change is involved here. Matter and the individual soul are his real manifestations. In the material world, only the existence aspect is manifested, while his aspects of knowledge and bliss remain obscured. In the individual souls the aspects of existence and knowledge are manifested whereas the bliss remains obscured. The individual's soul as part of God is essentially identical with it, but appears as different from him.

To sum up: both Śaṃkara and Vallabha argue that differences are mere appearances. Rāmānuja argues for identity in and through difference or identity qualified by difference. Difference does not and cannot exist independently of identity to which it belongs. Accordingly, identity is primary. Nimbārka argues for identity and difference; both are equally real.

ABSOLUTISM VERSUS NONABSOLUTISM (*ANEKĀNTAVĀDA*)

Jainism introduced a new dimension to metaphysical discussion. All other metaphysical views about the nature of reality may be regarded as views claiming to characterize reality fully and completely in their own terms whether it is nondualistic Vedānta, which regards reality as unchanging and differenceless, or Buddhism, which regards reality as changing. Both—as also other systems like Vaiśeṣika—claim to give exhaustive account of what reality is. The Jaina philosophers are the only ones who hold that since reality has infinite aspects, metaphysics has to be *anekānta* or nonabsolutistic. At the end of this chapter on metaphysics, we need to review this controversy.

Since a real has infinite aspects and cannot be summarily described under any of these aspects, the Jaina philosophers developed a method of describing reality from different perspectives and eventually of synthesizing seemingly inconsistent attributions. The logical aspect of this theory is known as *syādvāda.* One and the same thing, a jar for example, may, from one point of view, be regarded as permanent, and from another, impermanent. The matter or stuff of which the jar is made is permanent, while the form—namely the jar form—is impermanent. The jar has both these natures. Both the Vedāntin and the Buddhist are right, each from his or her own perspective. Furthermore, neither total destruction of a thing nor absolutely new origination is possible. What is cannot turn into nothing; what is not cannot become existent. What originate and are destroyed are forms, modes, or, to put in the Jaina language, *paryāyas.* The stuff that continues is *dravya* or substance. So the Jaina will say that everything is permanent from the standpoint of substance and is at the same time impermanent from the standpoint of form or mode. But this only shows that neither absolute permanence nor absolute impermanence is true. What is true is permanence-cum-impermanence. In the same manner, the Jaina synthesizes "existence" and "nonexistence." Everything exists as having its own qualities and is nonexistent with regard to an alien nature. If John is a philosopher and not a poet, then he exists as a philosopher, but does not exist as a poet. Thus for the Jaina philosopher, existence and nonexistence both belong to everything, only from different standpoints.

In this way, the Jaina developed a method known as *syadvāda,* by which the truths of opposing predications may be synthesized, their one-sided truth claims rejected, and a perfect knowledge of the totality of reality arrived at. Each such predication is conditional, relative to a standpoint, but if that condition is included in the predication, the judgment becomes unconditionally true.

This chain of thinking leads the Jaina philosopher to develop a systematic theory of standpoints (*nayas*). A *naya* is a partial truth, while a *pramāṇa* must grasp the total truth. The Jaina list of *nayas* is an inventory of philosophical standpoints, and thus provides an interesting metaphilosophical theory. The Jainas also develop an interesting theory of sevenfold predication (*saptabhangi*), according to which with regard to any property F and anything X, the question "Is x F?", has seven kinds of possible answers. These are:

1. from a standpoint, x is F;
2. from a standpoint, x is not F;
3. from a standpoint, x is and is not F;
4. from a standpoint, x is indescribable;

5. from a standpoint, x is F and indescribable;
6. from a standpoint, x is not F and is indescribable; and
7. from a standpoint, x is F, is not F, and is indescribable.

With slight transformations, this amounts to saying that the sentence "x is F" has seven truth values: true, false, true and false, indescribable, true and indescribable, false and indescribable, and true, false, and indescribable.

The Jaina theory of *anekāntavāda,* also translatable as "non-one-sided doctrine," by virtue of its willingness to accommodate all possible standpoints and to assign to each a truth value while rejecting the claim of any to absolute validity, is a model for philosophical liberalism. It was opposed by all others, each of whom was a one-sided doctrine (*ekāntavāda*)—including the nondualist Vedānta and the Buddhist. Śaṃkara launched a critique of the Jaina position—insisting that the Jaina raised his own position to the status of absolute truth—that is important but quickly dismissive. The Jaina position remains one of the finest achievements of the Indian mind.

One of the main problems for the Jaina philosophy remains, however, the very notion of "synthesis" of the different perspectives, and the resulting idea of "totality." Being a realist, "the Jaina philosopher" speaks as though the thing as the totality is already there; but he also gives the impression as though he develops a method by which the different perspectives can be "synthesized." One wavers between an ontological and an epistemological notion, between regarding "totality" as constitutive and regarding it as "regulative."

Part 3

Philosophy of Politics, Law, and Morals (*Dharma Śāstra*)

Chapter Six

State, Society, and Law

STATE

Ancient Indian texts such as the Upaniṣads, the epics *Rāmāyaṇa* and *Mahābhārata,* sciences of *artha* (or political economy), such as Kautilya's and the commentaries on it; sciences of ethics or *dharma,* such as those by Gautama, Parāśara, and Nārada; Śukra's digest of principles (or *nīti*); as well as poems and dramas such as Bhatti, Daśakumāracarita, Kādambari, Kirātārjunīya, and Śiśupālabadha, contain numerous, often seemingly endless and repetitive discussions of the duties of a king toward his advisors, army, subjects, friendly countries, and enemies as well as responsibilities for the treasury, for the poor, and for the maintenance of law and order. In this chapter, I will not rehearse these but will briefly recapitulate two ancient texts.

In *Chāndogya Upaniṣad* 5/11/5 we find the following account. The King Aśvapati Kaikeya, who studied the Universal Self, tells the *brahmins* who visited with the king about his kingdom. "In my kingdom," he says, "there is no thief, no miser, no drunkard, no one who does not have a sacrificial fire, no ignorant person, no adulterer or adulteress."

In chapter 77 of the "Śāntiparva" of the epic *Mahābhārata,* the same king says that in his kingdom there are no ignorant *brahmins,* all *brahmins* are engaged in studies, all are truthful and of gentle nature. The *kṣatriyas* also study, but do not teach; they protect the *brahmins* and are not hesitant to fight. The *vaisyas* are all truthful, in control of their senses, active, and engaged in agriculture, animal husbandry, and trade. The *sūdras,* without any jealousy for the three upper castes, accept their patronage and support. Regarding himself, the king goes on to say that he protects the *dharma* of the family (*kula*) and the *dharma* of the country (*deśa*) and gives away money to the poor, helpless, old, weak, and women. He never eats food without sharing it with others, he never commits adultery, and does not indulge in licentious games. He does not show disrespect to the scholars, the old, and the ascetics, and aims at fostering learning by spending money, collects wealth truthfully, and follows his teachers by serving them. He wages wars only if they are in the cause of *dharma.* His subjects live in his kingdom as freely as do children in the home of their father.

This picture, clearly, is of an ideal king, and of an ideal society in terms of the four castes. The Hindus favored monarchy, and high-flown praise of kingship, along with the idea of its divine origin, abounds in most ancient texts. Again the *Mahābhārata's* "Śāntiparva" (chapter 59) provides a typical account of the origin of kingship. Yudhiṣthira, the eldest of the Pāṇdavas, asks the "grandfather" Bhiṣma to explain how the word *rājā* ("king") came into being. One would have thought he was asking for the origin of the word. But the question takes a different shape. How is it, he asks, that although the king's body, mind, birth and death, pleasure and pain, are just like those of the subjects, the king nevertheless rules over all others? Bhiṣma's answer gives a version of the divine origin theory. At the beginning, he says, there was neither kingdom, nor king, nor punishment, nor anyone who deserved punishment. People protected each other by following *dharma.* But gradually, they lost their sense of *dharma,* became greedy, passionate, attached to things, and would rather steal the other's property. They lost their sense for the distinction between what ought and what ought not to be done. Under these circumstances, it is the gods—not humans—who approached Viṣṇu to find a solution of the problem. The solution, of course, consisted in writing a work on *dandanīti,* which laid down all the principles of social, economic, and political life, and produced from his own body a king. The mythology, whatever else it may suggest, accords a priority to *dharma* over any mundane authority, and accords well with the general Hindu view that the king is subordinate to dharma, has to obey it, and cannot violate it with impunity.

It is not therefore true that, on the ancient Hindu view, *dharma* is created by the state. It is more plausible that according to the predominant view in Hindu texts, not the king, but the royal function itself is divine in origin. That is why the king could not legislate. Nārada says (XVII.9) that the king can change laws that are unreasonable. According to Kātyāyana (verse 42) he can abolish practices that are repugnant to reason.

While the monarchical form has been most advocated by the Hindu authors, the Buddhists opposed monarchy and defended a sort of republican government. Buddhist rejection of monarchy, it should be emphasized, accords with, indeed is a consequence of, Buddist opposition to all eternal, and, even enduring substances, and rejection of universal entities in favor of changing particulars alone. Here metaphysics and political theory hang together—as with German idealism. The Hindus—especially the Nyāya-Vaiśeṣika and Mīmāṃsā—believed in real universals; the Vedantins defended a sort of conceptualism. A monarch as a real sovereign, or rather the kingly function (*rājadharma*) as what welds individuals together from above, goes well with the metaphysics of universals. The Buddhist nominalism, and conventionalism with regard to the way things are unified, and eventually the thesis of emptiness, deprives the monarch of any place in the scheme of things.

Nevertheless, it would be a mistake to identify the Hindu monarchy with the specific concept of sovereignty that arose in Western political thought in the fifteenth century, which was the result of a search for an ultimate and absolute political authority. Such a source was necessitated by the breakdown of the concepts of natural law and of the theological worldview. In India, the concept of *dharma* maintained its superiority over that of the king, making the emergence of the idea of "sovereignty" impossible. If the Hindu idea of kingship remained under the authority of *dharma,* to that extent it was, quite unlike the medieval European conception, free from theological influence, and the locution of origin of the king from Viṣṇu or Prajāpati is more mythological than theological.

Some authors have drawn attention to the prevalence of the elected king, evidenced in the *Aitareya Brāhmaṇa* (I.3.14), and in several well-recorded historical practices. And the text Śukranīti advances a purely positivistic notion of kingship, resting on the physical, military, and intellectual power of the ruler.

As everywhere else, the Hindu philosophers looked for the categories—like forms that structure the domain of *rājya* (*regnum*). Kautilya lists these as seven limbs or elements of the political organism. These are *svāmi* (master), *amātya* (minister), *suhṛt* (friend or ally), *koṣa* (treasury), *rāṣtra* (territory), *durga* (fort), and *vala* or *danda* (army). Various writers establish analogies with different limbs of the body and defend a mutual interdependence of the seven elements, thus making the *regnum* a living organism, such that each element is indispensable in its own place and serves its own purpose, which cannot be taken over by any other.

SOCIETY

Just as various texts describe kingship as an ideal institution, so do they describe an ideal society in which the four castes follow their respective duties. The questions about the origin and nature of the caste system among the Hindus is difficult to determine. Since the word "varṇa" is used for "caste" and since "*varṇa*" means "color," it has led scholars to find behind the system a division of humans according to their colors and so an attendant "racism." According to others, the hierarchy of castes is one of grades of purity and impurity, while still others find here a gradation of power. More notably, Dumont finds a more complicated intertwining of hierarchy of purity-impurity and power relations. While in its actual practice, the caste system is enormously complicated, as a whole, in its philosophical conception, I find in it an anticipation of Plato's scheme as laid out in the *Republic*, where the intellectual power, military power, and economic power are sharply separated and made to rest in different groups of people. The differences between the Hindu system and the Platonic are obvious. The fourth caste of *śudras* is absent in the Greek plan, but the Greeks had their slaves, while the *śudras* were free citizens, not slaves. In the Platonic scheme, the scholars were to be the rulers, in the Hindu scheme they are the advisors to the king who comes from the *kṣatriya* (i.e., the warrior) class who, unlike in the Greek scheme, could and did hold private property. The Platonic utopia was never put to practice; the Hindu scheme was indeed applied and has gone through thousands of years of vicissitudes and at least two major transformations. For one thing, the distinctions among castes seem originally to have been more flexible, determined not by birth but by aptitude, qualities, and acquired merits; it gradually was rigidified into lines of birth and heredity. For another, each *varṇa* differentiated into many caste (*jāti*)-clusters, so that excepting in the case of the *brahmins,* the other *varṇas* lost their significance, being overtaken by a myriad of *jātis* whose trademark has been economic differentiation of productive skills, trade and commerce, and labor, and whose hierarchies have been fluid and local.

While the society remained more stable over time than the state, one of the purposes of the state, under a king, is to preserve the local social customs if they do not come into conflict with the then rational standards. This independence of society from the state continues to influence Indian thinking on this matter even up to this day, as is evidenced in the writings of the poet Tagore and the communitarianism of Mahātmā Gandhi.

LAW

The word *dharma* is, to say the least, ambiguous, in our present context (i.e., leaving out other, more metaphysical and religious meanings) between ethics and law. The law, on the Hindu theories, was not made by God and not by the state either. It was not the command of the sovereign (excepting for special cases), nor was it based on anything like the natural law. It does not derive from legislative act or from judicial decisions. Thus the Austinian conception of positive law was not recognized by the Hindu legal scholars.

Manu gave four sources of law. These are Veda, *smṛti, sadācāra,* and *ātmaṇaḥ priya,* meaning, in that order, the Vedic scriptures, memory/tradition, good custom, and the approval of conscience (or, on an alternate reading, satisfaction of the self).

Limiting the role of the scriptures, Bṛhaspati adds: determination of the legal merits should never be made depending only upon the scriptures, one should also take recourse to *yukti* or reasoning. I will briefly talk about legal reasoning and then about the role of tradition and custom.

Almost all the major law books, such as Nārada and Yājñyavalkya, emphasized the role of reasoning. The word *nyāya* that is used in this context signifies justice, equity, and logic all three. Nyāya is to be taken recourse to especially when there are conflicting traditions. An example of such conflict is marriage with maternal uncle's daughter is *dharma* in the south and *a-dharma* in the north.

The question therefore was, which one was *yukti-yukta* or more logical? In such interminable discussions, one often appealed to a curious hybrid concept, "reasoning based on practice."

Custom was generally eulogized as the highest *dharma*. Manu's dictum "*ācarāḥ paramo dharmaḥ*," somewhat grandiosely rendered by Sir William Jones as "immemorial usage is transcendental law," encapsulates this point of view. Custom is distinguished from conventional rules. Custom is not due to conventional agreements. Custom eludes human memory. As Kātyāyana writes, custom is observed simply because it is, it is groundless. However, when it came to separate this immemorial custom from law, Manu fell back on the idea of *sadācāra* (i.e., customary practice of the good and the virtuous). In this sense, customary law was also part of the ethical reality Hegel called *Sittlichkeit*.

It is good to keep in mind that the position assigned to custom served to limit the power of the king on the one hand and the scriptural texts on the other. The king, on all accounts, could not interfere with custom. Scriptural *dharma* acquired its juridical function by its agreement with customary rule and customary rule by its agreement with "good conscience" (i.e., if it is *ātmanaḥ priyaḥ*—or, satisfying to the self). Even if of immemorial origin, a custom could go out of existence. Customs may change. In order to account for the role of time and history, the law books propounded the doctrine of *kali-varjya*, which, according to Kane, is a "peremptory argument" against the idea that *dharma* is immutable: ancient laws could be nullified in case they are against contemporary social ideas. As Lingat puts it, this theory is a fiction "to mark the effect of time" and "to legitimize the disappearance of certain customs."

One should note in this context what the king could or could not do. The king could pass orders, or ordinances, but law was not an order. It must have, to be law, a general and permanent application. The king could not interfere with morals or with custom (i.e., with *Sittlichkeit*). He could, according to some, especially Nārada, reform "inequitous" laws. According to Kātyāyana, he could abolish customs repugnant to reason, while on most accounts he should leave custom untouched. He could make a legal determination of an issue, not by himself, but in consultation with a council of advisors.

We have referred to two ways law, though grounded in custom, could change: legal reasoning by which conflicts were resolved, and *kali-varjya*, which allowed certain customary laws to pass into oblivion. Another procedure was "interpretation." In general, one could say, Hindu law was not enriched by judicial decisions, but by scholarly commentaries. The commentators and digest writers worked toward evolving consistent juridical frameworks by new interpretations. As a consequence, rules of interpretation, not of legal texts alone but for all texts, were laid down, and a science of hermeneutics, known as Mīmāṃsā, came into being. The importance of interpretation assured the development of law to cope with changing situations, even when the basic texts remained the same.

PRINCIPLES OF INTERPRETATION

In interpreting texts, it was not necessary to appeal to the intention of the author. The expression alone and its context, together with grammar, logic, rhetoric, and Mīmāṃsā, were taken to be adequate for determining the meaning of a text. Among various rules of interpretation, the following may be of some interest:

1. Every act contrary to the law is forbidden.
2. Everything not forbidden is permitted.
3. The same word is not to be taken in two different senses in the same sentence.
4. Singular includes plural.
5. What is said of a male applies to a female (unless otherwise specified).
6. A rule of *dharma* has greater weight than a rule of *artha* (i.e., pertaining to acquisition of wealth).
7. Where different texts of equal authority are in conflict, decide either by majority or by some reasoning.
8. When a *vidhi* (i.e., an injunction) conflicts with a statement of fact, then there is really no conflict, the injunction overrides.
9. When two *vidhis* (i.e., injunctions about the same matter) conflict, they should be so interpreted that they become complementary. One may express a general rule, the other an exception, or each has its own domain of application.
10. Where two scriptures conflict and the conflict cannot be interpreted away, that which is more logical (*yukti-yukta*) shall prevail.

Besides these and many rules as to how to complete a sentence, how to bring out the latent sense, and how to clarify a vague meaning, there were also rules about application of texts. These include principles of distinguishing between obligatory, quasi-obligatory, and nonobligatory texts; principles of showing to whom an imperative (*vidhi*) text is applicable; the principle of *krama* or order of application of a text; the principle of *atideśa* or that by which rules regarding one matter are extended to another matter; and the principle of *uha* or adaptation (i.e., modifications necessary to extend the domain of application).

The commentators tried to organize customs into a juridical framework, when two texts conflict and the conflict cannot be interpreted away. Nārada recommends (I, 40) that that which is *yukti-yuktaḥ* or more rational should prevail. *Yukti* clearly means "reasoning," although some have taken it to mean "equity."

SOME FUNDAMENTAL LEGAL IDEAS

At this point, it may be of interest to introduce more specific legal doctrines. Manu lays down seventy-eight causes for legal dispute. To give some idea of these, the list includes debt, selling property that has no owner, taking back gifts made, breaking a promise, breaking a contract to buy and sale, conflict between master and servant, killing, insulting, violence, not doing one's personal duty, inheritance, partnership transaction, partition, gambling and betting, and adultery. It is in the laws regarding these that the fundamental ideas of rights and duties may be discerned.

Since the ideas of property, contract, and evidence are so fundamental to justice and democracy, I will briefly recapitulate some of the basic features of laws regarding them.

Property

The basic principles in this area are only the owner can dispense with property; ownership can never be in abeyance so that property must be vested in some one, real or ideal; ownership is extinguished by sale, gift, death, change of religious order; property is for enjoyment and religious purpose; everyone can acquire and hold property; no ownership resides in the king to the soil of his dominion. Property belongs to the family, in which context one notices a vague idea of a trust in the interests of the living members of the family, of the dead as well as of the future members. Under Mitākṣarā law, the rights of a family member are like the rights of the members of a corporation; under the other school of law—the Dāyabhāga—a co-sharer can dispose of his share of the property as well as his self-acquired property.

The philosophers of law between the twelfth and the fifteenth centuries focused a great deal on the concept of property. A definition of "property," to begin with, was *yatheṣta-viniyoga-yogyatva*, (i.e., a property is that which can be used at the pleasure of the owner). Another widely used definītion was *vyavahāra-viṣayatva* (i.e., what may be the subject matter of legal transaction). The metaphysical realists regarded "being one's own" (*svatva*) as a further irreducible property, while the metaphysical idealists tended to regard it as existing only in the mind. But, then it was asked, how could babies (and lunatics) own property when they do not have the consciousness "This is mine"? Others such as Rāmabhadra Sārvabhauma construed "property" as a relational feature (i.e., as a relation that exists in both the relata together, the owner and the thing owned, not in any of them separately).

One of the questions that was much debated was, Does the king own the soil of the land? The majority of writers held that the real ownership of the land vested in the landlords (*bhaumikas*), the king had only the right to collect revenues.

Can property inhere in an indefinitely large class, where the latter class is larger than a family? "Being a property of x" contradicts "being a property of y" where x and y are different (*tad puruṣiyasvatvaṃ prati tadanyapuruṣiyasvatvasya pratibandhakatvaṃ*). However, one could donate property for "everyone's enjoyment."

Contract

Contracts by drunken, the infants, and men past eighty, and one without consideration, are not valid (*Manu,* VIII, 163). Contracts effected by a person who is not the rightful owner have no rightful consequence. The law of contract included laws for deposits. The depository was not allowed to entrust the deposited thing to someone else (*Sūkra,* IV.5.316). The holder of the deposit cannot be its possessor. The holder should exercise sufficient diligence to preserve the thing, and he cannot use the thing without permission of the depositor.

Evidence

Evidence is either human or divine. Human evidence is either by witness, or by written documents or by inference. Of these, Bṛhaspati gives the following assessment of their relative strengths: Witnesses are superior to inference, document superior to witness because of faulty memory, and three generations of undisturbed possession to all three. Nārada writes: a document is always strong, witnesses are strong as long as they are alive; possession becomes stronger with time. Of written documents, one written in one's own hand is valid even in the absence of a witness; one written in other's hands is valid when corroborated by witnesses. What is written under compulsion is never valid.

Punishment

Danda or punishment is praised in high-flown language. A typical praise is to be found in the Mahābhārata, Śāntiparva chapter 15: "Punishment rules all creatures, punishment preserves them all. When all others sleep, punishment keeps awake. The learned know punishment as *dharma.*" Manu offers the following praise: everyone follows his own *dharma* because of (fear of) punishment. A person who is pure without punishment is indeed rare. All social order will be destroyed if there is either absence of punishment or wrong application of the principles (7.22). The laws of punishment clearly bear testimony to the tension between a demand for equality before the law and the hierarchical society. The questions that were discussed are, Should the degree of severity increase with decrease in caste rank, or should exactly the opposite be meted out insofar as the higher castes were expected to be more law-abiding and moral?

Law and Justice

In spite of the fact that the Hindu philosophers attached great importance to the ideas of justice and impartiality (*Manu,* VIII. 173), their ideas were vitiated by the belief in inequality among castes and sexes.

To understand the nature of justice in Hindu thought, one must avoid two extreme views widely prevalent. At one extreme, there is the view espoused by Hegel—that in the Orient (including India) only one was free. This idea of "oriental despotism" is a myth. Neither politically nor legally nor economically, a Hindu emperor was a despot. As a matter of fact, there was more freedom and less "despotism" under the great Moghuls than under most European emperors of that time. At the other extreme, there is a completely misleading view held by many Indian writers that the Vedānta metaphysics of identity of all selves provides the only possible framework for equality and justice. This way of looking at things is both misleading and self-deluding, for what is required for legal, political, and economic justice is not identity but equality among differents. While Śaṃkara propounded the Vedānta metaphysics, he also excluded the śudras and women from studying the Vedas. To appreciate the nature of Hindu political and legal thinking, we have to look at the facts as they are as far as they can be gleaned from social history, documentations, law books, and books on judicial and economic administrations. What we find there is a monarchical system severely subject to the constraints of social customs and moral ideas; a hierarchical conception of society at its best inspired by a conception much like Plato's Republic, but at its worst vitiated by racism, intolerance, and persecution of the conquered peoples—in between marked by different degrees of social mobility up and down and egalitarianism; and a judicial system characterized by a large measure of procedural justice, a large degree of equality among all members of the society, inequalities of caste rankings showing up in theory of punishment—sometimes for relatively higher ranks punishment being lighter, sometimes just the opposite inasmuch as the higher your rank the higher was the expectation of your moral worth.

Since law was fundamentally not the command of the king but founded on social ethos, custom and scholarly law books—the royal command filling in gaps and fulfilling *ad hoc* needs—and since with the development of the social ethos law developed by way of a severely intellectual, commentarial, and interpretative tradition, ideas of freedom and justice were always on the horizon.

If one were to locate the idea of justice expressed in Hindu laws in terms of contemporary Western thought, one could place it closer to Michael Walzer's idea of "complex equality" and his pluralistic theory of social justice—the idea, namely, that the conventions and shared understandings that make up a society do not treat all goods as subject to the same principles of distribution. This does not rule out the possibility, within each society, that there is a *telos* toward the goal of "simple equality," as the hierarchical notion, not pluralism per se, gives place to modern idea of equality. It is here that the Hindu metaphysical ideas may come in handy for an urgently needed application (e.g., opening the opportunities to all members of the society to share the goods available, including Vedic learning).

Chapter Seven

Moral Philosophy

THEORY OF ACTION

Indian ethical theories developed elaborate theories of action, and without a correct understanding of the latter theories one may miss important aspects of those ethical theories. The theories of action have linguistic, psychological, and eschatological aspects. In their linguistic aspect, the theories are concerned with action sentences. In their psychological aspect, they look at the motives for acting and the springs of action. In their eschatological aspect, they consider the effects supposedly especially of spiritual actions, some of these effects flowing over into the afterlife. Although the various schools differed among themselves regarding the details of their theories, they all worked within a general framework, and there was considerable agreement among them. This general framework (on which there were variations) may be represented as the causal chain:

> Knowledge (*jñāna*), desire (*cikirṣa*), willing to do (*pravṛtti*), motor effort (*ceṣṭā*), the action (*kriyā*).

The differences that arose in the theories that developed concerned the precise nature of each member of the chain. Philosophers also differed in their interpretations of the verbal form in which imperatives expressing moral duties are expressed. Leaving aside many niceties of discussion, we can distinguish between various approaches as follows.

The philosophers of the Nyāya school held that the knowledge that brings about the desire, and then the will to do, is knowledge by the agent-to-be that the desired goal is achievable and that performance of the action will bring about some good to the agent (without causing greater harm), this good being acquiring *sukha* (or happiness) and getting rid of *duḥkha* (or pain).

Philosophers of the Bhāṭṭa school of Mīmāṃsā considerably simplified the requirement: an imperative sentence "you ought to do Ø," when heard, gives rise, in the auditor, to the cognition "This wants me to do Ø," which leads to the belief that the desired goal can be reached by doing Ø. This belief eventually leads the auditor to act.

A still simpler theory is proposed by the Prābhākara school of Mīmāṃsā. According to this school, conduciveness to future good is not a sufficient condition for desire and effort. Things past and things already present may be conducive to future good, but one does not act with regard to them. Neither is conduciveness to bring about a good necessary for activity. Only when an action requires a great deal of painful exertion does one need the assurance that the effort will result in happiness. The Prābhakara point is that even when an action is conducive to good, its "being something to be done" (*kāryatva*) and its "being conducive to production of good" are different entities. All that is needed to act is the belief that it should be done. The imperative sentence's very grammatical form especially when the sentence is a Vedic injunction has the power to generate this belief.

Thus we have two different theories of action, especially of actions that follow from imperatives: one which assigns a necessary mediating role to the thought of the good that will come out of doing the action, the other recognizes the resulting good but does not assign a mediating role to the thought of it. For the second theory, first espoused by Bādari, given a classic, popular statement by Kṛṣṇa in the *Bhagavadgītā,* and finally revived by Prabhākara, the idea of duty is what mediates between hearing an imperative and performance of the course of action recommended.

One way of resolving the conflict between the opposed theories is to show that the teleological-cum-consequentialist theory holds good of the actions directed toward the first two goods (i.e., toward *artha* and *kāma*), while the second, Kantian-type deontological theory holds good of actions inspired by the idea of *dharma.* Neither of the two theories, therefore, holds good of all actions. Actions that aim at the acquisition of wealth (*artha*) and enjoyment of pleasure (*kāma*) *naturally* must be preceded by the thought of the happiness that they would bring about, while it is plausible to hold that ethical actions, actions that follow upon moral imperatives (the scriptural injunctions, for example), although they *may sometimes* be performed by agents who think of the happiness that would accrue to them as a result, do not necessarily presuppose any such thought. Since in the case of *dharma* actions the result is regarded, in the Indian tradition, to be supernatural (i.e., merits accruing to the soul, to bear wholesome effects in the next life), thought about such results, unlike thought about the empirical pleasure likely to arise from wealth and pleasurable objects, is emptily symbolic, lacks intuitive content, and so could not stimulate action unless the idea of duty intervenes. Both kinds of action may be brought under a consequentialist theory. In that case, it may be maintained that even in the case of *dharma,* not unlike *artha*-directed and *kāma*-directed actions, actions are regarded as generating happiness *here and now* for the agent. This latter indeed is not an entirely implausible view—the view, namely, that leading a life in accordance with the scriptural recommendations brings about a certain kind of happiness that, to be sure, is very different from the happiness that results from the other two kinds of action. In that case, the thought of this happiness which is neither the pleasure of wealth nor the pleasure of erotica nor the supernatural well-being of the soul after death, may be an ingredient of the thought of duty that, on all accounts, must play a role in the causal chain leading from hearing an utterance of the imperative to performance of the appropriate action. This would be an Aristotelian way of combining happiness with virtue. But can it be combined with a theory of *dharma?* Let us then turn to the conception of *dharma* as it figures in the moral context.

WHAT IS *DHARMA*?

I will develop the concept of *dharma* in several stages. It is well-known that the word *dharma* stands for various things: sometimes for the harmonious order of the cosmos, sometimes for the essential functions of things ("The *dharma* of water is to flow downwards"), sometimes for the ultimate elements of things (as in early Buddhism), sometimes for ethical duty, and sometimes for laws in the legal sense. To look for a meaning common to all these usages would be a difficult project, and I will not attempt that here. For my present purpose, I will here take *dharma* in the sense of ethical rules of action and moral virtues.

The first stage of my explication of *dharma* in this sense is to attempt a formal definition of it. There are at least four such definitions in the philosophical literature. First, the *Mīmāṃsā-sūtra* of Jaimini defines *dharma* as *codanā lakṣaṇa* (i.e., as being of the nature of an injunction). One can construe that expression also as meaning what is known by the imperative sentences, which incite a person to act. The *Vaiśeṣikasūtra* of Kaṇāda defines *dharma* as that from which prosperity and the highest good result (*yato 'bhyudayaniḥśreyasaṣiddhiḥ*); this definition clearly excludes those injunctions that may be against any moral sensibility. A third definition restricts the term to Vedic injunctions alone, which also specify the high goal achievable by acting in accordance with them. A fourth definition gives up the attempt to define and ends up by conceding that *dharma* is that which the cultivated persons (*āryāḥ*) praise when it is done and *a-dharma,* the opposite of *dharma,* is that which they condemn when it is done.

The second stage of explication of *dharma* would consist of giving an account, however cursory, of the different kinds of *dharma.* The injunctions in the scriptures may be either obligatory (*nitya*) or occasional (*naimittika*) (i.e., those that are to be followed on appropriate occasions). Still others are optional (*kāmya*) (i.e., performed if so desired). All of these may pertain to one's caste (*varṇa*) or to one as a member of a family (*kula*), or may be for all humans, irrespective of caste or family, therefore common or *sādhāraṇa.* Some may pertain to one's stage in life history ("student," "householder," "forest dweller," and "renunciant"). These different ethical rules may come into conflict. A famous case is that of Arjuna, portrayed in the epic *Mahābhārata,* in the opening chapter of the *Bhagavadgītā:* facing the "other side" on the battlefield where he saw his own family members lined up to fight against, Arjuna realized that the *dharma* of his caste required him to fight for a righteous cause against the forces of evil while the *dharma* of his family forbids killing his own family members and the common (*sādhāraṇa*) *dharma* forbids taking any life. The teachings of Kṛṣṇa set out to resolve this moral dilemma.

Lists of the most important *dharmas* will be given later in this chapter. *Yājñavalkya's Smṛti* lists nine such: noninjury, truthfulness, honesty, cleanliness, control of the senses, charity, self-restraint, love, and forbearance. These are said to be meant for everyone. Manu mentions ten characteristics (*lakṣaṇa*) of *dharma:* fortitude, patience, restraint, abstention from wrongly appropriating another's property, purity, culture, control over the senses, correct discernment, truthfulness, and sweet temper. *Mahābhārata* adds, among others, modesty, forgiving disposition, serenity, and meditative temper. Clearly, we have here a theory of virtues as contrasted with a mere ethics of imperatives, As a matter of fact, the opposition set up by many philosophers between moral rules and moral virtues is simply misleading. This leads me to the third stage of understanding the idea of *dharma.* The question at this point concerns the correct interpretation of this doctrine. Now in the secondary literature, not the Sanskrit commentaries but in the Western-language secondary interpretative literature, there appear to be several lines of interpretation. First, there is a metaphysical interpretation that connects the ethical with a metaphysical theory of *dharma* as the cosmic order of things. Suggestion for such a connection are to be found in texts, like the *Bhagavadgītā,* which describe the cosmic order as a system of sacrifices (*yajña*). But to think that the ethical is deduced from the cosmic is just wrong. What rather takes place is that, once the ethical ideas were available, the cosmos was represented in analogy with them. Second, there is a functional interpretation that looks upon one's *dharma* as deducible from one's place in the order of things. But no such deduction has been given or is possible. One refers to the well-known four stages in the life of a person: the young student, practitioner of the *brahman* (*brahmacāri*); the householder, the forest dweller, and the renunciant. Each of these has *dharmas* attached to it. But none of these stages in any sense is a reflection of man's place in the universe; at most it is the picture of an ideal journey through life on one's way toward *mokṣa* or freedom from *karma*–rebirth, toward the Highest Good. This account, which contains the account of *dharma,* does not itself reflect some deeper-lying functional place in the universe, although as closely connected with the idea of *varṇa* or caste, the doctrine of *dharma* connects with an individual's place in society, and as connected with the rebirth-*mokṣa* structure, it points beyond society in two directions: one determining the "rationality" of social (world) and of individual desserts, the other pointing beyond the social toward attainment of a place above the social, a free, spiritual individuality. A third interpretation is religious in the narrow sense, (i.e., *ādhidaivika*). Practice of *dharma* is intended to please the appropriate deities, to go to heaven or a higher world, a practice of *a-dharma* leads to hell or nether worlds, which may be the way many practising Hindus today look at *dharma*. But Pūrva-Mīmāṃsā, as a traditional system of interpretation of Vedic rituals, offers a minimal interpretation that makes no ontological commitment regarding the existence of deities, rather instead considers deities as posits for making sense of appropriate practices. Practices are fundamental; ontological commitment is derivative.

The metaphysical interpretations are maximal interpretations. They want to justify practice by embedding it in a large metaphysical theory. A minimal interpretation, which is preferable, concedes autonomy to practice, looks for its own, for example, for practical rationality rather than grounding it in a theoretical system. The maximal interpretation is to be found in the *Purāṇa* literature, the minimal in the Mīmāṃsā and the *dharmaśāstra* tradition. For the interpretation that is being suggested here, use may be made of a concept that Hegel has emphasized, namely, the concept of *Sittlichkeit* or social ethics as contrasted to *Moralität* or individual morality. The *Sittlichkeit* of a people is the concrete ethical self, the actual norms, duties, virtues, and goods that a community prizes. It also includes the habitualities, customs, social practices, and law that Hegel regards as the medium for concrete freedom as contradistinguished from the abstract morality, the purely subjective inner freedom, which one may pursue in opposition to, or away from, concrete, objective freedom. We have here no need of the Hegelian systematic concepts of "spirit," "history," and dialectic. It is enough for our present purpose to regard the doctrine of *dharma* as constituting the Hindu *Sittlichkeit* whose origins lie shrouded in impenetrable past (*dharmasya tattvam nihitam guhāyām*), which is not a static, self-complete, unchangeable identity, but that has continued to change, to permit new interpretations while still preserving a sense of identity.

Many contemporary writers have contended that the idea of moral rules needs for its grounding the idea of a lawgiver (i.e., God), and that since that idea is not any more part of moral thought, we need an ethics of virtues rather than an ethics of rules and laws. This, however, is not justified. Rules and laws need not be commands of a lawgiver or a sovereign authority. Rules and laws may be components of a tradition brought about by customary usage. This seems to be the case with *dharma* whether understood as moral rules or as laws. Law, in the Hindu legal theory, is not the command of a sovereign, but found in tradition and customary usage.

There is also a view, at one time widely held but fortunately less likely to be defended today, that ethics as a philosophical discipline needs to provide a community's ethical beliefs with a philosophical metaphysical or epistemological grounding, and, consequently, that since Hindu ethical writings abound in producing lists of virtues and duties but do not provide theoretical groundings, such as the Kantian and the Utilitarian, one should not speak of "ethics" in the context of Indian thought. Contemporary writers on moral philosophy have come to recognize that the project of a theoretical derivation of moral laws and principles should be abandoned. Given the enormous complexity of moral life, such projects are doomed to failure. Moral philosophy in the sense of a descriptive work with regard to the enormously variegated field of morality is possible, but not a grounding in the classical sense. In this sense, Aristotle's *Nichomachean Ethics,* rather than the Kantian *Metaphysics of Morals,* should be the guide.

From this renewed perspective of phenomenological and communitarian virtue ethics, the *dharma* theory fares much better. No attempt need be made to ground the theory in a metaphysics. The different metaphysical systems from realistic pluralism of the Nyāya to idealistic monism of the Vedānta, notwithstanding their differences, accept the *dharma* theory as the handed-down *Sittlichkeit.* The only legitimization that is offered is epistemological. The scriptures record that tradition, and the epistemological authority (*prāmāṇya*) of the scriptures with regard to codes of conduct and virtues to be praised, is zealously defended by philosophers. The main point of the defense consists in arguing that a text's possible flaws are to be traced to possible defects in the author's competence, and that the scriptures that record a tradition are not authored by a personal author, and the tradition is beyond, and more original than any authorship, and so free from possible sources of error.

MORAL PSYCHOLOGY: FRUIT (*PHALA*) AND SPRINGS OF ACTION

In order to understand the moral theories yet to be presented, it is necessary, at this point, to be acquainted with the psychological framework within which the theories are formulated. In this psychological framework, the ideas of pleasure (*sukha*) and pain (*duḥkha*) play central roles. Pleasure is often defined as that which is desired for its own sake (*svataḥicchāviṣyaḥ*) and pain is defined as what is hated for its own sake (*svataḥ dveṣaviṣayaḥ*). Another way of defining pleasure is: whatever is favorably regarded by all (*sarveṣāmanukūlavedanīyaṃ*); the opposite being the case with pain. In order that these definitions of "pleasure" do not extend to "absence of pain" (or "decrease of pain"), which is also desired for its own sake and favorably regarded by all, it may be necessary to add the clause "whatever is a positive entity (i.e., not a mere negation)" to the definitions.

For ontology, pleasure and pain (along with desire and hatred) are, according to the Nyāya theory, qualities of the self. On the Vedānta theory, they are simply mental states and do not belong to the self. Epistemologically, two questions were asked by the Indian philosophers. For one thing, are pleasure and pain themselves modes of awareness? For another, closely related to the above question, do pleasure and pain have their own objects? According to the Nyāya-Vaiśeṣika school, pleasure and pain are not, by themselves, modes of awareness, while on the Buddhist theory, they are. The Buddhist philosopher Dharmakīrti argues that pleasure and pain arise out of the same causal conditions as awarenesses such as perceptions, and so are themselves awarenesses. On the Nyāya theory, their causal conditions are different. On the Nyāya theory, pleasure and pain become objects of inner awareness. As such, pleasure and pain do not have their own objects. They derive their objects from some cognition or other.

From the point of view of theory of action with which we are concerned in this chapter, pleasure and pain are the ultimate fruits of actions. This conception of fruit will influence the way morality is understood in the systems.

The Sāṃkhya distinguishes between three modes of feeling: pleasure (*sukha*), pain (*duḥkha*), and *moha* (confusion and stupidity). Pleasure is the feeling of "restful freedom," of lightness; pain is the feeling of "restless, freeing activity" giving rise to willing to be free; *moha* is the feeling of "affective insensibility," of indifference, ignorance, and indolence.

The idea of pain is fundamental to the worldview of much of Hindu and Buddhist thought. K. C. Bhattacharyya, writing on the Sāṃkhya philosophy, remarks that "[T]he exemplar of objective reality is (then) pain," and that the other feelings are intelligible only in reference to pain. Bhattacharyya's argument is that only pain is given as utterly distinct from the self. Furthermore, to be reflectively aware of pain is to wish to be free from it; the necessary wish is the necessary idea of the pain being foreign to and therefore ceasing to consciousness.

The Buddhists also tend to regard all feelings, including pleasure, as but modes of pain. What is called "pleasure" is but lesser pain; contrasted with greater pleasure, a state of pleasure is painful. It is also painful inasmuch as a state of pleasure is evanescent. We have only more or less pain.

An opposite view may be ascribed to Vedānta. Since, on the Vedānta theory, consciousness is, in its intrinsic nature, blissful (*ānanda*), pain is but a limitation imposed on blissfulness.

Various kinds of pain are distinguished in the different systems. Praśastapāda distinguishes between three kinds of pain: sensory feeling of pain, pain arising from memory, and pain arising from expectation. Sāṃkhya distinguishes between inner (*ādhyātmika*) pain, pain caused by men and other animals (*ādhibhautika*), and pain caused by gods and demons (*ādhidaivika*). Buddhism distinguishes between different kinds of *duḥkha:* ordinary suffering as in birth, sickness, and death; getting what one does not want and not getting what one wants is suffering due to the impermanence of things; and suffering due to the aggregate nature of things, especially of the ego, and the consequent thirst or craving.

Are there neutral feelings besides pleasure and pain? According to the Nyāya-Vaiśeṣika, there is no neutral feeling, the so-called indifference being not a feeling but a cognitive state. Buddhism and Vedānta accept a neutral state. The self, according to Vedānta, is intrinsically indifferent (*udāsīna*). The Buddhists call this neutral feeling *upekṣā* or equanimity in all situations and for all beings.

What are the springs of action? *Nyāyasūtra* 1.1.17 says that the causes of action are called *doṣas* or faults. These faults are attachment (*rāga*), hatred (*dveṣa*), and error or false cognition (*moha*). The third, i.e., false belief about the self, underlies the other two. Both good and bad actions arise from these causes. The attached person performs those actions that yield for him either pleasure or pain. Likewise with the one who is hateful. The *sūtras* continue to define "fruits" that are generated by actions and the faults, the fruits being pleasure and pain.

Rāga or attachment is of five kinds: sexual craving (*kāma*), jealousy (*matsara*), desire for acquisition (*spṛhā*), will to live (*tṛṣṇā*), and greed (*lobha*). These are all cravings for pleasure or for objects of pleasure.

Dveṣa or hatred is of six kinds: anger, envy, malevolence, resentment, violence, and egoism. These all express antipathy to pain or the objects of pain.

Moha or false cognition includes error, doubt, pride, and jealousy. Essentially, this is clinging to life and the consequent fear of death.

Buddhism recognizes three primal cravings: will to live, sex instinct, craving for wealth and power. Jainism recognizes four instincts: eating food, fear, sex, and acquisitive desire. For Patañjali, will to live leads to fear of death.

This psychological framework shared by all schools, with minor differences, forms the basis of the moral theories advanced. We shall follow the moral theories under two headings: theories of virtue and theory of duty. Both virtues and duties come under *dharma.* One could say virtues are ought to be, duties are ought to do.

VIRTUES: HINDU AND BUDDHIST

Virtues are excellences of character. They are states of one's being, transformations of one's nature by practice and effort. The Vedas praise the virtues of truthfulness, charity, self-control, gratitude, fidelity, forgiveness, nonstealing, noncheating, and noninjury. The *Chāndogya Upaniṣad* lists austerity (*tapas*), charity (*dāna*), simplicity (*ṛjutā*), nonviolence (*ahiṃsā*), and truthfulness (*satyavacana*) (III, IV, 34). The *Āruṇikopaniṣad* recommends self-control (*brahmacarya*), nonviolence (*ahiṃsā*), nonpossession (*aparigraha*), and truth (*satya*). All these virtues can be cultivated and preserved by repeated effort (*abhyāsa*). The *Bhagavadgītā's* list of virtues includes the following: fearlessness (*abhayaṃ*), nonviolence (*ahiṃsā*), nonhatred (*adveṣaṃ*), nonanger (*akrodhaṃ*), simplicity (*ārjavaṃ*), charity (*dāna*), forgiveness (*kṣamā*), compassion (*karuṇā*), friendship (*maitrī*), peace (*śāntiḥ*), truthfulness (*satyaṃ*), purity (*śaucaṃ*), austerity (*tapas*), detachment (*vairāgyaṃ*), and equanimity (*samatvaṃ*). It is easy to determine which of these are self-regarding (e.g., truth, austerity, fearlessness, detachment) and which are other-regarding (forgiveness, compassion, friendship, nonhatred, equanimity). One may also classify them, following an ancient mode of classification, into virtues of the body, virtues of speech, and virtues of the mind. In the *Gītā* the highest virtue would seem to be *samatvaṃ* or equality which includes equanimity. (I owe this view to Bina Gupta's unpublished manuscript on Hindu ethics.)

Some of these virtues can be reformulated as rules of action. Thus, to "charity" corresponds the rule "unconditionally give to the needy." Some virtues are not actional but are modes of the inner being. These are simplicity, compassion, and detachment. But all virtues pertain to character.

The Buddhist ethics especially emphasize virtues to be cultivated by effort and practice. The Buddha's so-called Noble Eightfold Path is traditionally divided into three groups: *śila* (ethical practice), *samādhi* (mental discipline), and *prajñā* (wisdom). The foundation of *śila* is love and compassion and, in the traditional list, includes right speech, right action, and right livelihood. Each of these again consists of a number of abstentions. Right speech consists in abstaining from telling lies; from slander and hateful speech; from rude, harsh, impolite, and malicious talk; and from idle gossip. What remains is truthful and appropriate speech, appropriate to the occasion and promoting goodness in the speaker as well as in the auditor. Right action includes abstaining from killing, stealing, dishonest actions, and illegitimate sex. Right livelihood rules out certain means of earning livelihood such as selling arms, drinks, or poisons; butchery; and cheating. The Buddhist work *Dhammapada* mentions a lot of virtues, some of which coincide with the virtues eulogized in the *Gītā*. Some of these virtues are to be energetic, attentiveness, purity, self-restraint, diligence, self-mastery, rightly directed mind, to be unshaken by praise or blame, tranquility, peace, patience, forbearance, freedom from hatred, contentment, freedom from lust, and detachment.

If the highest virtue in the *Bhagavadgītā* is *samatvaṃ* or equality/equanimity, the highest virtue in Buddhism is compassion (*karuṇā*). One distinguishes between *karuṇā* as means and *karuṇā* as the goal. Three levels of Buddhist practice are recognized, each having a certain ideal as its goal. These ideals are the *śrāvaka,* the *pratyeka-buddha* or the lonely *buddha,* and the highest *buddha* or *samyak-buddha.* The *śrāvaka* aims at removing the suffering of individuals. He follows the fourth of the four noble truths (i.e., the truth about the path or *mārga*). The *śrāvaka* attains the knowledge that the individual self is not real and comprehends the truth of dependent origination. His compassion arises from the perception of the suffering of all beings. This level of compassion is called *sattvāvalambanākaruṇā* or compassion that depends upon the truth (of suffering) of all individual beings. The next level of compassion is that of the *pratyeka-buddha,* who realizes the impermanence and so suffering nature of all elements of being. His compassion is called *dharmāvalambanākaruṇā,* compassion that follows from knowledge of impermanence of all things. Finally, there is the highest buddha (*samyak-buddha*) whose compassion has no grounds; his compassion is inseparable from emptiness (*śūnyatā*), like *śūnyatā* compassion is also transcendent (*lokottara*). It is uncaused. The highest buddha lives always in the service of humankind.

It does seem that Buddhism defines what is good (*kuśala*) in terms of its conduciveness to the production of happiness (*sukha*) and what is bad (*a-kuśala*) in terms of its conduciveness to the production of suffering (*duḥkha*). Sensory pleasure was brought under the category of suffering in view of its impermanence, relativity, and eventually bringing about discontentment.

The early Mahāyāna developed the idea of six perfections (*pāramita*) by adding two to the Sarvāstivādin list of four (giving [*dāna*], morality [*sīla*], vigor [*vīrya*], and wisdom [*prajñā*]). The two that were added are patience (*kṣānti*) and meditation (*dhyāna*). Four more were added: "skill in means" (*upāyakauśalya*), vows (*praṇidhāna*), strength (*bala*), and knowledge (*jñāna*), bringing the list to ten.

In all this, what is usually called the ethical is only a part that is mingled with cognitive and spiritual stages of advancement.

JAINA ETHICS

In a certain sense all Indian—Hindu, Buddhist, and more so the Jaina—accounts of ethical life regard it as a process of self-purification and self-cultivation. This statement is less true of those schools of Indian philosophy, like the Vedānta, for whom the self is always pure, what needs to be purified being the mind, or also of Buddhism, for whom the self is not an ontologically real entity needing to be purified. The idea of purification of the self is more true of Jainism.

The process includes right conduct consisting of five vows: nonviolence (*ahiṃsā*), truthful and pleasant speech (*sunṛta*), not taking what is not given to one (*asteya*), chastity (*brahmacarya*), and nonpossession (*aparigraha*). All of these are ultimately founded on *ahiṃsā,* which is the unique and cardinal virtue in Jaina ethics. And *ahiṃsā* itself is founded upon a panpsychical metaphysical theory according to which everything possesses sentience, though in different degrees. The idea of nonviolence is extended even to intellectual life, it being a moral obligation to respect and try to understand the other's point of view before rejecting it outright. This follows from the Jaina logical theory, known as *syādvāda,* to the effect that every proposition is true from a certain perspective and false from another.

To be able to practice this virtue, one needs to overcome the four passions that overpower the soul; these are anger (*krodha*), vanity (*māna*), insincerity (*māyā*), and greed (*lobha*).

Given the importance of *ahiṃsā* in Jaina ethics, few words about it are in order. Although *ahiṃsā* or nonviolence figures as a major virtue in all the systems of Indian thought considered here, it is only in Jainism that it remains the highest virtue and is recognized without any constraint imposed on it, although in practice the requirement is relaxed in the case of ordinary persons. In Hindu ethics, however, in spite of according to *ahiṃsā* a place in the list of universal virtues, many thinkers raised the question whether some *hiṃsā* or violence was not desirable, acceptable, and legitimate. It is rather clear that there was a tension between the Vedic rituals involving animal sacrifice and the recommendation of *ahiṃsā* as a supreme virtue. The Mīmāṃsākas such as Kumārila sought to argue for the *hiṃsā* involved in Vedic rituals and yet to make room for the practice of *ahimsā*. No satisfactory solution seems to have been arrived at. Many readers have found even in such a late work as the *Bhagavadgītā* a defense of *himsā* or killing of the enemy in a righteous war and yet inclusion of *ahimsā* among the supreme virtues. One way of reconciling them is to relativize the two claims to two interests and hold that a warrior should not hesitate to kill his enemy in case the cause he fights for is just, while one who is striving after attaining *mokṣa* should practice *ahimsā*. No ethical rule, in this sense, is unconditionally binding.

THE IDEA OF THE GOOD IN INDIAN THOUGHT

If the good is what men desire or strive after, the Indian thinkers very early on developed a theory of hierarchy of goods. These are *artha, kāma, dharma,* and *mokṣa.* Leaving aside the question about how precisely the first two in this list have to be ranked, one may want to suggest that the first two are what human beings do strive after while the last two are what they ought to strive after. Such a distinction between what men do desire and what they ought to strive after is indicated in a verse of *Kaṭha Upaniṣad,* although it may have to be conceded that the is-ought distinction did not come to the forefront of Hindu moral thinking. One may as a matter of fact construct an argument to prove that even *mokṣa* is not a mere ought to be. The argument would run as follows: men do want to get rid of pain and to have a state of happiness. This natural desire by implication may be extended to a complete freedom from pain and enjoyment of an uninterrupted state of bliss (even if no one ordinarily posits this as his or her goal). It is only on reflection, and as a result of being disappointed by reaching the first two and yet being dissatisfied with them, that one self-consciously posits the last two goals, the third to begin with, and as a result of a similar dissatisfaction with the third after reaching it, the fourth and the highest good, which is not a mere ought to do, but an ideal state of being. If the English phrase "the highest good" translates into *nihśreyasaḥ* (in Sanskrit), then *mokṣa* is that state of excellence in which there is nothing greater and that leaves, upon attainment, nothing else to be desired (*yam labdhvā nāparaṃ*. . .).

While the Upaniṣads gave various descriptions of this state of being, the systems of philosophy developed their respective accounts consistently with their general philosophical positions. Let us first look at some of the descriptions to be found in the Upaniṣads. The *Muṇḍaka Upaniṣad* says one who knows the *brahman* becomes the *brahman* ("*Brahmavid brahmaiva bhavat*i" II.ii.9). *Mokṣa* is described as a state in which all fear disappears, all duality vanishes. Yājñavalkya tells Janaka that one who knows Atman becomes full of peace, self-controlled, patient, and self-composed, that evil does not consume him while he consumes all evil (*Bṛhadāraṇyaka Up.* Iv.4.22–3).

Possibly, the most decisive text of antiquity on the topic of the highest good is Yājñavalkya's speech addressed to his wife Maitreyi. The text deserves to be quoted at length.

> When Yājñavalkya announced to his wife that he was about to renounce his life as a householder and assured her that he was going to divide his possessions between her and his other wife Kātyāyani, Maitreyi replied: "If now, Sir, this whole earth filled with wealth were mine, would I be immortal thereby?" When her husband said "no," Maitreyi asked, "What should I do with that through which I may not be immortal? What you know Sir, that, indeed, tell me!" In reply, after saying of various things that are desired and that are dear of such things as one's husband, wife, sons, wealth, gods, and beings, that they are not dear for their sake, i.e., for the sake of loving them, but only for the sake of the Self, Yājñavalkya concluded: "Lo, verily, it is the Self that should be seen, that should be hearkened to, that should be thought on, that should be pondered on, O Maitreyi." (*Bṛhadāranyaka Up.* IV. 5.6).

It is to this concept that we shall eventually attend. There is no doubt that this concept has loomed large before the Hindu mind, providing it with a practical end as well as a theoretical explanandum such that the various *āstika* philosophies may be regarded as providing theoretical justifications for the possibility (and desirability) of such an end. This of course does not imply either that there was agreement about the nature of the goal or that the theories that justified them were all alike. However, despite enormous internal differences and disputations, some large goal attracted the Hindu mind, and this goal may be called "*mokṣa.*" Before reflecting on the unity and the differences in understanding it, let me turn to the more mundane striving.

I said more mundane for the four ends of man easily fall into two groups: the first three into a group that may be called ordinary, natural ends, the fourth being an extraordinary, supernatural goal. It is quite reasonable to surmise that the first three were identified earlier, and, with the rise of reflective philosophies, the fourth was added. Be that as it may, that distinction between ordinary and extraordinary goals does not coincide with the distinction between "is" and "ought." All the four goals are pursued *as a matter of fact.*

The third is pursued by lesser numbers than the first two and the fourth is pursued only by very few. It may in one sense be claimed of the first two goals that they are striven after, never fully reached (i.e., reached with unsurpassable satisfaction). The same can be said of the third as well. In other words, one can make a reasonable case for the claim that the first three goals can be reached only in degrees, "more or less," never to an unsurpassable degree. Only the fourth, striven after by so few and reached by still fewer, is reached with finality, without any scope for more or less or in degrees, i.e., excluding the possibility of gradual progress (*kramonnati*). The familiar is-ought distinction derived from Western moral theory just does not apply.

Nevertheless, if we are to find here, in Indian thinking of these matters, a moral theory, we must, as we already have done, focus on theory of action. It may, however, be that what we have is a theory of value in a wider sense, which includes moral theory inasmuch as moral values are a subset of all values. In a specific sense, all ought pertains to actions and values, which can be striven after through actions. In a larger sense, there are values making a claim on our *being* to be actualized, values that ought to be, without it being possible to find a correlative duty. The distinction between these two kinds of values, actional and ontological, and correlatively between two kinds of "ought," the "ought" of duties and the ought to be will—in spite of the breakdown of the is-ought distinction—help us to sort out things in the complex field of Indian ethics.

FROM *DHARMA* TO *MOKṢA*: THE ETHICAL THEORY OF THE *BHAGAVADGĪTĀ*

The idea of *mokṣa* transcends the claims of *dharma.* On the one hand, *dharma* is advanced as a means to *mokṣa;* on the other, *dharma,* with its elaborate hierarchical social-caste-family structure, is also recognized to be a hindrance for *mokṣa.* The conflict between the two ideals pervades the history of Hindu thought as much as attempts to resolve the conflict. *Mokṣa* itself is construed differently in different systems of thought, but no matter what concept of it one takes into account, the conflict and the tension remain. In general, one can say, orthodoxy argued that *dharma* as embodied in the words of the scriptures had absolute validity even for the person who attained *mokṣa.* Śaṃkara gives strong arguments why *mokṣa* and *dharma* are so radically different that the former cannot presuppose the latter. *Dharma* is a course of action whose performance or nonperformance depends upon the will of the agent. *Mokṣa* is a state of being, consequent upon knowing the nature of things. One philosophical issue is: can knowledge be the subject matter of an imperative of the form "you ought to know"?

Liberalism holds that *dharma* is relative and changeable. The books of *dharma* are not *śruti,* the heard texts (i.e., those texts which are absolutely authoritative for the Hindus); they are rather *smṛti,* texts whose authority can be overridden and whose doctrines conflict among themselves. You need some *dharma* or other for social cohesion, but there is no absolutely valid set of *dharmas.* The *dharma* regarding *varṇa* or caste has played out its role and needs to be replaced by a more universalistic, nonhierarchical ethics.

What, then, is the connecting link between *dharma* and *mokṣa?* Or, is there a connecting link at all, or, should one desirous of pursuing *mokṣa* make a Kierkegaardian leap?

I think it is undeniable that although one often speaks of *artha* being a means to *kāma,* there is no necessary means-end relation between them. One pursues *artha* for the sake of the erotic pleasure that *kāma* signifies. Likewise, there is no necessary link between *kāma* and *dharma.* A person may devote his or her life to the pursuit of the two lower ends without being inspired to a life of virtues. But, given the inspiration, derived either from some frustrating feature of the first two pursuits, or from study of the scriptures, or from the influence of a virtuous person, he or she can turn toward *dharma* and practice of *dharma* may eventually lead either to abandonment of the first two pursuits, or to regulating them in accordance with the requirements of *dharma.* Likewise, a person may spend his or her life practicing *dharma,* trying to lead a *dhārmika* (i.e., virtuous) life but may not be led to a pursuit of *mokṣa.* As Śaṃkara said, practice of *dharma* is not a prerequisite for asking the sort of questions, for example, for desire to know the *brahman,* which, on the Vedānta theory, leads to *mokṣa.* Again, there is no necessary link.

It is here that the teachings of Kṛṣṇa in the *Bhagavadgītā* become relevant. The *Gītā* is widely admired as a work on ethics and spirituality, and people of many different ethical persuasions have confessed to their indebtedness to this unique text. For my present purpose I will look upon it as precisely focusing upon the link between *dharma* and *mokṣa.* Arjuna's "despondency," as the first chapter's title goes, may be understood as arising out of the internal conflict between different parts of the total *dharma:* the *varṇadharma* (i.e., the *dharma* of caste) points in one direction, and the *kuladharma* (i.e., the *dharma* of family) in another, and the *sādhāraṇadharma* (i.e., the *dharma* common to all persons in all contexts) in still another. As a member of the caste of warriors, Arjuna knows he ought to fight a battle if the cause is righteous. As a member of a family, he ought not to kill his grandfathers, uncles, and cousins. In any case, he is subject to the universally binding rule of noninjury (*ahiṃsā*). How to reconcile these conflicting demands? Faced with this collapse of the system of *dharma,* Arjuna refuses to fight. Kṛṣṇa undertakes to bring Arjuna back to his senses and to fight for an undoubtedly just and righteous cause (i.e., to do his duty). But how must he do his duty so that practice of *dharma* will be conducive to attainment of *mokṣa?* Kṛṣṇa does not explicitly opt for one of the sides, although the situation and his task required that the *dharma* of the warrior had to override that of the family. But he does not likewise say that the *sādhāraṇadharma,* the universal *dharma,* should override the *dharma* of the warrior, for then Arjuna should have been advised to practice nonviolence (as Gandhi would have him under his symbolic interpretation of the battlefield). Leaving that conflict untouched, Kṛṣṇa advises Arjuna against giving up his duties and the life of action and insists that true freedom is achieved not by giving up all action (which, in any case, is not feasible) but by giving up all attachment to the fruits of one's actions. Actions are ordinarily performed as motivated by some desire. When performed, an action either satisfies or frustrates the desire and so causes either happiness or pain. It is this causal chain that is the source of attachment to the mundane order (*saṃsāra*). *Mokṣa* means minimally (for it may also mean more) freedom from this attachment. A necessary condition for it is desirelessness, which is the same as absence of attachment to the fruits of one's action. This concept of fruits of an action (*karmaphala*) must be correctly understood. Any consequence of one's action is not here called its fruit. If a physician treats a patient he or she is not asked to be disinterested in the consequence (i.e., in the patient's well-being or lack of it). "Fruit" means the consequences in or for the agent of his actions: success or failure, pleasure or pain, etc. It is these that are the source of attachment. Kṛṣṇa urges the aspirer after *mokṣa* to do his or her duty without desire for pleasure, success, fame, etc. He does allow impersonal motives such as good of all or preservation of mankind (*lokasaṃgraha*). If one performs *dharma* with this detachment and desirelessness, then one is truly free. Thus Kṛṣṇa attempts to save the *varṇadharma* as against Arjuna's temporary and occasional skepticism, and at the same time suggests a way beyond *dharma* toward quite another goal—*mokṣa,* which is the highest good.

It is natural to ask, at this point, How can anyone act without any desire? The bulk of Kṛṣṇa's discourse is devoted to show how this is possible, and for this purpose Kṛṣṇa makes use of metaphysical concepts deriving from Sāṃkhya and Vedānta. This is one place where a metaphysical grounding is offered, not so much for the *dharmas* as for the idea of desirelessness and nonattachment. If the former corresponds, as suggested earlier, to Hegel's *Sittlichkeit,* the latter corresponds to what Hegel calls *Moralität,* the Kantian inner good will, right intention. The former provides the content, for which the latter provides the form and the spirit. The two together—*dharma* practised with inner freedom—lead to *mokṣa.* The content needs and permits no grounding save in the idea of tradition. The form is grounded by Kṛṣṇa first in the Sāṃkhya distinction between self *(puruṣa)* and nature (*prakṛti*), then in the Vedāntic idea of the *ātman-brahman,* and finally in the theistic idea of the supreme self (*Puruṣottama*). From the first, it follows that the three *guṇas (sattva, rajas,* and *tamas),* which motivate and drive persons to action, are parts of nature and do not touch the self, so that the true self of a person is not an agent, nor is it an enjoyer (*bhoktā*); from the second, it follows that the sense of otherness that underlies ordinary ways of acting, giving rise to desires and other emotions, is false, all being one at bottom so that the wise man perceives all in himself and himself in all; from the third, it follows that acting in the true spirit (i.e., with desirelessness and nonattachment) is also acting in the spirit of "offering your actions and their fruits" as offerings—replacing flowers and fruits and incense—to the highest deity (i.e., Kṛṣṇa himself). The three *Yogas—karma* or action, *jñāna* or knowledge, and *bhakti* or devotion—join together, just as the three systems, Sāṃkhya, Vedānta, and theistic religion, are grafted together. Kṛṣṇa offers Arjuna some advice: "go beyond the three *guṇas"* (*nistrayirguṇyo bhavārjuna*), "do your actions, while settled in *yoga*" (*yogasthaḥ kuru karmāṇi*), "take refuge in your intelligence" (*buddhou śaraṇamanviccha*), "be only an occasion" (*nimittamātraṃ bhava*), "think of me, be my devotee" (*manmanā bhava madbhakto*). These instructions are calls to transcend moral distinctions (i.e., the qualities or the *guṇas*), to do one's duties with an inner freedom, to work with clear and enlightened intelligence, and to act as if you are an instrument of God's purpose.

There are several tantalizing questions that inevitably arise. What does one mean by saying that the wise man transcends moral distinctions? Some statements by

Kṛṣṇa seem to suggest that the wise man can do what he wants, not being bound by moral rules and obligations. But how are we to understand this "freedom" not only from evil (*pāpa*) but also from good (*puṇya*)?

Louis Dumont has interpreted the difference of *mokṣa* from the first three ends (which he takes to be profit, pleasure, and religious duty respectively) to consist in the difference between the individual outside the world and man in the world. By so understanding *mokṣa,* Dumont takes the world of caste as a world of relations in which the particular man has no substance, no reality, no "Being" (as he puts it), but only empirical existence. The person who attains *mokṣa* just becomes thereby a true individual who stands outside the relational structure of the world and society and transcends morality, which is tied to that structure.

But the transcendence into *mokṣa* leaves *dharma* unaffected, and we will wonder if the form of "nonattachment" is only prefixed to the already available *dharma.* Are there any contents (that is, any actions) that are just incompatible with the form of "nonattachment?" Many writers have sought to deduce some moral rules and virtues such as love, nonkilling, and toleration from the Vedāntic thesis of a fundamental identity among selves and would argue that certain actions, which by their very nature entail egoistic and selfish desires and destructive emotions such as lust and anger, preclude nonattachment. While this sort of deduction may be an interesting project, it seems clear that the Hindu tradition did not critically examine the entire *dharma* tradition in this manner in order to weed out many *dharma* rules that are amoral or immoral. As a result, a large part of that tradition remained untouched by critical reflection.

Let us consider a *dharma* that passes the critical test. What is the difference between practicing nonkilling on the part of a virtuous person who has not attained *mokṣa* and practicing the same on the part of one who has? The latter person is said to be beyond the three *guṇas,* beyond good and evil, and yet he or she follows the moral rule "don't kill." What difference then does transcending morality do? A comparison with Kant may help. One begins with unconditionally submitting one's will to the moral law out of a sense of duty and ends with the recognition that the law has its source not in an external authority but in one's own rational nature. As a result, the sense of constraint is replaced by a sense of freedom and spontaneity. Can we say that the person who attains *mokṣa* likewise follows the moral law out of an inner freedom (and not out of, say, a fear of punishment)? But this Kantian-type answer can only be partly true. The *dharmas* of tradition do not flow from my rational nature. The idea of the moral agent being self-legislative is not there in Indian thought. The *dharmas* belong to the social ethos that exert a hold on me insofar as I belong to the tradition. My rationality consists in respecting that tradition's wisdom. *Dharma,* in the Hindu tradition, is ultimately relative and contingent, and only used as a means to a goal that transcends it. It must be added that this last remark is not true of the Buddhist and the Jaina traditions.

We may even make a stronger assertion. In Hindu ethics there is no categorical imperative, no unconditional moral principle. All moral laws have the "hypothetical" form: If you wish to attain such and such a goal, then these rules and virtues are binding. The lesson of the *Bhagavadgītā* is: if you want to attain *mokṣa,* then perform *dharma* with nonattachment. Thus there is a sort of separation among the goals, which gives pursuit of *dharma* an autonomy, and yet allows for, in a sense demands (without necessitating) transition to the pursuit after *mokṣa.*

It is important to bear in mind that the *dharma* texts do not have the authority of "heard" texts (*śruti*) but are only records of tradition or are "remembered" (*smṛti*), which implies that philosophical thinking can subject the *dharmas* to criticism when that criticism is internal (i.e., based upon the doctrines of the *sruti*). From within, there are at least two ways of criticizing the tradition: for one thing, the critic can argue that the existing *dharma,* or some component of it (for example, the caste hierarchy) is not consistent with some fundamental conception of the Upaniṣads, and so needs to be either revised or rejected in toto for, after all, the *śruti* is "stronger" than the *smṛti.* For another, one may criticize the received *dharma* by reinterpreting the texts as Gandhi did famously with regard to the *varṇa* theory when he interpreted the theory to mean not a hierarchy of castes but a system of family inherited skills of production, so ordered as to avoid a competitive economic system.

It is to be regretted that philosophical thinking of the *darśanas* focused primarily upon *mokṣa,* and the *dharma* tradition was unquestionably passed over and taken for granted. Yet life was more determined by the *dharma*-s while *mokṣa* remained in the distant horizon, unreachable but worthy of praise.

Mokṣa is regarded, in the Hindu tradition, as the highest good. Several questions need to be asked about this claim. First, if the good is what is desired (*iṣta*), can it be said that *mokṣa* is a possible object of desire? If so, is it not the case that one is desiring desirelessness? Second, can one say that the idea of *mokṣa* is simply the idea of an experiential equivalent of a system's metaphysical theory? To take an example: the nondualistic Vedāntin holds that all differences are unreal. The idea of *mokṣa,* on this theory, then is but the practical, experiential implication of the theory, a realization in one's experience, of that identity between *ātman* and the *brahman*. One may also ask why such an experience is to be called the highest good. The difference between this end and the other three ends (i.e., *artha, kāma,* and *dharma*) is not one of degree, but rather one of qualitative otherness. *Mokṣa* simply lies on another dimension. It is not an ought to do, but at most an ought to be, suggesting a radical transformation of one's mode of being. On some conceptions of it, especially Śaṃkara's, the locution "my *mokṣa*" (or "she attained *mokṣa*") would be a contradiction inasmuch as the possessive "my" (or the nominative "she") ascribes an ego that would seem to contradict the very idea of *mokṣa.*

Two other questions were discussed in connection with the nature of *mokṣa* (also with regard to the idea of *nirvāṇa* among Buddhists). One of these questions is, Can the highest *mokṣa* (or *nirvāṇa*) be attained while one is alive in a bodily state or does attainment of such a goal require giving up of the body? It is interesting to note that philosophical theories that regard body and the world to be real hold that the highest state of *mokṣa* requires cessation of bodily existence, while those who regard body and the world to be unreal, as Śaṃkara does, regard liberation to be possible in a living body. Clearly, only a living "liberation" (*jivanmukti*) can be called the highest good.

The other question that was discussed is: Is it possible for one person to achieve the highest state of *mokṣa* while the others are in bondage? Or, is it necessary that the highest *mokṣa* for one is also liberation for the others? Of these two alternative positions known as *eka-mukti* and *sarvanmukti,* Śaṃkara and Mahāyāna Buddhism opted for the latter.

A NOTE ON THE CONCEPT OF *SANNYĀSIN* (RENUNCIANT)

A *sannyāsin* or renunciant who appears at the end of the four-phase ideal-typical life history of an ideal person (i.e., after the practitioner of "austerity," the married householder, and the retiree into the forest for the purpose of contemplation have played out their roles), is a figure who is free from the constraints of social roles and rules. He has no caste; is not bound by rules; and has no home, no family, and no kith and kin. A life determined by social roles comes to an end, he becomes free and spontaneous; in him all previous ethics are negated and deconstructed, opening the prospects of being outside the world. This figure yields a new perspective from which being in the world acquires meaning and surrenders its claim to unlimited validity.

IS THERE A HINDU MORAL THEORY?

Classical Western moral philosophy has taken upon itself the task of legitimizing and grounding our moral beliefs and intuitions with the help of fundamental principles. These principles have been God as the lawgiver, the principle of universalizability, and the utility principle. In this sense, Hindu thinking on *dharma* does not, it is often contended, provide a moral theory. Besides, the concept of *dharma,* like the German *Recht,* covers a large variety of different, even if loosely connected, phenomena. However, today moral thinking, by returning to the more descriptive Aristotelian virtue theory and recognition of various dimensions of human excellence, has broken loose from the constraint of the Kantianism-Utilitarianism framework. From this new perspective, the *dharma* theory fares well. Part of it is a theory of moral rules, part of it a theory of virtues, another part communitarian, and added to all these, there is a layer of Kantian-like duty for duty's sake subserving a transcendent goal of *mokṣa,* where ethics transcends itself. Are we in the domain of religion?

Part 4

Religion and Art

Chapter Eight

Philosophy of Religion

There is a widely held view that philosophy in the Indian tradition was inseparable from religion just as religion was deeply philosophical. This book, up until this stage, must have amply demonstrated that the first part of that belief is just not true. Whether the second part of the belief is true may emerge out of the discussions in this chapter.

There is no doubt that in the traditional Sanskrit doxographies there is no special term for philosophy of religion. However, in some works, there are chapters entitled *Īśvaravāda* (i.e., the doctrine of God). In this chapter we will not be discussing the major Indian religions such as Hinduism (or the *Vaidic dharma*), Buddhism, Jainism, and Islam but only philosophy of religion (i.e., such philosophical questions as arose from reflection on the religions themselves). Sometimes these questions have been dealt with from within the tradition, sometimes the questions are raised from outside.

NATURE OF THE VEDIC TRADITION

Not being a historical religion that is founded by a prophet, based on a book, at an identifiable point of time, the Vedic religion may best be called a natural religion. The corpus of the texts of this religion is much unlike the Bible or the Q'ran. The texts, rather, record everything that the community knew (*vid* = to know) and serve as the founding texts from which the entire culture began. Not having an author, the texts—compiled into the various Vedas in course of time—came to be characterized as *apauruṣeya.* Meaning "not having a human author," this concept was construed in many different ways by the later thinkers, among them being an understanding of the texts as the words originating from the mouth of the primaeval creator *Brahmā.* More appropriate is the construal that the texts can be understood—following the rules of interpretation—without bringing in "authorial intention." The texts then are claimed to be free from all possible defects that originate from the deficiencies of human authorship. But for that reason, one need not understand the "heard" texts (*śruti*) as revelations, for we have no idea of who revealed them and to whom. Nor are they all records of the so-called spiritual experiences of mystic sages, which would be to read into them our later ideas of "experience." What we have is a primacy of the texts themselves.

From the perspective of religion, it is necessary that we point out a few remarkable features of the Vedic religion. On the surface, the hymns of the Ṛg-Veda appear to be a sort of "naturalistic polytheism," which then matures, through stages of internal development, successively into a "henotheism," a monotheism, and finally an agnostic monism ("who knows that One Being?"). But this reading, combined with the ritualism one ascribes to the Vedic religion, makes use of more modern ideas of "nature" and "naturalism," and also of "rituals." It may be more appropriate to use conceptualizations that are prior to the Cartesian divide between nature and spirit and also prior to the anthropologist's idea of "rituals." Luckily, in more recent times, our understanding of the Vedic language has been deepened. As Sri Aurobindo has brought out, the key Vedic words such as *Agni*, *Indra*, *Marut*, and *Varuṇa* signify, on the one hand what may look like our familiar natural elements and powers such as fire, raincloud, wind, and the waters, but on the other, even etymologically, carry inner, deeply psychological meanings. Spanning the divide between the outer and the inner, these "deities" or *devas* (or "shining ones") show both the inseparability of man from his world and the sacredness of both. It is not worship of nature as opposed to spirit, of the outer as opposed to the inner, for those distinctions were not yet available. It is recognition of the intentional threads that bind the inner to the outer, such that each *deva* may be construed as such an intentional nexus. Is there then, the hymns go on to ask, any one being underlying these multiple *devas*, a fundamental unity, a unitary being, whose self-differentiations are the specific unities of subjective functions and their objective correlates ?

Taken as a religion, the Vedic thought and practice develop into a three-tiered program. At one level, it is worship, celebration, and recognition of the deities as constituting the ways the individual is tied to the cosmos. At another level, it is practice of the roles and the rules, the *dharmas,* which connect the individual to the community. At a still another level, in one sense the most esoteric level, it becomes a search for knowing one's innermost self—who one is—as the unity prior to the subject-object split.

All three levels of religion were interpreted with reference to some abiding beliefs that were rather pan-Indian: that human life is characterized by suffering, that *karma* and rebirth are at the source of that suffering, and that religion aims at opposing that experience of suffering with a celebration of the presence of the gods in our body, life, and mind in relation to the world, and eventually conquering the bondage of *karma* and rebirth by discovering the innermost universality of existence.

As religion developed from these basal notions and experiences, every ritual, every deity, every action took on a symbolic meaning. The object of religious worship and devotion, the form, the figure, all acquired significance that goes beyond the given datum. Not even that symbolic meaning was a fixed concept. It grew and developed with experience and history—all pointing to the ultimate unity of subject and object, meaning and reference, self and deity, individual and cosmos. Theological myths sprang around these symbolisms, myths of creation and destruction; conceptual systems articulated the metaphysics; rituals brought home to the practitioner multivalent and inexhaustible possibilities of self- (and other) interpretation; all facets of life from birth and death, even before and after, acquired meanings. Eventually all symbolisms came to be represented in art. The religion, originally poetic, originating in the Vedic hymns, became artistic. Figurative art sought to rigidify the forms that arose out of the fluidity of poetic experience. Music, including singing and chanting, sought to capture the fluidity of the process behind the rigidity of the figurative art.

THE VEDĀNTIC TRADITION

The Upaniṣads initiated the conceptual frameworks, some of which we have, discussed purely philosophically in the other chapters of this volume. Two philosophical, and three practical, ideas must have emerged at some time. The philosophical ideas are the Vedāntic monism and the personalistic theism. The practical defined a path, but there was laid down the conception of three possible paths: a path of action (*karma*), a path of knowledge (*jñāna*), and a path of devotion (*bhakti*). These ideas, in their mutual opposition as well as in their interrelations, determined the religious life as well as religious thought. The text *Bhagavadgītā* owes its importance in Hindu religious life to the way it synthesizes these, and several other, distinct ideas. The *brahman* is both the impersonal source of all beings and the personal deity Kṛṣṇa whom devotees adore. The path to *mokṣa* is to be chosen by the aspirant in accordance with his best talents and capabilities. This widely conceived plan, in more modern interreligious garb, appeared in Calcutta's much revered Saint Sri Ramakrishna's saying "*yato mat tato path*" ("as many views, so many paths").

If philosophy of religion it is, the central metaphysical issue becomes the compatibility or incompatibility of the two aspects of God: the impersonality, ubiquitousness, and yet transcendence of being and yet the deity's presence, as an object of religious adoration, within as "the inner controller (*antaryāmin*). The metaphysical controversies briefly reviewed among the various interpreters of Vedānta become also of religious significance and had their equivalents in religious life and practice.

THEISTIC ARGUMENTS

With the rise of Buddhism on the one hand and of Hindu theism on the other, there were attempts to prove the existence of God on the part of Hindu philosophers. A classic text containing theistic arguments is Udayana's *Nyāyakusumānjali.*

The Naiyāyikas before Udayana, such as Śrīdhara and Jayanta, had advanced responses to the antitheistic arguments of the Buddhists and some Mīmāṃsakas. What the Naiyāyikas emphasised is the principle that whatever is an effect must be the effect of an intelligent cause—a principle that is not self-evidently true and has obvious counterexamples. A jar is made by a potter, where the principle is satisfied. But when a seed causes a sprout, we do not have an intelligent cause. What the Naiyāyika does is to include all such controversial and disputed cases under the scope of the minor term (i.e., *pakṣa*) of the inference, of which "being the effect of an intelligent creator" is sought to be proved with the help of the middle term (or *hetu*) "since it is an effect" and the undisputed cases such as "jar" as instances in favor. This strategy blocks the antitheist move to cite the disputed cases as counterexamples, which is just not permitted by the rules of the game: the counterexamples must also be agreed upon by both parties to the dispute.

What the Naiyāyikas want to prove is that even in those cases where there is no ostensive intelligent maker, such cause can be inferred. And this intelligent cause is none other than God (*Iśvara*). To the argument that the alleged God, not having a body, could not possibly be a cause, Śrīdhara replies that there is no such rule that an agent must be embodied, and, as a counterexample to that rule, cites the agency of the incorporeal self in causing movements in its body. He also rejects the view that desire and effort can arise in a soul only if the soul has a body.

The Buddhist denies the existence of God on the grounds, among others, that if God did exist, he would have been perceived. Nonperception of x is a good ground, on this reasoning, for inferring the nonexistence of x. Udayana rejects this argument. Nonperception of a thing proves the latter's nonexistence only if the thing is a perceptible entity, and God is not. The Buddhist cannot even deny the existence of God, for if, on his view, God is a fiction, it cannot even be the counter-positive of a meaningful negation. This last argument presupposes the Nyāya view that one can meaningfully negate only that which is real and exists in some locus other than where it is being negated. On this view, to deny "rabbit's horn" amounts to denying the existence of horns on a rabbit (though horns are on many other animals).

Among the causal arguments advanced by the Naiyāyikas, the following one suits best their conception of God. They want an explanation of what first makes the atoms that are material to move, so that they may, by joining together, produce bodies of larger extension. The first mover could not be a material body, for *ex hypothesis* no such material body other than the atoms then existed. To say that the atoms are self-moving would amount to ascribing to them sentience, contrary to the initial position. Finite souls can initiate movement only by moving their bodies, and in the present case we still do not have bodies. The only remaining alternative is God's will.

There are several other arguments in Udayana's work, which may be recalled here. They reveal some interesting aspects of the Indian theist's thinking. One argument starts with the premise that falling bodies can be supported only by volitional effort (as when I hold a stone on my palm and resist my palm from going down, or when a flying bird does not fall down, or also when a blade of grass held in a bird's beak does not fall down). The heavenly bodies are prevented from falling due to the volition of an infinite sentient being called God. This clearly is not a good argument, for there clearly is a good physical explanation of why the heavenly bodies stay on their respective orbits.

Another argument makes use of the relation between words and their meanings, which, on the Nyāya view, and contrary to the Mīmāṃsā view on the matter, is conventional in origin. Since the convention "Let this word have that meaning" could not have been introduced for natural language by any finite person, it must have been due to God's will. A similar argument traces the Vedic injunctions to God's commands and the infallibility of the Vedas to God's omniscience. Many Indian philosophers do not accept these arguments—not certainly the Mīmāṃsakas, who maintain that words and their meanings have a natural relation and the Vedas possess intrinsic validity of their own.

THE THREE PATHS

At least since the *Bhagavadgītā,* the idea of three paths—the paths of knowledge, action, and devotion, both as alternatives for religious life and as components of a grand synthesis—has dominated the Hindu understanding of religious life. The philosophies incorporate them all, or any two of them, or sometimes also tried to place the sole emphasis on any one. Nondualistic Vedānta place the sole emphasis on the path of knowledge, action, and devotion performed with nonattachment serving the preparatory goal of "purification of mind" (*cittaśuddhi*) necessary for being able to pursue knowledge with the attainment of which the other two fall away. The theistic Vedānta either emphasizes devotion exclusively or, in addition, takes note of the necessity of action only in the sense of ritualistic action intended to serve the deity. Or sometimes the theists such as Rāmānuja combined devotion with knowledge (*jñānamiśrābhakti*), but also stress that *mokṣa* needs the grace of God. The followers of Rāmānuja differed, however, as to how much effort on the part of the aspirant is needed to receive God's grace, some stressing completely passive self-surrender on the part of the devotee so that God "lifts" you up (as the mother cat picks up the kitten, *mārjāraśāvakavat*); others stressed some effort to cling to God (as does the little monkey cling to the mother). Various forms of the relation of the devotee to the deity are distinguished, each demanding a certain type of devotion: the deity may be loved as the beloved loves her lover, or as the child adores its parent, or as a friend loves her friend, or as a servant respects the master. Each such mode of *bhakti* corresponds to an aesthetic *rasa.* Religion comes close to aesthetics.

In all this, religious life remains dominated by feeling. As said earlier in this chapter, religion as worship of the deity is essentially aesthetic. The figure of the deity—in itself formless, God may be worshipped and thought of under any name and form—is a creation of the artist. The songs in his or her praise are compositions of poets, to be sung in accordance with the canons of music and often in communion with other devotees. Religious rituals performed in service of the deity involve subtle movements of the body, which transform the body into an aesthetic medium, not unlike as in Indian dance. Religion and art become inseparable.

But the idea of action is not to be restricted to religious rituals. Service to the others (the poor, the needy, and the suffering), when performed with no thought of benefit to oneself—as expressed in Prahlāda's prayer—is treated as offerings to the deity, as itself a form of worship, leading to the highest perfection.

The goal of *mokṣa* still looms large before religious life. Birth and death, desire and *karma,* pleasure and pain, are regarded as sources of bondage. Religion hopes to achieve this goal with the help of God. Only the extreme defender of the path of knowledge claims to be able to reach this radical transformation of existence by one's own effort. Religion and philosophy seem to part company.

One may very well ask, Is nondualistic Vedānta a religion? Or, does it transcend the religious attitude and quest in order to reach a philosophical knowledge of the truth? A satisfactory answer to this question would depend upon whether nondualistic Vedānta has room for the experience of something as sacred. Is the *ātman-brahman*, as the original source and stuff of all things, a sacred entity? Or, is its interpretation as a sacred entity due to its symbolization by an already available religious object.

THE IDEA OF *SĀDHANĀ*

The three paths referred to above may be construed as different means (analogous to the *pramāṇas* as means of knowing), practical means to be sure, for reaching the goal of religious life. The idea of such a practical means, involving disciplined pursuit, has dominated Hindu and Buddhist writings and practice of religion. If the essence of religion lies, as it does according to many Indian authors, in the immediate experience of the Divine, or the attainment of *mokṣa* or *nirvāṇa,* the different means are the different paths of *sādhanā* for reaching the goal. Faith (*sraddhā*), although recognized to be a preliminary component of *sādhana,* was not the end; it had to be transformed into a living experience (*anubhūti*). In its negative phase, a *sādhanā* involves cultivation of detachment from worldly concerns and attachments (*vairāgya*). In its positive aspect, it involves repeated practice (*abhyāsa*). As Vyāsa's commentary on *Yoga Sūtra* I.12 puts it, "Through detachment, the flow (of consciousness) towards worldly concerns is arrested; through repeated practice of 'discrimination' the flow towards spiritual progress is opened up."

The aspirant may focus on the object or on the subject. When the Absolute or God is posited as the object par excellence, the path is one of *bhakti* (i.e. loving devotion). When the focus is on the subject within, one may practice *yoga* in order to penetrate to the deeper layers of inner subjectivity. A third path is also open (i.e., the path of nondualistic Vedānta), the path of knowledge, which aims at knowing the universal spirit that transcends the distinction between individual subjectivity and God as the original other. As said above, the *Bhagavadgītā* attempts a synthesis of all these paths.

THE PROBLEM OF EVIL

At the end of this chapter, a few remarks may be in order on the so-called problem of evil. This problem, as it is formulated and sought to be resolved within the framework of the semitic religions, and consequently in the mainstream Western philosophy, cannot even be stated in the tradition of Indian thought. The question of how to reconcile the fact of evil (including pain and suffering) with the goodness, omniscience, and omnipotence of God presupposes the conception of God and his relation to human beings, which is not available in the Indian thought, not even in theistic religions. Even when the theistic religions in India describe God as omniscient, omnipotent, and all-good, these characterizations should be understood together with the role that the law of *karma* plays both in human affairs as well as in connection with God's creative act. God creates the world in conformity with the law of *karma,* and even if he could do otherwise he would not consistently with his moral nature. The moral law and the natural laws—both in cooperation—shape the world, which is both the world for sentient beings and the world ruled by inexorable natural laws.

The facts of evil (of moral evil or *pāpa*) and pain and suffering (*dukkha*) are the starting point of much of Indian thought. Philosophy is under obligation to account for them, in such a way that the account is consistent with the basic metaphysical conceptions, and also can "save" our fundamental moral intuitions. For examining how satisfying the Hindu and Buddhist understandings of evil are, one has to consider them system by system. To contend that they do not satisfy the requirements of the Western philosophies of religion is to miss the point. Here I can only draw attention to the main features of the understanding of evil in Indian thought in general.

For the Hindu theist, God is not responsible for evil. Evil arises, as much as goodness does, in accordance with the law of *karma* as operating through all the myriad sentient beings. Various *karmic* routes (of the worldly sojourns of all the souls involved in mundaneity), intersecting and crisscrossing each other—together with the natural laws and powers—provide causal explanations of the facts of evil. At the same time, the moral obligation remains for each soul, for himself as well as for all others, to eliminate evil by improving the *karmas* in any given life. The ideal of *mokṣa* (or of *nirvāṇa*) is not a selfish pursuit of one's own freedom from suffering, leaving the others to their fates. Rather, the path to one's own *mokṣa* requires cultivation of knowledge of one's basic identity with others, and/or compassion for all suffering creatures. The *arhat* becomes *boddhisattva.* One's own *mokṣa* requires *mokṣa* of all others. Our moral intuition in favor of working toward relieving others' sufferings is confirmed. Not depending upon God to free all creatures, each person can become a contributor to that goal of "freedom for all" (*sarvanmukti*). God is responsible neither for our suffering nor for our possible freedom from sufferings. In the long run the responsibility for both is only ours.

Chapter Nine

Aesthetics or *Rasaśāstra*

From the highly complex field of Indian aesthetics, we shall select and focus upon two key concepts. These are the concepts of *dhvani* and *rasa.* The former concerns the meaning of poetic words and sentences; the latter concerns the nature of aesthetic experience. While there have been many exponents of the two in Sanskrit literature, I will, for my present limited purpose, make use of Ānandavardhana's *Dhvanyāloka* (text from the ninth century A.D.) for "*dhvani,*" and Abhinavagupta's commentary *Bhārati* on Bharata's *Nāṭyaśāstra* (fourth or fifth century A.D.) and *locana* on *Dhvanyāloka* (Abhinavagupta himself belonging to tenth century A.D.) for the concept of *rasa.* We shall find that the two concepts eventually merge into each other.

DHVANI

The concept of *dhvani* or suggested meaning, sometimes also called *vyanjanā,* became a controversial matter in the Indian semantical theories. The Nyāya and the other schools admitted two kinds of meanings of words: the primary meaning or denotation known as *vācyārtha* and the secondary meaning known as *laksyārtha.* In the former case, as when the word "cow" denotes a cow, the relation between a word and its meaning is called *abhidhā,* and the denoted thing is sometimes called *abhidheyārtha.* In the latter case, as when the expression "the village on the Ganges" means the village on the banks of the river Ganges, the relation between the expression and its meaning is called *lakṣaṇā.* The secondary meaning is something that, though not the denotation, is related to the denotation. It is likewise with the expression "the lion amongst men," which means a person who is obviously not a lion, but who possesses the strength and courage of a lion.

Some philosophers admit a third meaning of words and sentences. This is called *vyangya*; the process of meaning it, or rather the function involved, is *vyanjanā,* sometimes translated into "suggestion." The literary theoreticians regard the poetic meaning to be neither the denotation nor the secondary meaning that is objectively related to the denotation, but rather as what is suggested but cannot be derived from the denotation. Ānandavardhana calls this suggested meaning *dhvani.* When a poet writes a sentence, each word of the sentence as well as the entire sentence has its primary meaning, but that is not what the poet intends to express. He wants to suggest a deeper meaning. The primary meaning is like a lamp, which manifests the poetic meaning. The word *vyangya*, by which the poetic meaning is designated, means "what is manifested." The literal meaning manifests, but does not designate, this poetic meaning. Both the meanings are simultaneously experienced. The literal meaning is apprehended, the poetic meaning is suggested; the former easily accessible to the reader, the latter only to the reader who is cultivated. Both, like light and darkness, coexist, as though in the dusk. The poet leaves the meaning unmanifested; it is not "said" or "denoted." The cultivated reader, with appropriate sensibility, experiences it. The unconcealment of the meaning is the function of *vyanjanā.*

Ānandavardhana defines a poetic sentence (*kāvya*) by saying that its soul is *dhvani.* Various writers before him had identified the essence of poetry to be something else. Thus Bharata regarded it to lie in the nine kinds of *rasa* (a concept to which we shall soon turn). According to Bhāmaha, it lies in the three excellences (*guṇas*): *mādhurya* or sweetness, *ojah* or energy, and *prasāda* or harmony. Bāmana emphasised *rīti* or style. Still others took the poetic character of poetry to consist in figures of speech (*alaṇkāra*). Ānandavardhana takes all of these into consideration, but while assigning to each of these factors its due place, insists that without *dhvani* there is no poetry, or rather true (or great) poetry, and concedes to Bharata by saying that this *dhvani,* or suggested meaning, is none other than *rasa,* about which Bharata had spoken. All the others—style, figures of speech, excellences—are merely external embellishments, and without *dhvani* the words do not rise to the level of true, and certainly great, poetry.

There were already theorists who rejected *dhvani* as superfluous on the grounds that *dhvani* can be subsumed under the primary and secondary meanings. We need not, in this brief exposition, undertake to review these anti-*dhvani* theories. Ānandavardhana recognizes the element of truth in each of these theories, but asserts that *dhvani* is an irreducible feature of great poetry. He likens it to the graceful beauty of a woman, which cannot be reduced to features of the various parts of her body, or to absence of defects or presence of embellishments such as jewelry. He recognizes that some varieties of suggested meaning may be conveyed by the primary meaning function of appropriate expressions, but what cannot be so conveyed is *rasa.* Hiriyanna is quoted as saying that *dhvani* is "failure that succeeds." Language fails to designate it, but this failure, in great poetry, succeeds in expressing, or rather suggesting, *dhvani* for the cultivated readers. Since the poetic (i.e., suggested) meaning, in its deepest layer, is *rasa,* let us now turn to the idea of *rasa.*

RASA

The most ancient source for the idea of *rasa* is Bharata's *Nāṭyaśāstra* or The Science of Dance. Various authors since Bharata have developed this concept, which reaches its high point in the writings of Abhinavagupta. *Rasa* lies neither in the mind of the author nor in the mind of the actor—Abhinavagupta is focusing on acting on the stage and the audience watching the drama—nor out there in the object (the poem, the performance, or the work of art). It is neither subjective nor objective. What then is it and where does it belong? *Rasa* arises, according to Bharata, out of the cooperation and interaction of three factors: *bibhāva, anubhāva,* and *vyabhicāribhāva.* The first, *bibhāva,* is the cognition or understanding that makes representations (words, gestures, and internal feelings) capable of being sensed. The second, *anubhāva,* is the actual sensing of these elements. The third, *vyabhicāribhāva,* consists in subsidiary facts that strengthen one's experience. These three together generate *rasa,* bringing a *sthāyibhāva* or a permanent mood to an actually relished state. Alternately, a *bibhāva* may be regarded as what makes a permanent mood capable of being sensed, an *anubhāva* makes it actually experienced, the third consists of the auxiliary conditions that strengthen it. If a permanent mood that is always there, to be sure potentially, in the human mind, is "love," representations of women and seasons (such as spring) are *bibhāva,* glances and embracing are *anubhāvas,* and the passing feelings of pleasure and pain are the auxilliary conditions that heighten the experience of the erotic *rasa* called *śṛngāra.*

The exact relation between these three factors and the *rasa* that comes to be experienced has been a matter of some disputation among exponents of the theory. Lollata regards *rasa* as causally brought about by the appropriate conditions. Śankuka took it to be inferred from the presence of the above mentioned three factors. Bhaṭṭa Nāyaka holds that the enjoyment of *rasa* is made possible by those factors. The *dhvani* theory of Ānandavardhana gives the theory a new twist. *Rasa,* on his view, is suggested so that Bharata's three factors simply manifest it. The result is an extraordinary state of enjoyment, according to Abhinavagupta; a state sometimes called variously *rasanā*, *āsvāda*, and *carvaṇā* (all signifying different intensities of tasting).

The theory holds that there are some—on the usual count, eight—permanent moods (*sthāyibhāva*) potentially in the mind. These are love, laughter, sadness, anger, enthusiasm, fear, repugnance and surprise. Each one of these, under appropriate conditions, is actualized upon reading a poem or watching a drama. A level of cultivation of sensibility is necessary for this actualization, as also, possibly, a community of cultivated minds (*sahṛdaya*). The enjoyment of *rasa* is said to unfold through various stages: other objects disappear from consciousness until *rasa* alone is left, the particular feeling is universalized (*sādhāraṇikaraṇa*) into an essence, and finally there is a state of restfulness (*viśrānti*). Aesthetic enjoyment then becomes somewhat like the contemplation of the *brahman.*

From the fact that every *rasa* experience aims at a state of mental repose, it is natural to draw the conclusion that all *rasa* experience culminates in the experience of *śānta rasa*, or the *rasa* of peace. Abhinavagupta placed *śānta* as the highest *rasa* because of its relation to the state of *mokṣa,* so that poetic experience may approximate to realization of the *brahman.* While thus Abhinavagupta led the theory of *rasa* to the proximity of Vedānta, another author, Rūpa Goswamī, in his *Ujjvalanīlamaṇi,* developed the theory into the domain of *bhakti* or loving devotion to Kṛṣṇa. In his work, the *śṛngāra rasa,* or love, becomes *bhaktirasa* with its various forms such as *śānta* (tranquility), *dāsya* (servitude or humility), *sakhya* (friendship), *vātsalya* (affection for a child), and *mādhurya* (sweetnss).

The *rasa* theory thus provides a connecting link between semantic theory, aesthetics, religion, and metaphysics. At the same time, its theory of *sthāyibhāva* or permanent moods connects aesthetic theory to physiology and psychology. The idea of universalization as a step in the constitution of *rasa* overcomes psychologism, while not falling into the opposite trap of Platonism.

SUMMARY

Table 9–1

Sthāyibhāvas		*Poetical Expressions*	
rati	delight	*śṛngāra*	erotic
hāsa	laughter	*hāsya*	comic
śoka	sorrow	*karuṇa*	pathetic
krodha	anger	*raudra*	furious
utsāha	heroism	*vīra*	heroic
jugupsā	disgust	*bibhatsa*	odious
vismaya	wonder	*adbhūta*	wonderful
bhaya	fear	*bhayānaka*	terrible
sama	serenity	*sānta*	serene, serenity

Of these permanent moods, Bharata recognized the first eight; Abhinavagupta added the ninth one.

Figure 9–1a The Traditional View of *Rasa* (Bharata, Lollata)

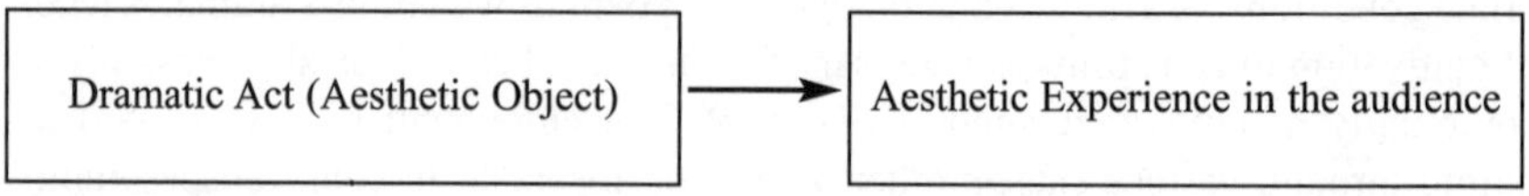

(*Rasa* as aesthetic object)

Figure 9–1b Later Theory of Rasa (Sankuka, Bhaṭṭa Nāyaka, Abhinavagupta)

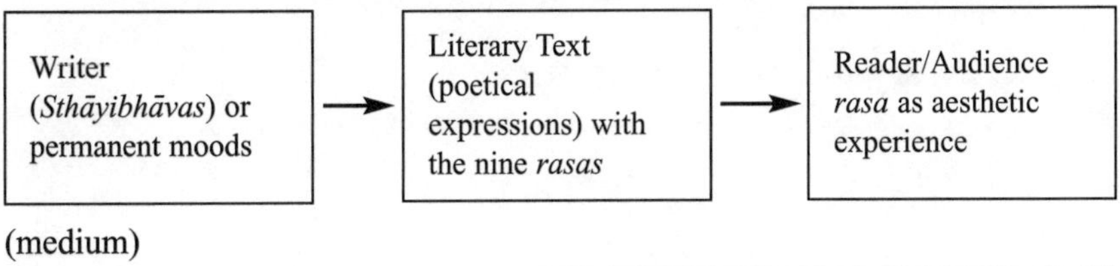

Figure 9–2 Vedāntic Foundation of Abhinavagupta's Aesthetics

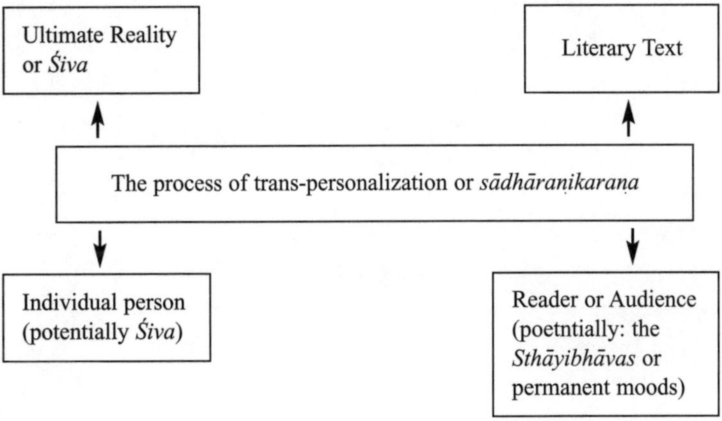

Part 5

Beyond the *Pramāṇa-Prameya* Distinction

Chapter Ten

Beyond the *Pramāṇa-Prameya* Distinction

In the preceding chapters, the basic structure has been the subject-object dualism, or, more specifically, the large distinction between the means of knowing and the object of knowing. Even in chapters on *dharma* and *rasa,* we are still considering domains of possible objects of knowing (namely, moral laws and aesthetic essence) and so means of apprehending them. While Indian philosophy is thus determined by the subject-object dualism, there is also a tendency on the part of the philosophers to overcome that dualism. From the time of the Upaniṣads, philosophers have pointed to the possibility of a kind of experience or even of knowledge that is beyond the subject-object dualism.

In some of the Upaniṣads, we have very well-known accounts of knowing the *brahman,* which reject the subject-object dualism and dispense with any conceptual mediation. Thus it was frequently emphasized that knowing the *brahman,* is also becoming the *brahman: brahmavit brahmaiva bhavati.* Of none of the means of knowing reviewed in the chapter on theory of knowledge (see chapter 2), this seems to be true—not even of the so-called indeterminate perception (*nirvikalpaka pratyakṣa*). This last mentioned cognition is not conceptual and linguistic but nevertheless is of an object that is distinct from the cognition, of something that stands over against the knower. But the Upaniṣads, in saying that by knowing the *brahman* one becomes the *brahman,* are talking about a kind of cognition that is radically different from any *pramāṇa*-generated cognition. The Greeks seem to have thought that the larger the object that one contemplates, since the soul assumes the form of the object it contemplates, the soul becomes more expansive and noble. In the Upaniṣads, if there is an object X such that by knowing X the knower becomes X, then the X must pertain to the innermost nature of the soul of one's own being. Furthermore, if knowing X transforms my being, and since knowing can remove only ignorance, the transformation of my being through becoming X must have to do with getting rid of wrong self-understanding and reaching the right self-understanding. Philosophers such as Henri Bergson have spoken of a mode of cognition that is higher than the intellectual, and have described it as one whereby the knower achieves an identification with the known. The Upaniṣads seem to point toward such a mode of knowing.

That this knowledge of the self is not intellectual, the Upaniṣads do not desist from emphasizing. The self, we are told, is that from which words return after not being able to reach it. The mind also fails to reach it ("*yato vācā nivartante aprāpya manasā saha*"). The texts also indulge in paradoxes: one who knows does not know, and one who does not know knows. Such paradoxical locutions suggest a mode of knowing that is different from the familiar modes of *pramāṇa,* and so—if the latter define "knowledge"—may amount to not knowing.

Within the Vedāntic framework, what all this amounts to is something like this. Knowledge as a process and as an achievement is nothing but the overcoming of ignorance. Once ignorance is removed, the knowledge that is of the nature of the *brahman* stands unconcealed. This knowledge is not produced, it is not acquired through the *pramāṇas,* it is self-revealing once its concealment is removed. To know in this sense is to be one with that knowledge. "Knowledge" in this sense has no object; it is not of something. Nor has knowledge in this sense a subject; it is not some one's knowledge. This knowledge is eternal, universal, ubiquitous, the foundation of all things. The goal of philosophy is to realize it.

Let it not be misunderstood. The sort of knowledge that involves subject-object dualism, which is acquired through a *pramāṇa,* is not unimportant, nor is it dispensable. It is also through such knowledge that ignorance can be removed, so that the other knowledge would be revealed. The one cannot take the place of the other. The Indian philosophies sought to keep both in their places.

A CRITIQUE OF SUBJECT-OBJECT DUALISM

The Vedāntic Critique of "Objectivity"

The nondualistic Vedāntin does not find any theoretical justification for concepts such as "means of knowing," "object of knowledge," and "real existence" as they are employed by the epistemologist. They consider various available definitions of "object," and argue that all of them apply to the contents of nonveridical cognitions such as hallucinations. The contents of such hallucinations as perceiving a snake where there is a rope are also "presented;" they also give rise to appropriate practical response. The only reason some contents are regarded as real is that they have not yet been contradicted. Replacing "truth" by "uncontradictedness," one can only, at best, speak of "uncontradicted as far as experience up to this point of time goes." The idea of real existence or nonexistence is here not of much worth. X is said to exist, just in case it is an object of a *pramāṇa* or veridical cognition, and the cognition is veridical just in case its object X really exists. It is not any better to say, as the Buddhists do, that X exists in case it is causally efficient. The nonexistent may also have causal efficiency; a particular nonexistent has its own distinctive causal efficiency. The cause should be defined, in that case, simply as the invariable antecedent, entity or nonentity. In any case, the effect arises only when the cause has ceased to exist. The Vedāntin goes on to critique the idea of an existent entity. The realist Naiyāyikas understand it as the relation between the putative entity and the universal "existence." The Vedāntin finds the very possibility of this relation unintelligible. The entity must then be nonexistent prior to the relation to "existence," and the realist must have to say how something nonexistent could enter into a relation. One may suppose that each object has its own individual self-existence, prior to the relation to the universal "existence." But that only means that the object must have its individuality, and the question of existence is redundant, giving rise to additional problems regarding the relation between individuality and existence.

Thus while the Vedāntin admits objects and their causal relations within empirical discourse, he or she resists the attempt to raise them to a metaphysical level. Metaphysically, the only reality is the *brahman*—pure consciousness, which alone is self-manifesting and that is beyond the dualism of subject and object.

The Mādhyamika's Critique of the Logical Categories

The Mādhyamika Nāgārjuna uses the Buddhist law of dependent origination (*pratītyasamutpāda*) to demonstrate the intrinsic emptiness or essencelessness of all things. If things arise through dependence on something else, nothing is real by its own right; nothing possesses its own essence (*svabhāva*). The argument, in its utmost generality, rules out the validity of the so-called *pramāṇas* or means of true cognition. One may then ask, What legitimizes their claim to validity? The validity of the *pramāṇas* cannot be established by any means other than other *pramāṇas,* for if they were capable of being legitimized without the use of *pramāṇas,* that would contradict the thesis of the epistemologist, namely, that all objects are established through *pramāṇas.* But if other *pramāṇas* are needed to legitimize the *pramāṇas* under consideration, then there would be an infinite regress. Could one reply, on behalf of the epistemologist, that the *pramāṇas* while legitimizing their objects are themselves self-validating? But this would involve something being both subject and object of the same act at the same time. Since the subject and object, *pramāṇa* and *prameya,* depend upon each other, neither of the two can be autonomous. If a cognition necessarily refers to its object, then the cognition cannot be self-validating while the object is not.

Can it be said that a cognition comes into being depending upon its object? But to say that X depends upon Y is to admit that X already exists, for only an existent X could be said to depend upon another thing. But then, in case X exists, to say that it comes into being is redundant.

Nāgārjuna concludes that the *pramāṇas* are neither established by themselves nor by one another, nor by their objects. The same holds good of objects as well.

This refutation of subject-object dualism, or of *pramāṇa-prameya* dualism, has a different implication than the Vedāntin's. The Vedāntins want to assert a reality or an experience, which is none other than the self-shining consciousness, that is beyond that dualism. Nāgārjuna does not want to assert any such position, thereby leaving room for various possibilities of interpretation of his intentions—ranging from a complete nihilism to simply an antirealism, which just lets everything be what it is without metaphysically reifying it. But, be it noted, the logical categories in this critique are exposed with the help of logic, just as the poison of a disease is removed by poison (i.e., the medicine) or a thorn in one's foot is removed by another thorn. Nāgārjuna is not simply doing a deconstructionist reading of texts. He is demonstrating the logical incoherence of the categories (*padārthas*).

MOKṢA AND *NIRVĀṆA*

It is in this context that we need to take a fresh look at the soteriological concepts of *mokṣa* and *nirvāṇa*. The concepts are, without doubt, very important for Indian thought, not merely for the religions. One would misunderstand their roles in Hinduism and Buddhism, respectively, if one holds any of the following two extreme positions. One extreme position is to claim that all Indian thinking is geared toward this large soteriological goal, thereby bolstering the claim that Indian philosophy is deeply religious. At the other extreme, there is a possible view that the ideas of *mokṣa* and *nirvāṇa* are entirely outside the domain of philosophy. They belong to religion, and even there to a mystical dimension. Both these are mistaken interpretations.

As a matter of fact, the following seem to hold good. In the first place, the idea of *mokṣa* is understood differently in various systems of Indian philosophy—in Nyāya-Vaiśeṣika, in Sāṃkhya, and in the different schools of Vedānta. These differences both reflect and are reflected in the metaphysical theories of the systems. Second, one may want to say either that the *mokṣa* is the experiential equivalent of the theoretical position of a system, or that the theoretical position of a system is intended to provide for the possibility of actualizing that ideal. Both ways of describing the situation are valid. As regards the former: to begin with the example of the Sāṃkhya system, spirit and nature are in this system ontologically and essentially separate, and *mokṣa* (or aloneness, *kaivalya* as they call it) consists in realizing that distinction. In nondualistic Vedānta, the *brahman* and *ātman* are identical, the individual self is identical with the *brahman,* and the world is a false appearance, and *mokṣa* consists in realization of that truth. In Rāmānuja's system, the individual selves and the world are parts of the *brahman* conceived both as the all-comprehensive absolute whole and as a person above all, in which case *mokṣa* would consist in knowing that dependence and through *bhakti* incurring the grace of God and enjoying his eternal company. One could extend the same relation between theory and practice to Buddhism. For Buddhism, there is no eternal self, no substance, the putative ego being but a series or an aggregate of momentary states, and such other theses as follow from these. *Nirvāṇa* then would arise from bringing your conduct and life in consonance with the accurate understanding of and conviction in these truths. Even for the Naiyāyika, liberation (*apavarga*) arises from knowing the categories listed by Gautama, especially the nature of the self and its distinction from the body. So, one could say it is as though there is no common goal of *mokṣa* to which there are different paths. But it is more appropriate to say that all the concepts of *mokṣa* do have a common core—namely, freedom from suffering, *karma,* and rebirth—while the total understanding of *mokṣa* varies from system to system, and each system's theoretical position determines its total conception of that goal. The nondualist Vedāntins *mokṣa* is severely criticized by the followers of theistic Vedānta, so is also the Naiyāyika's *apavarga.*

One can also say—as suggested earlier—that each system of philosophy provides the condition for the possibility of *mokṣa*. If a philosophical system is such that it makes freedom from suffering, *karma,* and rebirth impossible, then—in accordance with the spirit of Indian tradition—that system may be charged with the material fallacy of *anirmokṣaprasaṇga* (i.e., the impossibility of *mokṣa*). Thus the exact relation between a *darśana* and its built-in conception of *mokṣa* needs to be correctly understood, setting aside a lot of misleading rhetoric that abounds in Western language expositions of Indian philosophy.

There is a misleading inference made from the etymology of the word *darśana* (which stands for philosophy) that since *darśana* derives from the verbal root *dṛṣ* (= to see), philosophy, on the Indian view, has something to do with "seeing." Does then each philosophical system represent, articulate, and conceptualize a way of seeing? Not too far removed from the last misconception is the view that philosophy, in the Indian tradition, was intuitive, not intellectual and discursive. The exposition of Indian philosophy in this book must have shown that this is far from the truth. Philosophy was an intensely intellectual, rigorously discursive and relentlessly critical pursuit. However, this activity was supposedly trusted and relied upon to lead to a kind of knowledge that would *become transformed* into a transformation of the thinker's mode of being. How this could happen was explained, accounted for, within the system. Belief in *mokṣa* or *nirvāṇa* was belief in the *possibility* of such transformation. *Mokṣa* thus provided a distant horizon that loomed large before the Indian mind, giving meaning to all one's mundane pursuits—from *kāma* through *artha* and *dharma.* A person's being is not depressingly being in the world, but a being in the world that is grounded in the possibility of a transcendence into the beyond.

Appendix One

A Note on Navya-Nyāya Analysis of Cognition

The Navya-Nyāya system developed out of the old (i.e., classical Nyāya). Its founder is Gangeśa's Upādhyāya of the twelfth century. The Navya-Nyāya developed a highly technical language, which was most effectively used to formulate and solve problems in logic and epistemology. After the discussion of theory of knowledge (Part 1), it may be appropriate to present a brief account of the Navya-Nyāya analysis of cognitions—a sort of analysis that was employed by philosophers of different schools to their own advantage.

First of all, the analysis that will be presented, in very general outlines (leaving out many, many levels of sophistications), holds good only of cognitions that are expressible in language—for example of conceptual, judgmental, and linguistic perceptions (*savikalpa pratyakṣa*), of inferences as well as of word-generated (*śabda*) cognitions.

Even if the cognitions to be analyzed are said to be linguistically expressible, the Navya-Nyāya does not hold that the cognitions themselves are linguistic. The cognitions are rather *guṇas* (qualities which are also occurrent events of the knowing self) as has been explained earlier in chapter 2. Although linguistically expressible, on the Navya-Nyāya theory, there would always and necessarily be components of a cognition that are not "mentioned" (i.e., are *anullikhita*). For example, if my cognition of that thing in front of me is expressed in "that pot," the cognitive component "pot" has an "unmentioned" qualifier "potness" whose presence is understood even if not expressed. However, on the Navya-Nyāya theory, only relations, as components of a cognition, cannot be expressed; for, if expressed, they become terms. Thus in the cognition "that blue lotus," the relation between "blue" and "lotus," which, on the Nyāya theory, is "inherence" (*samavāya*), is not expressed, but is nevertheless "understood."

When Navya-Nyāya gives an analysis of the structure of the cognition "that blue lotus," the expression that analyzes it is not the same as the expression of the cognition. The analysis is carried out on the basis of a reflective focusing on the cognition and with the help of a meta-language that uses technical expressions adapted to the structural components that are discovered in the original cognition.

Analysis of a cognition is not analysis of the object in the ontological mode, but rather of the content in an epistemological mode. All these epistemological contents can be brought under one category, namely, *viṣayatā* or objecthood. We shall not, for our limited purpose, discuss the question whether this epistemological entity called *viṣayatā* is identical with the object or is identical with the cognition or is a relation between the two—a topic to which the great logician Gadādhara Bhattacharyya devoted his work *viṣayatāvāda* (Theory of Objectivity). If I have a cognition *of* a pot, one can say that an epistemic content refers to a pot: the Navya-Nyāya prefers to say there is a *viṣayatā* that attaches to the pot (*ghata-niṣṭha*).

Epistemic contents are of three kinds: *viṣyatā* or qualificandumness, *prakāratā* or qualifierness, and *samsargata* or relationness. According to Navya-Nyāya, all linguistically expressible cognitions have, to begin with, these three contents. The cognition expressed by "that blue lotus" then has the following components (*viṣayatās*):

(1) a qualificandumness attaching to "lotus,"
(2) a qualifierness attaching to "lotusness,"
(3) a qualifierness attaching to "blue,"
(4) a qualificandumness attaching to "blue,"
(5) a qualifierness attaching to "blueness,"
(6) a qualifierness attaching to "that,"
(7) a qualificandumness attaching to "that," and
(8) a qualifierness attaching to "that-ness."

Eight qualifies 7; 7, so qualified, qualifies (hence 6) the lotus (1). Five qualifies 4; 4, as so qualified, serves as a qualifier of the lotus (1). The qualificandum in (1) is also qualified by "lotusness" as in (2). All these entities thus form a relational whole (the relations relating these entities have to be epistemological relations, not ontological relations). A full expansion would thus be a string of names for these epistemological contents, making use of two epistemic relations: "limitor-limited" (*avacchedaka-avacchinna*) and "*nirūpaka-nirūpita*" (determinant-determined). All these contents, appropriately related and nested into each other, would in the long run qualify the cognition (being analyzed), which again must be located in the knowing subject's self. A brief, highly simplified, example would be: The cognition (located in the self of S) whose qualificandum is lotus as qualified by lotusness, and thatness (*tatta*), the qualifier of which is the blue color as qualified by blueness, and the relation by which the lotus is qualified by blue is the relation of inherence.

Appendix Two

Some General Features of the Indian Theories of Knowledge

1. The Indian epistemologies are through and through causal theories. The *pramāṇas* are defined, as we have seen, as what cause the true cognitions. The distinction, common in Western thought, between the causal question and the question of justification, was not made by the Indian theories. True cognition is said to be not only what corresponds to its object, but also is produced in the right way. This would be a way of avoiding the so-called Gettier paradoxes.

2. The methods that the theorist generally applies, both while defending her own position and critiquing her opponent are: (i) appeal to ordinary linguistic usage (*lokavyavahāra*); (ii) consider the evidence of experience, ordinary as well as not-so-ordinary; (iii) and, finally, consider the evidence of one's own introspection into one's cognitive life. Thus, while analyzing a cognition, the Navya-Nyāya appears to be analyzing the linguistic expression of the cognition, while all the while we are asked to check the validity of the analysis by looking at the introspective data. So we can say that the Indian epistemologist gives a theory of cognition, not merely of linguistic expression of cognitions, nor of what the Western logicians call "propositions." This is particularly striking in the case of Indian theories of inferential cognition.

3. Cognition is also looked upon by the Indian theorist as leading to conative activity. A cognitive theory—as, for example, in the case of theories of false cognition—is tested by its ability to account for appropriate conative response.

4. Connected with (2) above is the fact that all Indian theories of meaning (of words and sentences) are referential—with the sole exception of the Buddhist theory of *apoha*. A word *means* what it designates. A sentence *means* a complex state of affairs. Consequently, the meaningfulness of empty terms such as "sky flower" and of false sentences remained problematic. The former was accounted for by the Nyāya in a manner reminiscent of Russell's theory of descriptions. The latter proved recalcitrant to the theory of *śabda* as a means of knowing, discussed earlier in chapter 2.

5. Perhaps the emphasis laid on *śabda* as a *pramāṇa* (i.e., on knowledge that is generated by words alone), is a distinctive feature of the Indian epistemological theories. The idea also serves them well to give an account of our moral knowledge (i.e., of knowledge of what one ought and ought not to do).

6. Logic, as theory of inference, is a part of theory of knowledge. The Indian logician's interest is in inference as a mode of *knowing*. As noted before, logic remains a logic of cognition. Consequently it remains in the vicinity of a psychology of inference. Yet the ruinous consequences of "psychologism" are avoided by showing how, in the absence of specific faults (*doṣas*), the psychological process leads to logically valid conclusions. If logic is psychologized, one may say, so is psychology logicized. The psychological process of inference and the logically valid structure coincide—at least insofar as first-order logic is concerned. Besides, one should note that inasmuch as the logic is concerned with cognitions and uses the language of properties and "limitors" (in place of quantification), it is intensional. But insofar as it presupposes a purely referential theory of meaning, it is extensional.

7. With regard to the empirical world, a primacy of perception holds good. All other *pramāṇas* presuppose perception. Although *śabda*—specifically extraordinary (*alaukika*) *śabda*—tells us about moral injunctions and prohibitions, *śabda* no less depends upon perception. The utterances of the speaker must be *heard*. (Alternately, texts must be *read*.) But the scope of perception as a *pramāṇa* is much wider than in the Western theories. One perceives not only sensory qualities such as colors, but also substances that possess those qualities. One also perceives the universals of which they—the qualities and the substances—are instances. One also perceives the internal states such as pleasure and pain. If Western epistemology, up until recent times, remained under the pressure of a large distinction between "reason" and "experience," the Indian thinker had no such distinction before her. Her question is: Is the object under consideration known exclusively by any of the *pramāṇas* or by all of them together? Only the Buddhist argued for a one-to-one correlation between the *pramāṇas* and objects or for what is known as *pramāṇavyavasthā*. Thus, for example, according to the Buddhist, the object of perception and the object of inference cannot be the same. The former is a bare particular (*sva-lakṣaṇa*), the latter a universal object (*sāmānya-lakṣaṇa*). All the other schools held that different *pramāṇas* could possibly know the same object, a position known as *pramāṇa samplava* or "mixture of *pramāṇas*." What is perceived, could have been inferred, and may be the subject of verbal instruction as well.

8. It is also necessary to note that epistemology, as theory of *pramāṇa*, is not entirely independent of metaphysics, as theory of *prameya*. This is so because *pramāṇas* as well as the cognitions they produce are themselves also *prameyas*, for example entities that can be known. This mutual dependence of the two parts of philosophy is discussed at the end of this book, and may have radical consequences for philosophy as a whole.

9. Like the opposition between reason and experience (as alleged sources of knowledge), certain other distinctions connected with it are absent in Indian theories of knowledge. These are that between the *a priori* and the *a posteriori*, between analytic and synthetic judgments, and also between necessary and contingent truths. To reflect on why they are absent, where, if at all, they tend to emerge and in what form, and what could be the consequences of these "lacks," would take us beyond the confines of this book. It needs, however, to be emphasized that the talk of "lacks" here must not be construed as defects, but rather as pointing to another possibility, from which we may learn the lesson that none of these distinctions is essential for philosophy.

10. Finally, it must be noted that there is the prospect of a kind of *knowledge* that transcends the subject-object (and so the *pramāṇa-prameya*) distinction, and so is as much knowing as *being,* which looms large before both the theorist of knowledge and the metaphysician, and for which they have to make room. To this possibility—and to its possible actuality—we have turned in the concluding part of this book. But it is important that we do not obliterate the distinction between what we are doing now and that far-off prospect on the horizon and that we do not abandon this immediate task at hand for that sublime end.

Appendix Three

The Classical *Darśanas* (Systems)

Because the text's exposition follows the guidelines of concepts, problems, and theories, it was deemed desirable, in order to help beginning students of Indian philosophy, to add this appendix, which gives an inventory of the principal philosophers, texts, and doctrines of the major schools of Indian philosophy for ready and easy reference. Approximate dates of authors and of texts are also given, where possible.

BUDDHISM

Basic Texts:

Samyutta Nikāya (third century B.C.E.)
Visuddhimāgga (400 C.E.)
Lankāvatārasūtra (first century B.C.E.)
Mādhyamīkakārikā (by Nagarjuna, c. first century C.E.)
Abhidharmakoṣa (by Vasubandhu, c. fifth century C.E.)
Vijñaptimātratāsiddhi (by Vasubandhu, c. fifth century C.E.)
Pramāṇasamuccaya (by Digñāga, c. sixth century C.E.)
Nyāyabindu (by Dharmakīrti, c. seventh century C.E.)
Kṣaṇabhangasiddhi (by Ratnakīrtī, c. tenth century C.E.)

Doctrines:

No soul theory.
The empirical self consists of five aggregates.
The theory of Dependent Origination.
The theory of instantaneousness of all being.
The *pramāṇas:* perception and inference.
The theory of *pramāṇavyavasthā:* the object of perception is the bare particular, the object of inference is the universal.

CĀRVĀKA

Basic Text:
Tattvopaplavasimha. (by Jayarāśi, seventh century C.E.)

Doctrines:
Perception, the only means of valid knowledge.
Matter is the only reality.
No afterlife, no *karma.*
Pleasure, the only thing desirable.

JAINISM

Basic Texts:
Prameyakamalamārtanda (by Prabhāchandra, ninth century C.E.)
Pramāṇa-Mīmāṃsā. (by Hemachandra, twelfth century C.E.)
Pravacanasāra. (by Āchārya Kuṇḍakuṇda, fourth century C.E.)
Syādvādamanjari (by Mallisena, thirteenth century C.E.)
Tattvārthādhigamasūtra (by Umāsvati, fourth century C.E.)

Doctrines:
Reality has infinite aspects.
All truths are relative to a standpoint.
Every judgment is true from a certain standpoint, false from another.
Perception, inference, and verbal testimony are the only means of valid knowledge.
There are souls in every living beings.
Each soul is capable of developing infinite consciousness, power, and happiness.
No God.

SĀṂKHYA

Basic Texts:
Sāṃkhya Sūtra (author not known)
Sāṃkhya Kārikā (by Īśvarakṛṣṇa, c. 200 C.E.)
Tattvakaumudī (by Vācaspati Miśra, ninth century C.E.)
Pravacana Bhāṣya (by Vijñāna Bhikṣu, sixteenth century C.E.)

Doctrines:
Ontological dualism: spirits and nature.
The doctrine of three *guṇas*: *sattva, rajas,* and *tamas.*
A doctrine of evolution of the *tattvas* or principles.
Theory of *satkāryavāda,* namely that effect already was contained in the cause.

Pariṇāmavāda: the effect is a transformation of the cause.
Highest liberation: a state of aloneness (*kaivalya*) brought about by discriminating knowledge (*vivekajñāna*).
Consciousness is self-manifesting.
Knowledge is a modification of the intellect in which consciousness is reflected.
Both truth and falsity are intrinsic to a cognition.
Means of true cognition: perception, inference, and verbal utterance.

YOGA

Basic Texts:

Yogasūtra (by Patañjali, c. second century C.E.)
Yogasūtrabhāṣya (by Vyāsa, c. 400 C.E.)
Tattvavaiśāradi (by Vācaspati Miśra, c. ninth century C.E.)
Yogavārttika (by Vijñāna Bhikṣu, sixteenth century C.E.)

Doctrines:

Theoretical doctrines, in the main, are the same as those of Sāṃkhya.

VAIŚEṢIKA

The philosophers of this school are generally called the Vaiśeṣikas.

Basic Texts:

Vaiśeṣika Sūtra (by Kaṇāda, second century B.C.E.)
Bhāṣya on *Vaiśeṣika Sūtra* (by Praśastapāda, ninth century C.E.)
Nyāyakandalī (by Śridhara, c. tenth century C.E.)
Kiranāvalī (by Udayana, tenth century C.E.)

Doctrines:

Six categories: substance, quality, action, universal, particularity, and inherence.
Two *pramāṇas:* perception and inference.
Truth = Correspondence.
Both truth and falsity are extrinsic to cognitions.
Atomic theory of the material world. God as the efficient cause of the world.

NYĀYA

The philosophers of this school are called the Naiyāyikas. Since about 600 C.E., the school is often joined with the Vaiśeṣika as forming one system.

Basic Texts:

Old Nyāya

Nyāya Sūtra (Gautama, second century C.E.)
Bhāṣya on the *Nyāya Sūtra* (by Vātsyāyana, fourth century C.E.)
Varttika on the *bhāṣya* (by Uddyotakara, seventh century C.E.)
Tātparyatīkā on the *Vārttika* (Vācaspati Miśra, ninth century C.E.)
Pariśuddhi on the *Tātparyatīkā* (by Udayana, tenth century C.E.)
Nyāyamanjari (by Jayanta, ninth century C.E.)
Kusumānjalī (by Udayana)
Ātmatattvaviveka (by Udayana)

New Nyāya

Tattvacintāmaṇi (by Gangeśa Upādhyāya, 1200 C.E.) Commentaries on the above by Raghunātha Śiromaṇi (1500 C.E.), Mathurā Nātha Bhattacharya (1580 C.E.), Gadādhara Bhattāchārya (1650 C.E.), and Jagadīśa Bhattāchārya (1590 C.E.)
Bhāṣāparichheda with *Siddhāntamuktāvali* (by Visvanātha, seventeenth century C.E.)
Tarkasaṃgraha (by Annambhaṭṭa, seventeenth century C.E.)
Tarkabhāṣā (by Keśava Miśra, twelfth century C.E.)

Doctrines:

Four *pramāṇas*: perception, inference, comparison, and verbal utterance.
A seventh category added to Kaṇāda's list, absence (*abhāva*).
With regard to the rest, mainly in agreement with Vaiśeṣika.
The New Nyāya introduced a host of abstract entities into its ontology.

PŪRVA MĪMĀṂSĀ

The philosophers of this school are called the Mīmāṃsakas. There are two subschools: the followers of Prabhākara, known as the Prābhākaras and the followers Kumārila Bhaṭṭa, known as the Bhāṭṭas. There was also a third school traced to one Murāri Miśra, known as the Miśra school.

Basic Texts:

Mīmāṃsā Sūtra (by Jaimini, c. 200 B.C.E.)
Bhāṣya on *Mīmāṃsā Sūtra* (by Śabara, c. first century B.C.E.)
Bṛhati *tīkā* on Śabara's *Bhāṣya* (by Prabhākara, eight century C.E.)
Prakaraṇapañcikā (by Śālikanātha, eighth century C.E.)

Ślokavārttika (by Kumārila Bhaṭṭa, c. eighth century C.E.)
Śāstradīpikā (by Pārthasārathi Miśra, c. ninth century C.E.)
Bhāṭṭacintāmaṇī (by Gāgā Bhaṭṭa, sixteenth century C.E.)

Doctrines:

Five *pramāṇas*: perception, inference, verbal utterance, comparison and postulation according to the Prābhākaras; the Bhāṭṭas admit a sixth, nonperception.
Knowledge is immediately known, according to the Prābhākaras, but is inferred according to the Bhāṭṭas.
Knowledge is a quality of the soul according to the Prābhākaras, but is an act of the soul according to the Bhāṭṭas.
For all the subschools, knowledge is intrinsically true, but falsity is extrinsic.
According to the Prābhākaras, there is no false cognition.
The self is known by a mental perception such as "I am happy," but according to the Prābhākaras, it is known as the knower together with the object that is known as the object.
Realistic metaphysics. Recognize a new category "power," of which supernatural potency called *adṛṣṭa* is a type.
Ambivalent with regard to God's existence, but reject the theistic arguments.

VEDĀNTA

Śaṃkara Vedānta: = ADVAITAN VEDANTA

Basic Texts:

Ātmabodha (by Śamkara, 788–820 C.E.)
Bhagavadgītābhāṣya (by Śamkara)
Brahmasūtrabhāṣya (by Śamkara)
Upaniṣadbhāsyas (by Śamkara)
Upadeśasāhasī (by Śamkara)

Doctrines:

Reality or the *brahman* is nondual (*advaita*).
The world is a false appearance due to *māyā.*
Finite individuals are not different from the *brahman.*
Realization of the *brahman* (*mokṣa*) is the ultimate goal of human life.
Mokṣa is the realization of one's true nature.
In order to realize the *brahman,* one must follow the path of knowledge (*jñāna-yoga*).
Six *pramāṇas* are perception, inference, verbal utterance, comparison, postulation, and nonperception.

Rāmānuja's Qualified Nondualism

Basic Texts:

Śrībhāṣya (by Rāmānuja, eleventh century C.E.)
Gītābhāṣya (by Rāmānuja)
Vedārthasaṃgraha (by Rāmānuja)

Doctrines:

The *brahman,* about the same as the god of theism, contains internal differences.
The world rooted in the *brahman* is as real as the *brahman.*
Both matter and selves are parts of the *brahman.*
Ignorance is the root cause of our bondage.
Freedom from ignorance is possible through devotion.

Appendix Four

Glossary of Important Sanskrit Terms

abādhita	noncontradicted
adharma	demerit; sin
ābhāsa	appearance
abhāva	absence, negation; the negative
abhihitānvaya	relating the separate meanings of the words of a sentence
adṛṣṭa	unseen, unobserved; unseen merit and demerit; *karmic* potencies lying hidden and acting as determinants; fate
advaita	nondual, nondualism; one, "monism"
advaitin	nondualist; monist
advaya	nondual, one
āgama	that which has come down by tradition; name of any of the texts of sectarian religious philosophies like the Pāñcarātra; also the Vedas
agraha	noncognition
ahaṃ	I
ahaṃkāra	ego
ahaṃpratyaya	the I-consciousness
aitihya	historical evidence; tradition; belief handed down
ajātavāda	the doctrine that the world was never created
ajñāna	ignorance
ajñāta	unknown
ākāśa	space; sky; ether
akhyāti	absence of erroneous cognition
akhyātivāda	the doctrine that the object of illusion is due to the noncognition (of the difference between the seen and the remembered objects)
ālaya-vijñāna	receptacle, storehouse

anekānta-vāda	the doctrine that reality has many aspects, that there is no absolute reality
anirvacanīya	indescribable, indefinable
anirvacanīya-khyāti-vāda	the doctrine that the object of illusion is indescribable in terms of being and nonbeing, reality and unreality, existence and nonexistence
antaḥkaraṇa	internal instrument, inner sense
antaḥkaraṇavṛtti	modification of the inner sense
antaryāmin	inner controller
aṇu	atom, absolutely small
anumāna	inference; syllogism
anupalabdhi	noncognition, nonapprehension, nonperception
anuvyavasāya	reflective cognition as in "I know that I know X"
anyathākhyāti-vāda	the doctrine that illusion is the perception of an object that is not here but elsewhere
anyonyābhāva	mutual absence, difference
aparokṣa	direct, immediate
apramā	invalid cognition
apūrva	supernatural; merit in the form or state of latency or potency; another name for *adṛṣta*
artha	meaning; object; wealth; purpose, aim
arthakriyā	purposive action
arthakriyā-kāritā	ability to successfully fulfill the purpose
arthāpatti	presumption, presupposition; one of the means of valid knowledge
asat	nonbeing, nonexistence; the nonexistent, the unreal; false, untrue
asatkārya-vāda	the doctrine that the effect is nonexistent in the cause
asatkhyāti-vāda	the doctrine that the object of illusion is nonexistent
āśarma	a stage of life
āśrava	inflow of *karma* in Jainism
ātman	spirit; self; soul
āvaraṇa	veil
avidyā	same as ajñāna; nescience, ignorance
avidyāvṛtti	modification of nescience
avyakta	unmanifest; the unmanifest; at times used as a synonym for *prakṛti* and *māyā*
bhedābheda	identity-cum-difference; identity-in-difference
bodhisattva	an enlightened being who works for the salvation of others
bhrama	error, illusion, hallucination

brahman	the Absolute; the Supreme Spirit
buddhi	reason; mind
cit	consciousness
citta	apperceptive reason; that which gathers and integrates knowledge
darśana	view; vision; philosophy; system
devas	the shining ones
dhārāvāhika-jñāna	a serial cognition as in "That is a rose, that is a rose, that is a rose" and so on; it is a repetition of the same cognition, only having a different temporal location
dharma	that which supports; ethical law; duty
dhyāna	meditation, concentration
dik	space; direction; *see* ākāśa
doṣa	defect
dravya	substance
duhkha	pain, suffering, misery, grief, sorrow, unhappiness
dvaita	dual; duality; dualism
guṇa	quality; property; that which binds
hetu	cause, reason, ground
hetvābhāsa	fallacy; pseudoreason
hīnayāna	the lower vehicle; a name given to the southern schools of Buddhism
indriya	sense organ
Īśvara	God
jaḍa	the insentient; the inorganic; matter
jāti	genus; universal; also means one of the wrong ways of arguing, raising a futile objection to a position; birth; caste
jīva	empirical self
jñāna	consciousness; knowledge; cognition
jñānātman	buddhi, rational consciousness
jñātā	the knower (*jñātṛ*)
jñeya	the knowable
kaivalya	aloneness; salvation
kāla	time
kāma	desire; love; pleasure; enjoyment; passion
karaṇa	instrument; the cause

kāraṇa	cause; reason
karma	action; activity; process; past actions in their potential forms or states
kevala	alone; absolutely direct (knowledge) in Jainism
khyāti-vādas	doctrines of illusory perception
kośas	sheaths; collections
kṣana	instant; moment
kṣanika-vāda	doctrine of momentariness
lakṣana	mark; character; definition
mahāyāna	the higher vehicle of Buddhism; a name for all the northern schools of Buddhism taken together
manana	reflecting
manas	mind
mārga	way, path; the path to salvation
māyā	illusion; a synonym for *prakṛti, avyakta, pradhāna, avidyā, ajñāna,* and so on
mīmāṃṣā	discussion; debate; criticism; critical interpretation; one of the six Vedic systems
mithyā	the illusory, false, nonexistent; illusion
mokṣa	liberation, salvation, emancipation
mukti	same as *mokṣa*
nayavāda	doctrine of tropes, of modalities, of points of view
nididhyāsana	meditation
nigamana	conclusion
nirguṇa	without qualities, without characteristics, without attributes
nirvāṇa	freedom from suffering; peace; salvation
nirvikalpa	indeterminate, formless, absolutely direct cognition
nirviśeṣa	without any determinations
nirvṛtti	withdrawal from outward activity; turning inwards
niyama	vow; self-imposed and accepted restriction
pakṣa	minor term
para	higher
parāmarśa	consideration, recollection, reflexion
paramārtha	ultimate, highest, absolute; the absolute reality or truth
pāramārthika	pertaining to the highest being
pariṇāma	change, transformation

phala	result, fruit
pradhāna	the primary, the important, the basic; a synonym for *prakṛti*
prakāra	form; universal; method; qualifier in Nyāya
prakṛti	nature; root; synonym for *pradhāna*, *māyā*, and so on
pramā	valid knowledge; valid cognition, obtained through measuring by senses, mind, and reason
pramājñāna	true cognition
pramāṇa	cognition, means of true cognition
prāmāṇyavāda	doctrine of the validity of knowledge in answer to the question whether cognition is valid by itself or made valid by something else
pramātā	cognizer
prameya	the knowable; object of cognition or knowledge
prāṇa	life, vital principle
pramiti	true cognition
pratibhāsa	appearance
prātibhāsika	apparent, seeming; false
pratijñā	thesis; hypothesis
pratītya-samutpāda	dependent origination
pratyabhijñā	recognition
pratyakṣa	sense perception; perception
pravṛtti	activity; the life of action
pudgala	the psycho-physical person in Buddhism
puruṣa	ātman; person; man
rajas	one of the attributes of *prakṛti*, manifested in activity
śabda	sound; word
sādhya	major term (of a syllogism)
saguṇa	with qualities or characteristics
sākṣin	witness
sākṣī-caitanya	witness consciousness
sākṣijñāna	witness-cognition (awareness)
śakti	energy, power, force
samādhi	trance, ecstasy; the final stage in Yoga
sāmānya	the common characteristic; the universal
saṃsāra	the flux of the world; the world
saṃskāra	impression; instinct; traces of past experience; potency
saṃyoga	contact; conjunction
sannikarṣa	contact

śānta	without agitation, peaceful
sat	being, existence, reality
satkārya-vāda	the doctrine that the effect preexists in the material cause
satkhyātivāda	the doctrine that the object of illusion is also real
satya	truth, reality; the true, the real; a derivation from *sat*
savikalpaka	determinate; with form or shape; conceptual
skandha	aggregate, group
smṛti	memory; what is remembered
sphoṭa	the original seed state of a word before its letters are uttered in a sequence; a word or sentence as an ideal entity
śravaṇa	hearing
śruti	what is heard; a synonym for the Veda
sukha	happiness
śūnya	void, empty; the zero; the void, the empty
śūnyatā	voidness, emptiness, vacuity
suṣupti	deep or dreamless sleep
sūtra	thread, string; aphorism
svabhāva	one's own nature
svataḥ prāmāṇya	intrinsic validity
svayamprakāśa	self-manifestation
syādvāda	the doctrine of conditioned predication
tādātmya	same-self-ness
tamas	one of the attributes of *prakṛti* manifested in inertia; indolence; darkness
tanmātras	subtle elements
tarka	argument; logic; arguments using counter-factual conditions
tathā	such, so, thus, in that way
tathāgata	one who has gone thus, attained the simple thusness; a name of Buddha who has gone the way of reality
tathatā	suchness, thusness
tejas	light; psychic energy; the light of the dream, which constitutes also the objects of the dream, including the dreamer
turīya	the transcendent, or the 'fourth' experience
udāharaṇa	example
upādhi	a condition vitiating a generalization
upamāna	similarity; comparison; cognition of similarity

vaidika	pertaining to the Veda
vairāgya	detachment; withdrawal from the world
vaiśadyam	clarity
varṇā	color; caste
vāsanā	perfume, smell; impression, imprint, trace, vestige; *see samskāra*
vidhi	injunction; law; rule; ethical command
vibhu	all-pervading; infinite; endless
vidyā	knowledge, learning
vijñāna	consciousness; determinate consciousness
vikalpa	empty verbal cognition without a corresponding object; idea, image; distortion
vikṣepa	projection, throwing out
viṣaya	object of cognition; subject of discourse; topic
viśeṣa	the particular as distinct from the individual and the universal; any distinguishing mark
viśeṣaṇa	adjective
viśiṣṭajñāna	determinate cognition
vivarta	apparent transformation
vivartavāda	theory of apparent transformation
vṛtti	mental modification
vṛttijñāna	cognition, which is a mental mode
vyāpāra	activity of the instrumental cause
vyāpti	major premise; concomitance of the major and middle terms in a syllogism
vyavahāra	activity; custom; convention
vyāvahārika	the empirical; the conventional, the customary
yama	self-control; control
yoga	yoking, binding, tying

Bibliography

RECOMMENDED GENERAL WORKS ON INDIAN PHILOSOPHY

Brahma, Nalini Kana. *The Philosophy of Hindu Sādhanā.* Delhi: Motilal Banarsidass (1st Indian edition), 1993.

Chatterjee, Satischandra, and Dhirendramohan Datta. *An Introduction to Indian Philosophy.* Calcutta: University of Calcutta, 1960.

Dasgupta, Surendranath. *A History of Indian Philosophy.* 5 vols. Cambridge: Cambridge University Press, 1922–1955.

———. *Indian Idealism.* Cambridge: Cambridge University Press, 1933.

Edgerton, Franklin. *The Beginnings of Indian Philosophy.* London: George Allen & Unwin Ltd., 1965.

Halbfass, Wilhelm. *Tradition and Reflection: Explorations in Indian Thought.* Albany: SUNY Press, 1991.

Hiriyanna, Mysore. *The Essentials of Indian Philosophy.* London: George Allen & Unwin, 1932.

———. *Outlines of Indian Philosophy.* Bombay: George Allen & Unwin, 1973.

Maitra, Sushil Kumar. *Fundamental Questions of Indian Logic and Metaphysics.* Calcutta: University of Calcutta, 1974.

Mohanty, J. N. *Reason and Tradition in Indian Thought.* Oxford: Clarendon Press, 1992.

Potter, Karl. *Encyclopaedia of Indian Philosophies.* 6 vols. Delhi: Motilal Banarsidass, 1970–1993.

———. *Presuppositions of India's Philosophies.* Englewood Cliffs, NJ: Prentice Hall, 1963.

Radhakrishnan, Sarvepalli. *Indian Philosophy.* 2 vols. London: George Allen & Unwin, 1923, 1927.

Radhakrishnan, Sarvepalli and Charles A. Moore, eds. *A Sourcebook in Indian Philosophy.* Princeton, NJ: Princeton University Press, 1957.

Smart, Ninian. *Doctrine and Argument in Indian Philosophy.* London: George Allen & Unwin, 1964.

Zimmer, Heinrich. *Philosophies of India.* Edited by Joseph Campbell. London: Routledge & Kegan Paul, 1952.

RECOMMENDED SECONDARY WORKS ON INDIAN PHILOSOPHICAL SYSTEMS

Vedas and the Upaniṣads

Belvalkar, S. K., and R. D. Ranade. *The Creative Period.* Poona, India: Bilvakunja Publication House, 1927.

Gambhirānanda, Swāmī. *Eight Upaniṣads with the Commentary of Śaṅkarācārya.* 2 vols. Calcutta: Advaita Ashrama, 1965.

Hume, R. E. *The Thirteen Principal Upanisads.* Oxford: Oxford University Press, 1923.

Keith, A. B. *Religion and Philosophy of the Vedas and the Upanisads.* Cambridge, MA: Harvard University Press, 1925.

Macdonell, Arthur Anthony, trans. *Hymns from the Ṛg Veda.* 2 vols. London: Oxford University Press, 1922.

Müller, F. Max. *Upanisads.* London: Constable, 1926.

Panikkar, Raimundo. *The Vedic Experience: Mantramañjarī.* Los Angeles: University of California Press, 1977.

Radhakrishnan, S. *The Principal Upanisads.* London: George Allen and Unwin, 1953.

Ranade, R. D. *A Constructive Survey of Upanisadic Philosophy.* Poona, India: Oriental Book Agency, 1927.

Buddhism

Anacker, S. *Seven Works of Vasubandhu.* Delhi: Motilal Banarsidass, 1984.

Bahm, A. J. *Philosophy of the Buddha.* New York: Harper, 1958.

Barua, B. M. *History of Pre-Buddhist Indian Philosophy.* Calcutta: Calcutta University, 1921.

———. *Prolegomena to a History of Buddhist Philosophy.* Calcutta: Calcutta University, 1918.

Bhattacharya, Vidhusekhar. *The Basic Conception of Buddhism.* Calcutta: Calcutta University, 1934.

Conze, Edward. *Buddhism: Its Essence and Development.* New York: Philosophical Library, 1954.

Coomaraswamy, A. K. *Buddha and the Gospel of Buddhism.* London: Harper Torchbooks, 1928.

Davids, Rhys. *Buddhist Psychology.* New Delhi: Oriental Books, 1975.

De Bary, William Theodore, ed. *The Buddhist Tradition in India, China, and Japan.* New York: The Modern Library, 1969.

Guenther, Herbert V. *Buddhist Philosophy in Theory and Practice.* Maryland: Penguin Books, 1972.

Kalupahana, David J. *Buddhist Philosophy: A Historical Analysis.* Honolulu: University of Hawaii Press, 1976.

———, trans. *Mūlamadhyamakakārikā of Nāgārjuna.* Delhi: Motilal Banarsidass Publishers, 1991.

Keith, A. B. *Buddhist Philosophy in India and Ceylon.* Oxford: Clarendon Press, Oxford, 1923.

Kochumuttom, Thomas. *A Buddhist Doctrine of Experience: A New Translation and Interpretation of the Works of Vasubandhu the Yogācārin.* Delhi: Motilal Banarsidass, 1982.

Murti, T. R. V. *The Central Philosophy of Buddhism.* London: George Allen and Unwin, 1960.
Pruden, L., trans. *Abhidharmakośabhāṣyam.* 4 vols. California: Asian Humanities Press, 1988–1990.
Rahula, Walpola. *What the Buddha Taught.* New York: Grove Press, 1959.
Rhys Davids, C. A. F. *A Manual of Buddhism.* London: Sheldon Press, 1932.
Sprung, Marvin, trans. *The Lucid Exposition of the Middle Way.* London: Routledge & Keagan, Paul, 1979.
Stcherbatsky, Th. *Buddhist Logic.* 2 vols. New York: Dover Publications, 1962.
———. *The Conception of Buddhist Nirvāṇa.* Leningrad, Russia: Academy of Sciences, 1927.
Streng, F. J. *Emptiness: A Study in Religious Meaning.* Nashville: Abingdon Press, 1967.
Takakusu, Junjiro. *The Essentials of Buddhist Philosophy.* Delhi: Motilal Banarsidass, 1978.
Thomas, E. J. *History of Buddhist Thought.* New York: Barnes and Noble, 1951.

Cārvāka

Basham, A. L. *Ājīvikas.* London: Luzac and Co., 1951.
Chattopadhaya, Deviprasad. *Lokāyata.* Calcutta: Peoples Publishing House, 1959.
Dasgupta, S. *Obscure Religious Cults.* Calcutta: K. L. Mukhopadhyaya, 1969.
Jayarāśi. *Tattvopaplavasimha.* Baroda: Gaekvad Oriental Series, 1930.
Sastri, Dakshinaranjan. *A Short History of Indian Materialism.* Calcutta: Bookland Private Ltd., 1951.

Jainism

Āchārya, Guṇabhadra. *Ātmānuśāsana.* Lucknow: The Central Jaina Publishing House, 1928.
Āchārya, Kuṇḍakuṇda. *Nyāyasāra.* Lucknow: The Central Jaina Publishing House, 1931.
Bhattacharyya, H. M. *Jaina Logic and Ontology.* Calcutta: Bagchi & Co., 1994.
Hemachandra. *Pramāṇa-mīmāṃsā.* Bombay: Singhi Jaina Series, 1939.
Mallisena. *Syādvādamanjari.* Bombay: Bombay Sanskrit Series, 1938.
Mehta, M. L. *The Heart of Jainism.* London: Oxford University Press, 1915.
———. *Jaina Psychology.* Amritsar: Sohanlal Jaina Dharma Pracharak Samiti, 1957.
———. *Outlines of Jaina Philosophy.* Bangalore: Jaina Misssion Society, 1954.
———. *Studies in Jaina Philosophy.* Banaras: Jaina Cultural Research Society, 1951.
Mookerjee, S. *Jaina Philosophy of Non-absolutism.* Calcutta: Bharatiya Mahavidyalaya, 1944.
Panditacharya. *Prameyaratnālaṇkāra.* Mysore: Superindent, Govt. Branch Press, 1948.
Prabhāchandra. *Prameyakamalamārtāṇḍa.* Bombay: Nirnayasagar, 1941.
Schubring, Walther. *The Doctrine of the Jainas.* Delhi: Motilal Banarasidass, 1912.
Sen, Amulyachandra. *Schools and Sects in Jaina Literature.* Calcutta: Visvabharati Book-shop, 1931.
Shah, Nagin J. *Jaina Philosophy and Religion.* English trans. by Muni Shri Nyayavijayaji. Delhi: Motilal Banarsidass, 1997.
Tantia, Nathmal. *Studies in Jaina Philosophy.* Benaras: P. V. Research Institute, 1951.
Umāsvāti. *Tattvārthādhigamsūtra.* Mysore: Superindent, Govt. Branch Press, 1944.

Mīmāmsā

Bhatt, Govardan P. *Epistemology of the Mīmāṃsā School.* Banaras: Chowkhamba, 1962.

Devasthali, G. V. *Mīmāṃsā.* Bombay: Booksellers Publishing Co., 1959.

Jaimini. *Mīmāṃsā Sūtras. Mīmāṃsā Sūtras with the Commentaries of Śabara, Kumārila, Murāri, et al.* Poona: Anandasrama, 1931–1951.

Jha, Ganganath, trans. *Kumārila's Śloka Vārtika.* Sri Garib Das Oriental Series, No. 8. Delhi: Sri Satguru Publications, 1983.

Jha, G. N. *Pūrvamīmāṃsā in Its Sources.* Banaras: Banaras Hindu University, 1942.

Kane, P. V. *A Brief Sketch of the Pūrva-Mīmāṃsā System.* Poona: Aryabhushan Press, 1924.

Keith, A. B. *Karmamīmāṃsā.* Oxford: Oxford University Press, 1921.

Kumārila. *Ślokavārtikā.* Trans. C. N. Jha. Calcutta: Asiatic Society of Bengal, 1908.

Misra, Mandana. *Mīmāṃsā Darśana.* Jaipur: Ramesh Book Depot, 1954.

Radhakrishnan, S., ed. *Ganganatha Jha's Pūrva Mīmāṃsā.* Library of Indian Philosophy and Religion Series, Vol. 1. Banaras: Banaras Hindu University, 1964.

Rāmānuja. *Tantrarahaśya, a Primer of Prabhakara Mīmāṃsā.* Baroda: Oriental Institute, 1956.

Sastri, Gaurinath. *Mīmāṃsāparibhāṣā.* Banaras: Sarada Sanskrit Series, 1936.

Sastri, Pasupatinath. *The Pūrva Mīmāṃsā.* Calcutta: Ashokoath Bhattacharya, 1923.

Thadani, N. V. *The Mīmāṃsā.* Bharati Research Institute, 1952.

Nyāya-Vaiśeṣika

Athalye, Yashwant Vasudev, trans. *Tarka-Saṃgraha of Annaṃbhaṭṭa with Dīpikā and Govardhana's Nyāya-Bodhinī.* Bombay Sanskrit and Prakrit Series 55. Bombay: R. N. Dandekar, 1963.

Bhaduri, Sadananda. *Studies in Nyāya-Vaiśeṣika Metaphysics.* Poona: Bhandarkar Oriental Research Institute, 1947.

Bhattacharya, Kamleshwar, trans. *Vigrahavyāvartani.* Delhi: Motilal Banarsidass, 1986.

Bhattacharyya, Sibajiban. Part I of *Gadādhara 's Theory of Objectivity.* New Delhi: Indian Council of Philosophical Research, 1990.

———. *Gadādhara's Viṣayatāvāda,* Part 2 of *Gadādhara 's Theory of Objectivity.* New Delhi: Indian Council of Philosophical Research, 1990.

Dravid, Raja Ram. *The Problem of Universals in Indian Philosophy.* Delhi: Motilal Banarsidass, 1972.

Ingalls, Daniel H. H. *Materials for the Study of Navya-Nyāya Logic.* Cambridge: Harvard University Press, 1951.

Jhalkīkar, Bhīmācārya. *Nyāyakośa.* Bombay Sanskrit and Prakrit Series, No. 49. Poona: The Bhandarkar Oriental Institute, 1978.

Mādhavānanda, Swāmī, trans. *Bhāṣā-Pariccheda with Siddhānta-Muktāvalī.* Calcutta: Advaita Ashrama, 1977.

Matilal, Bimal K. *Epistemology, Logic and Grammar in Indian Philosophical Analysis.* Paris: The Hague Mouton, 1971.

———. *Nyāya-Vaiśeṣika.* A History of Indian Literature Series. Vol. 6, ed. Jan Gonda. Wiesbaden: Otto Harrassowitz, 1977.

———. *Perception.* Oxford: Claredon Press, 1986.

Mohanty, J. N. *Gangeśa Theory of Truth.* Shantiniketan: Centre of Advanced Study in Philosophy, 1966.
Mukhopadhyaya, Pradyot K. *Indian Realism: A Rigorous Descriptive Metaphysics.* Cacutta: K. P. Bagchi & Co., 1984.
Phillips, Stephen H. *Classical Indian Metaphysics.* Chicago: Open Court, 1995.
Śāstrī, Kuppuswami, trans. *A Primer of Indian Logic.* Madras: Kuppuswami Research Institute, 1961.
Śāstrī, S. and Gaurinath Sāstri. *Kirṇāvalī* (Hindi trans.). Banaras: Research Institute, 1980.
Tailanga, G. S., ed. *Vācaspati Miśra's Nyāyavārtikatātparyaṭīkā.* Vizianagram Sanskrit Series, No. 9. 1896.
Vidyābhusan. *History of Indian Logic.* Calcutta: Calcutta University, 1921.

Sāṃkhya-Yoga

Āranya, Hariharānanda. *Yoga Philosophy of Patañjali.* Trans. P. N. Mukerji. Calcutta: Calcutta University, 1977.
Bahm, A. J. *Yogastūtras.* New York: Frederick Ungar Publishing House, 1961.
Dasgupta, S. N. *A Study of Patañjali.* Calcutta: Calcutta University, 1920.
———. *Yoga as Philosophy and Religion.* London: Kegan Paul, 1924.
Jha, G. N. *Tattvakaumudi on Īśvarakṛṣṇa's Sāmkhyakārikās.* Sanskrit with English translation. Poona: Oriental Agency, 1934.
———. *Yogadraśana.* English translation. Bombay: Bombay Theosophical Publication, 1907.
Kapila. *Sāṇkhyapravacanasūtra.* Trans. Nandalal Sinha. Allahabad: Sacred Books of the Hindus, 1915.
Keith, A. B. *The Sāṇkhya System.* Calcutta: Y.M.C.A. Publishing House, 1949.
Larson, Gerald, M. *Classical Sāṃkhya.* Delhi: Motilal Banarsidass, 1969.
Patañjali. *Yogasūtras with the Commentaries of King Bhoja and Vyāsa.* Poona: Anandasram, 1932.
———. *Yogasūtras with the Commentaries of Vyāsa and Vācaspati Miśrā.* Trans. Ram Prasad. New Delhi: Oriental Books Reprint Corp., 1978.
Vijjñānabhiksu. *Sāṇkhyasūtra with his Commentary.* Banaras: Chowkhamba, 1909.
Woods, J. H. *The Yoga System of Patañjali.* Cambridge, MA: Harvard Oriental Series, 1927.

Vedānta

Advaita Vedānta

Apte, V. M., trans. *Brahma-Sūtra-Śhānkara-Bhāshya.* Bombay: Popular Book Depot, 1960.
Bhattacharya, Asutosh Sastri. *Studies in Post-Śaṅkara Dialectics.* Calcutta: University of Calcutta, 1936.
Bhattacharyya, Kalidas. *A Modern Understanding of Advaita.* Ahmedabad, India: L. D. Institute of Technology, 1975.
Bhattacharyya, Kokileswar. *An Introduction to Advaita Philosophy.* Calcutta: University of Calcutta, 1924.
Bhattacharyya, K. C. *Studies in Vedāntism.* Calcutta: University of Calcutta, 1909.
Chakraborty, Nirod Baran. *The Advaita Concept of Falsity—A Critical Study.* Calcutta Sanskrit College Sanskrit Series, No. 57. Calcutta: The Principal, Sanskrit College, 1967.

Chaudhuri, Anil Kumar Ray. *The Doctrine of Māyā.* Calcutta: Dasgupta & Co., Ltd., 1950.

———. *Self and Falsity in Advaita Vedānta.* Calcutta: Progressive Publishers, 1955.

Datta, Dhirendra Mohan. *The Six Ways of Knowing: A Critical Study of the Vedānta Theory of Knowledge.* 2nd rev. ed. Calcutta: The University of Calcutta, 1960.

Deutsch, Eliot. *Advaita Vedānta: A Philosophical Reconstruction.* Honolulu: University of Hawaii Press, 1968.

Deutsch, Eliot and J.A.B. Van Buitenen, eds. *A Sourcebook of Advaita* Vedānta. Honolulu: University of Hawaii Press, 1971.

Devanji, Prahlad Chandrashekhar, trans. *Siddhāntabindu of Madhusūdana with the Commentary of Purushottama.* Gaekwad Oriental Series, Vol. 64. Baroda: Oriental Institute, 1933.

Devaraja, N. K. *An Introduction to Śaṅkara's Theory of Knowledge.* Delhi: Motilal Banarsidass, 1962.

Gambhirananda, Swami. *Brahma-Sūtra Bhāṣya of Śankarācārya.* Calcutta: Advaita Ashrama, 1983.

———, trans. and ed. *Eight Upaniṣads with the Commentary of Śaṅkarācārya.* 2 vols. Calcutta: Advaita Ashrama, 1965.

Granoff, Phyllis, trans. *Śrī Harṣa's Khaṇḍanakhaṇḍakhādya.* Dodrecht, Holland: D. Reidel Publishing Co., 1978.

Gupta, Bina. *The Disinterested Witness: A Fragment of Advaita Vedānta Phenomenology.* Evanston, Illinois: Northwestern University Press, 1998.

Hiriyanna, Mysore, ed. *The Naiṣkarmya-Siddhi of Sureśvarācārya with the Candrikā of Jñānottama.* Bombay Sanskrit and Prakrit Series, No. 38. Poona: Bhandarkar Oriental Research Institute, 1980.

Jagadānanda, Swāmī, trans. *Upadeśa Sāhasrī of Śrī Śankarāchārya ("A Thousand Teachings").* Mylapore, Madras: Sri Ramakrishna Math, 1961.

Jha, Ganganath, trans. *Advaitasiddhi of Madhusūdana Sarasvatī.* Indian Thought, Vol. 6, 1914; Vol. 7, 1915; Vol. 8, 1916; Vol. 9, 1917.

Mādhavānanda, Swāmī, trans. *The Bṛhadāraṇyaka Upaniṣad: with the Commentary of Śaṅkarācārya.* Mayavati, Almora, Himalayas: Advaita Ashrama, 1950.

———, trans. and ed. *Vedānta Paribhāṣā by Dharmarāja Adhvarīndra.* Mayavati: Advaita Ashrama, 1983.

Mahadevan, T. M. P., ed. and trans. *The Saṃbandha-Vārtika of Sureśvarācārya.* Madras: University of Madras, 1958.

Nikhilānanda, Swami, trans. *The Māṇḍūkhyopaniṣad with Gauḍapāda's Kārikā and Śaṅkara's Commentary.* Mysore: Sri Ramakrishnan, Ashrama, 1955.

Śāstrī, S. S. Suryanarayana, trans. *Siddhāntaleśasaṅgraha of Appayya Dīkṣita.* Madras: University of Madras, 1935.

———, trans. and ed. *Vedānta Paribhāṣā by Dharmarāja Adhvarīndra.* Adyar: The Adyar Library, 1942.

———, and Raja, C. Kunhan, ed. and trans. *The Bhāmatī of Vācaspati: on Śaṅkara's Brahmasūtrabhāṣya* (Catussūtrī). Madras: Theosophical Publishing House, 1933.

———, and Saileswar Sen, trans. *Vivaraṇaprameyasaṅgraha.* Madras: The Sri Vidya Press, 1941.

Śāstrī, Srirama, trans. *The Pañcapādikā of Padmapāda.* Madras Government Oriental Series, Vol. 155. Madras: Government Oriental Manuscript Library, 1958.

Satprakāshānanda, Swāmī. *Methods of Knowledge.* Calcutta: Advaita Ashrama, 1975.

Sengupta, Bratindra Kumar. *A Critique of the Vivaraṇa School.* Calcutta: Dr. Bratindra Kumar Sengupta, 1959.

Shastri, Hari Prasad, trans. *Pañcadaśī. A Treatise on Advaita Metaphysics by Swāmī Vidyāranya.* London: Shanti Sadan, 1956.

Sundaram, P. K. *Advaita Epistemology.* Madras: University of Madras, 1968.

Thibaut, George, trans. *The Vedanta-Sutras with the Commentary of Śaṇkarācarya.* Ed. Max Müller. Vols. XXXIV and XXXVIII, Sacred Books of the East Series. Oxford: Clarendon Press, 1890 and 1896.

Veezhinathan, N., ed. *The Saṃksepaśāriraka of Sarvajñātman.* Madras: University of Madras, 1985.

Venkataramiah, D., trans. *The Pañcapādikā of Padmapāda.* Gaekwad Oriental Series, Vol. 107. Baroda: Oriental Institute, 1948.

Yogīndrananda, ed. and trans. *Citsukha's Tattavapradīpikā with Pratyaksvarūpa's Nayaṇaprasādini.* Banaras: Shuddarsana Prakasana Pratisthana, 1956.

Viśiṣṭādvaita

Ādidevānanda, Swāmī, trans. *Yatīndramatadīpikā.* Madras: Sri Ramakrishna Math, 1949.

Bhatt, S. R. *Studies in Rāmānuja Vedānta.* New Delhi: Heritage Publishers, 1975.

Carman, John B. *Theology of Rāmānuja.* New Haven, CT: Yale University Press, 1974.

Srinivasachari, P. N. *The Philosophy of Viśiṣṭādvaita.* Madras: The Adyar Library and Research Center, 1978.

Thibaut, George, trans. *The Vedānta Sūtras with the Commentary of Rāmānuja.* The Sacred Books of the East, Vol. XLVIII. Oxford: The Clarendon Press, 1904.

Van Buitenen, J. A. B., trans. *Vedārthasamgraha.* Deccan College Monograph Series, No. 16. Poona: Deccan College Postgraduate and Research Institute, 1956.

Varadachari, K. C. *Śrī Rāmānjua's Theory of Knowledge.* Madras: Tirumali-Tirupati: Devasthanama Press, 1943.

Other Vedānta Schools

Maitra, S. K. *Madhva Logic.* Calcutta: Calcutta University, 1936.

Nimbārka. *Vedānta Parijata Saurabha (Commentary on the Vedānta Sūtras).* Ed. Roma Bose. Calcutta: Society of Bengal, 1940–1943.

Sarma, B. N. K. *A History of the Dvaita School of Vedānta and Its Literature.* 2 vols. Bombay: Booksellers Publishing Co., 1960–1961.

———. *The Philosophy of Śri Madhvacharya.* Bombay: Bharatiya Vidyabhavan, 1962.

Srinivasachari, N. *The Philosophy of Bhedābheda.* Madras: Srinivasa Varadachari and Co., 1934.

Vallabha. *Anubhāsya* (Commentary on the Vedānta Sūtras). 2 vols. Bombay: Bombay Sanskrit Series, 1921–1926.

Index

About the Author

J. N. Mohanty, born in 1928 in India, holds an M.A. from the University of Calcutta and a Ph.D. from the University of Göttingen, Germany. Among the universities at which he has taught are the Universities of Calcutta and Burdwan in India, the University of Oklahoma, and the New School for Social Research in New York. At present he is a professor of philosophy at Temple University, Phildadelphia, and also Woodruff Professor of Philosophy and Asian Studies at Emory University Atlanta. His publications are in the fields of phenomenology and Indian philosophy.

A past president of the Indian Philosophical Congress, he has been a Visiting Fellow at All Souls College, Oxford, and is a member of the Institut Internationale de Philosophia, Paris. He is also a life member of the Indian Academy of Philosophy and a member of the board of directors of the Center for Advanced Research in Phenomenology. In 1992 he received the Humboldt forschungspreis and was awarded the Sir William Jones Memorial Gold Medal by the Asiatic Society.

About the Author